MW01622583

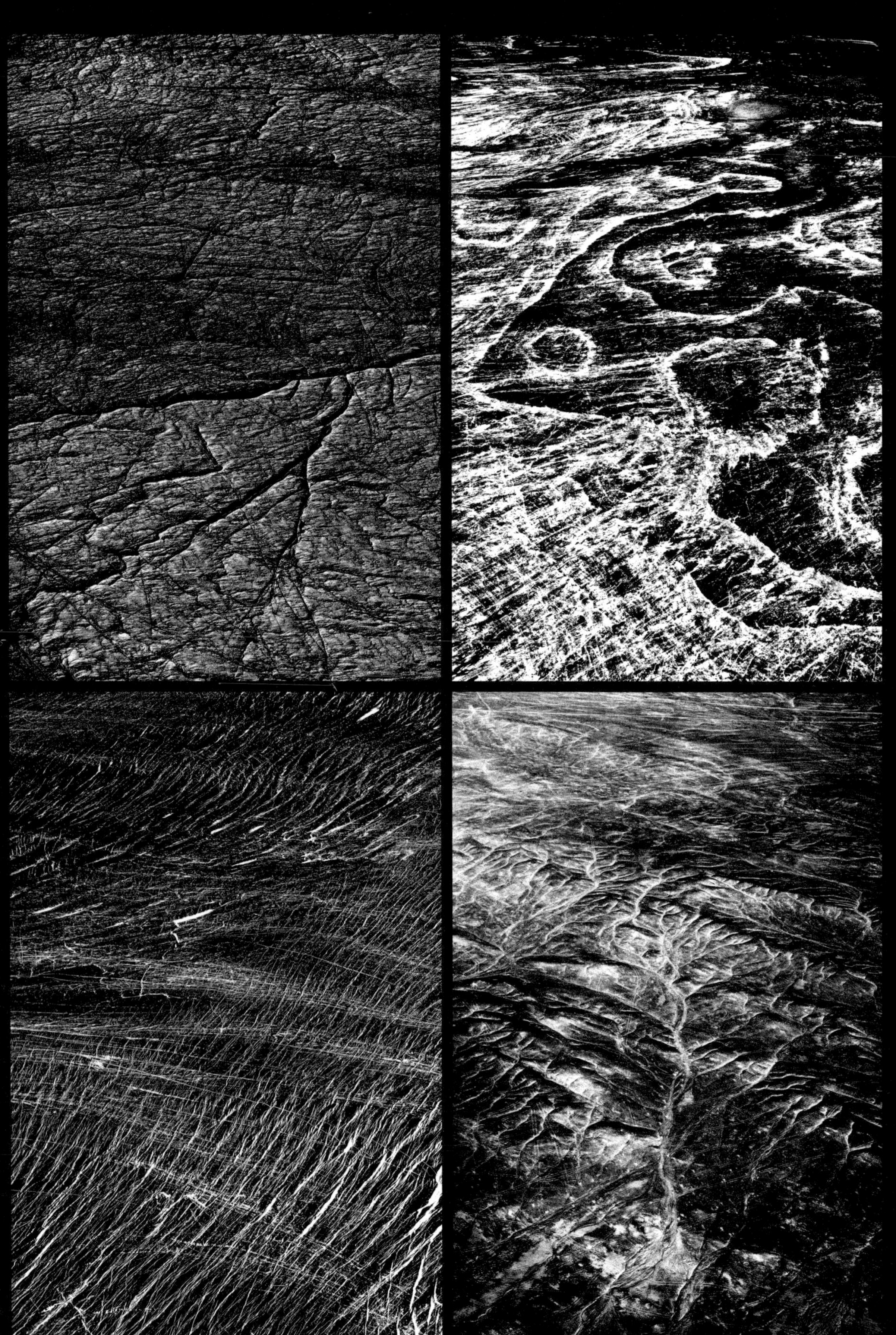

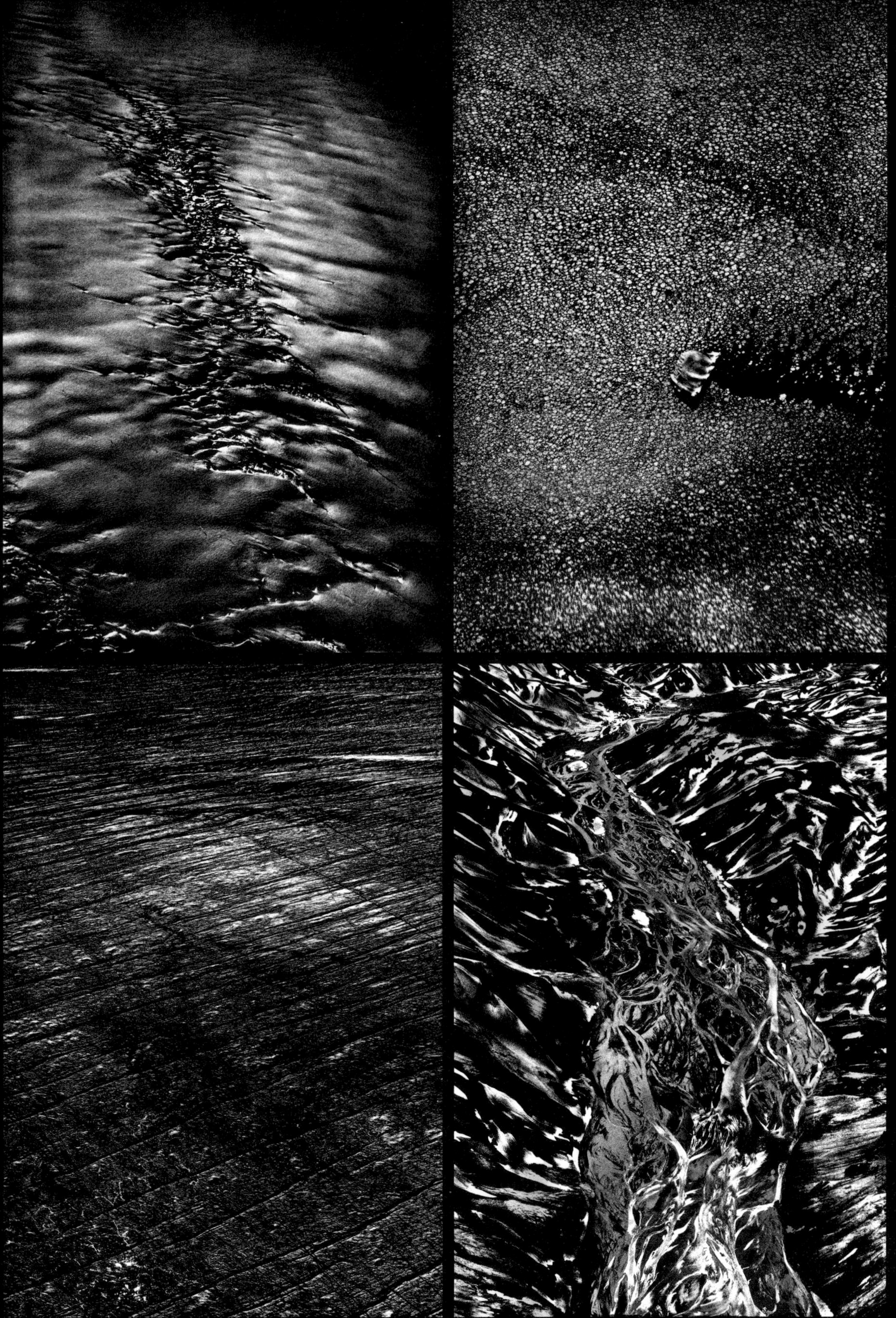

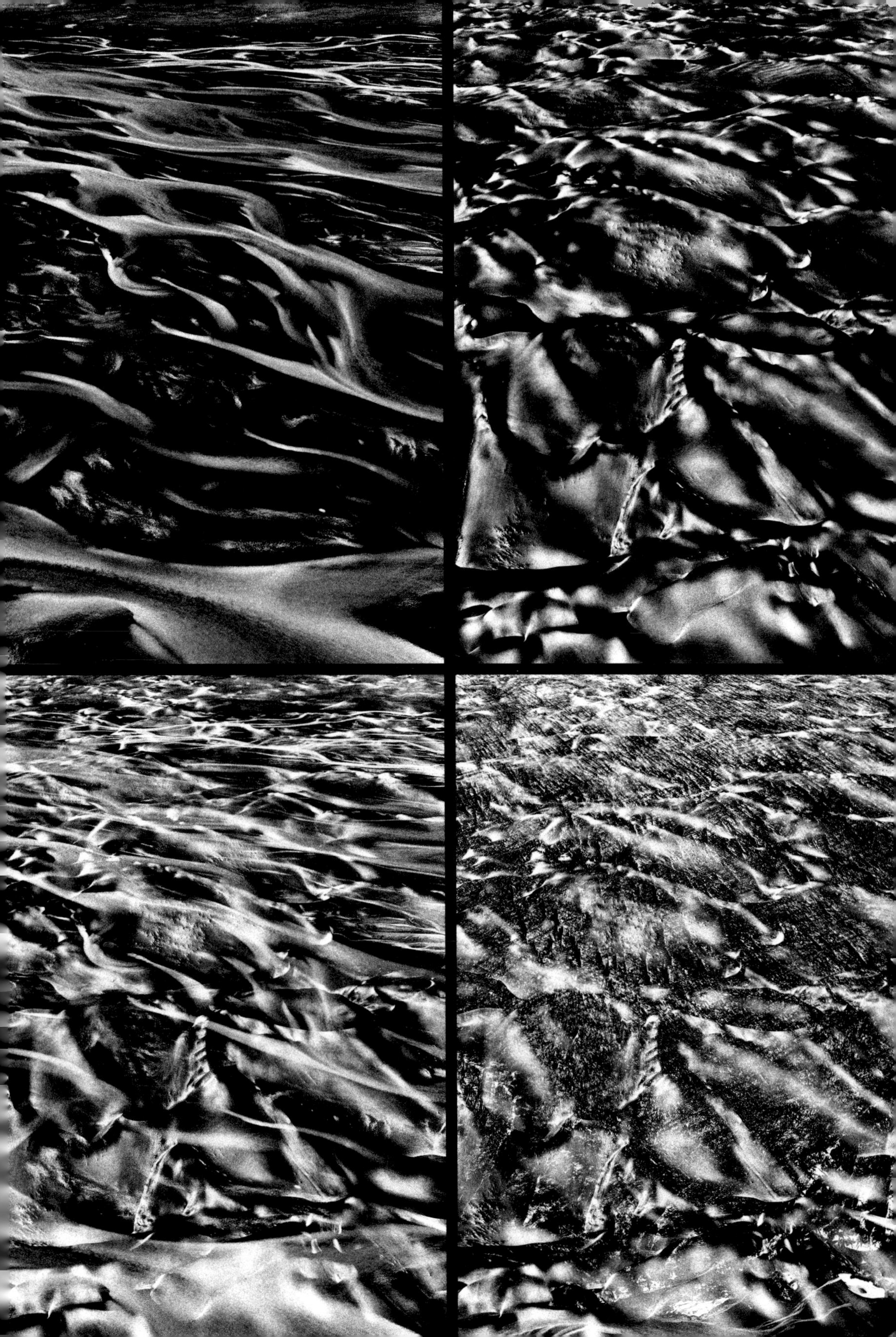

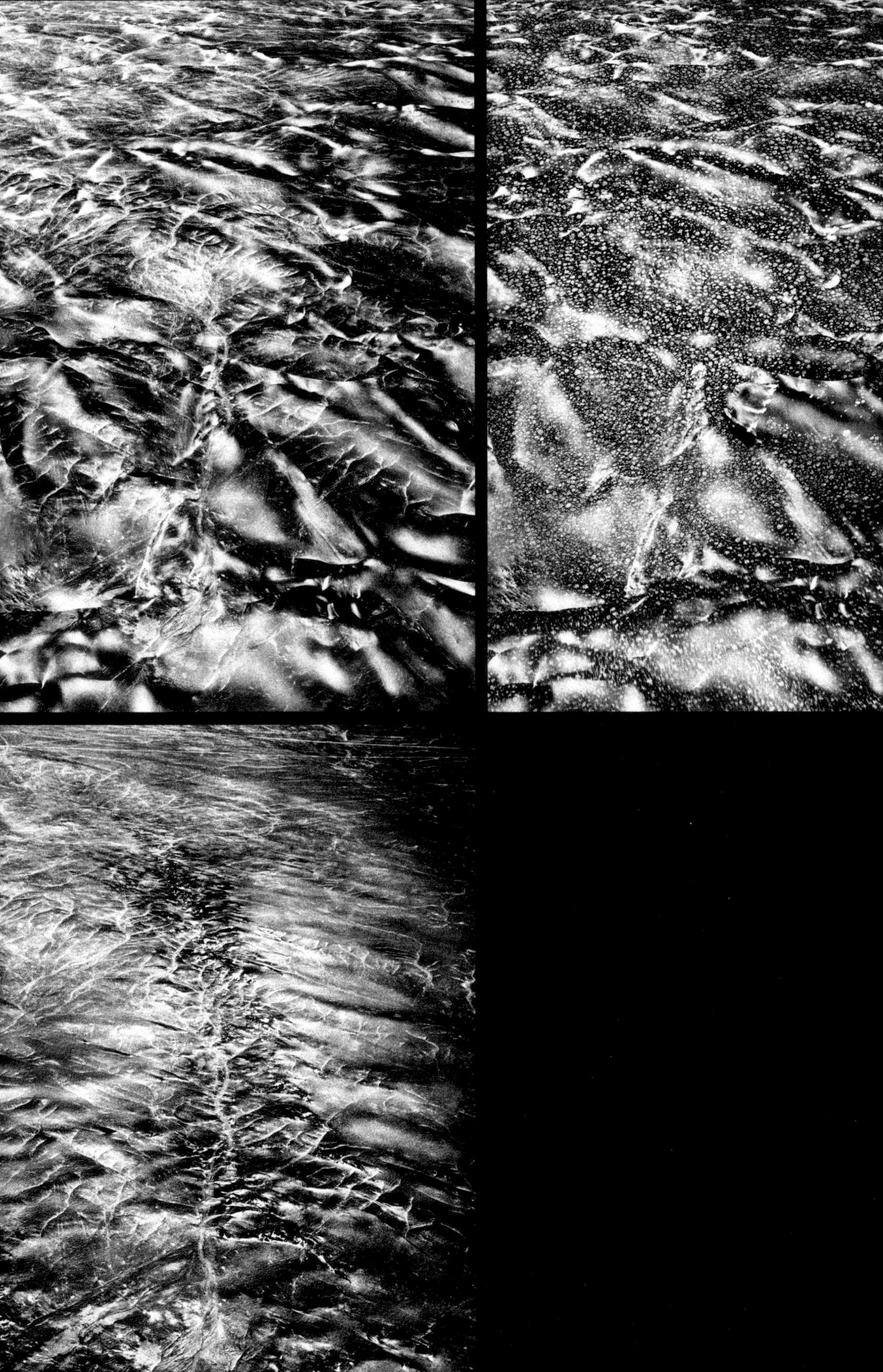

GALLERIE D'ITALIA
TORINO

Gallerie d'Italia | Skira

edited by Walter Guadagnini

Paolo Pellegrin. Fragile Wonder

A Journey through Everchanging Nature

Intesa Sanpaolo's fourth museum opens in Turin, in Piazza San Carlo.

Thanks to a brilliant intuition of architect Michele De Lucchi, the underground spaces of the magnificent seventeenth- and eighteenth-century rooms of Palazzo Turinetti have been enhanced: radically re-functionalized, they have become an extensive state-of-the-art exhibition area, which we have decided was to be dedicated to photography.

The Gallerie d'Italia that are already established and operating in the heart of Milan, Naples, and Vicenza correspond, each with their own identity, to a single comprehensive project, insofar as they reflect the vocation and cultural specificities of their host cities. The fact that the new museum in Turin is devoted to the culture of the image is in line with the leading role that this city has long played in promoting cinema and the most recent visual arts.

The Gallerie d'Italia in Piazza San Carlo therefore set out to operate as an international centre for the study and investigation, collection, and conservation of photography. Photography understood as a tool for learning about history (the permanent exhibition of Intesa Sanpaolo's Publifoto Archive is an important step in this direction) and to document and interpret the present. This twofold value inherent in photographic pictures corresponds to the bank's commitment to culture, in preserving the values and memory of the past while at the same time promoting innovation.

Photography is undoubtedly one of the main forms of art of the new millennium. Thanks to wonderful technologies, it can harness a communicative and suggestive power that allows it to present events, places, situations, and people in immediate and extremely engaging ways. An ability that makes photography an incredibly effective means to investigate and reflect on today's dramatic issues, from international conflicts to the pandemic, from the violation of human rights to social inequalities and the climate crisis.

Reinterpreting in a contemporary way the traditional practice of art patronage, the Gallerie d'Italia will ask leading world photographers to observe and read the most pressing themes of our time through their lenses. The outcome will be photographic narratives that are not just repertoires of images, but critical projects stemming from the author's sensitivity and talent. Narratives that will translate into

Giovanni Bazoli

exhibitions intended to increase public awareness about the momentous challenges humanity is facing. Thanks to its practice of artistic patronage, the museum in Piazza San Carlo will promote the collection and encourage the conservation of unpublished photographic documents that are to be the archives of tomorrow.

The opening exhibition *Fragile Wonder: A Journey through Everchanging Nature* is the result of our first commission to one of the absolute protagonists on the international photography scene, Paolo Pellegrin. Curated by Walter Guadagnini with the contribution of Mario Calabresi, the exhibition tackles the subject of the climate crisis, in line with our bank's strong commitment to sustainability and battle against climate change.

During an over one-year-long expedition, the Roman photojournalist travelled by plane, boat, and on foot across various countries of the world, capturing the marvellous and fragile spectacle of nature in his photographs: the glaciers of Greenland, the fires in Australia, the Costa Rican forest, the tsunami and earthquake in Japan, the Vaia storm in north-eastern Italy, Mount Etna, the volcanoes of Iceland, the wildlife of Namibia, the migration of starlings in the skies of Denmark.

His are deeply poetic photographs, and looking at them – in the words of the photographer – we feel a sense of beauty, of sublime, and of sacredness paired with dismay at the devastating consequences of climate change. Human beings, who have been the main protagonists of the photographic investigation Pellegrin has conducted so far, take a step back in these shots. Looking at these photographs we become spectators of Earth's magnificence and, at the same time, of the deleterious effects our action has on it.

"The photographs seem to show a kind of reality with no boundaries, with no need for transcription or translation", writes Giovanna Bertelli. The moving beauty of Pellegrin's pictures, while surging emotions, also channels a severe and universal message, urging us to rethink the relationship between humans and the environment, that is, to understand the pressing need to take care of our planet's sufferings.

After working as a sensitive and courageous witness to conflicts in Lebanon, Iraq, Palestine, Kosovo, and other countries, Pellegrin left for Ukraine just as the construction site for the Gallerie d'Italia in Turin was being set up, to document the events, destruction, and pain of an absurd war that is striking at the heart of Europe.

In an interview from the front, the photoreporter explained the meaning of his work: "I no longer ask myself the question: will one more photograph change the world? Maybe it will, maybe it won't, but the sense of duty that moves me in taking that picture stems from another conviction: that we must hand over records and documents to history".

Pellegrin's photographs, exhibited at Palazzo Turinetti and collected in this volume, are both a chronicle and a testimony, a cry and a warning to humanity. They are by no means an answer to the world's tragedies, but rather an incentive for each one of us to interrogate our conscience.

Giovanni Bazoli
Chairman Emeritus
Intesa Sanpaolo

A wall, a partition at the entrance, maybe it's all there: thirty sheets, thirty serigraphs opening the exhibition of a photographer. Thirty variations on a theme, many details forming a whole. Or perhaps not. Thirty full immersions into a vision, into a mysticism of image, so to speak, where all the references are lost. All but one. What those signs are, we do not know, we are unable to say. They are the marks of time on Earth's skin – perhaps roads, paths, traces, footprints, wounds: we are free to interpret them as we choose. Little do those places care of our modest human interpretation. But what if they were the remains of specific actions of the Earth, or even moments of a life that defines itself as movement and then stops, too hot or too cold, too fluid or too solid, we do not know, we can't tell. Just as we cannot tell – something we will experience many times throughout this project – the high from the low, the top from the bottom: farewell perspective and welcome horizon-less world, seen from above, or from too close up, in a dimension that is in any case extra-rational, with no certainty whatsoever, except that of the mythopoetic dimension of places and elements.

Silk-screen printing is a slightly earlier technique than Daguerre's photography, but in this case the reverse route is taken and photographs appear before silk-screen prints and silk-screen prints appear before the photographs visitors see upon entering the exhibition space. A kind of prologue, an enigma offered to the visitor who likes to imagine that everything will be revealed eventually. Also a kind of warning not to trust the intelligibility of nature too much, and to trust that of photography even less. *Et quid amabo nisi quod aenigma est*, what shall I love if not the enigma, asked the pictor optimus. Like a fragment made up of fragments, and it could not be otherwise, if it is true that this fragment is introducing us to an experience based on the four elements, a subject extensively explored by the Greeks: "Some, for instance, [regarding the matter of bodies, *Editor's Note*] postulate fire and earth: some add air, making three, and some, like Empedocles, reckon water as well, thus postulating four", said Aristotle.

Walter Guadagnini

The question is to what extent we can tell the presence of the four elements and the effects of their action in these images, and how willing we are to let ourselves be guided by the photographer's eye on the journey into the (almost) total otherness of nature.

The Iceberg

It is as if one were crashing into it, like a Titanic of the senses: the route is clearly defined, it has its own logic that does not respond to geography but to elements, and to an attempt to build a narrative around them. The main subject are human beings, even though they never appear. The main subject is the man behind the camera (or video camera) who accepts to interact with vastness. But let's take one step back: Paolo Pellegrin (Rome, 1964) is a photographer of stories, facts, and people, set in specific times and locations, facts which have clearly visible consequences on the people who are more or less voluntarily protagonists of his pictures (although he may follow events over very long periods of time, Pellegrin is certainly not a photographer who can be counted among the representatives of the so-called aftermath photography and this is perhaps the first project to be moving in this direction, at least metaphorically, because it has the very long, infinite timing of earth and sea, of fire and air, of plants and birds, of deserts).

Pellegrin's major anthological exhibition at MAXXI Rome in 2018 had already clarified that this operating method was no longer enough for the author to define his own role within the world of contemporary image: his stories were always there, but they were presented differently, with different techniques, and above all they were intertwined and interspersed with an obsessive reflection – no longer destined to remain private but made public – on the roots of this job, on the mechanisms of image creation, in a descent into the depths not of a profession, but of a relationship with the world. Entire walls lined with images that had never left the studio, reflecting in an installation structure that recalled the bow of a ship or the glacier we see in a famous painting by Caspar David Friedrich, certainly not a casual reference. And it was precisely glaciers, the polar caps, that closed that experience and opened a new one: with no fractures (even though fractures constantly appear in many of the images of glaciers and volcanoes, so much so as to hint at a not-too-veiled symbolic intention), with a continuity determined by an inflexible desire to communicate through images in order to reach as many people as possible. Using all possible languages, fearlessly extending the potential of the medium, with the awareness of being in the midst of a revolution that it would be foolish to try to stop, but of which we can exploit the new horizons it opens up – however difficult they may be to grasp and above all to handle for those born in a different era of mass media. By doing so, even individual work becomes more collective, not only in the operational or productive phase but also in the creative one.

Those dazzling white expanses Pellegrin photographed a few years ago were, more or less consciously, the beginning of today's series; they are the prologue to the prologue, the discovery of a necessity, that of talking about humans without showing them. However, the addition and the difference the images collected in this volume bring to the table is that in the face of certain subjects, the criterion of human measurement and discernment does not retain value, it no longer provides a reliable scale in order to understand nor let alone evaluate. The reaction to this condition of discomfort in the face of the incommensurability of nature and the fundamental impossibility of bringing it to a human scale is what led to the dawn, around the end of the eighteenth century, of the concept of "sublime", to which Pellegrin himself refers in his dialogue with Mario Calabresi in the following pages. The various and best-known definitions of sublime, from Burke to Kant and Schopenhauer, agree on the fascination produced by the immensity and uncontrollability of nature, which generates aesthetic pleasure and philosophical reflections on the relationship between humans and nature. So much so that Pellegrin seems to translate this feeling (the sublime is, in fact, a feeling) into photography itself, forcing it, in turn, to go beyond the limits historically attributed to this medium. Here it is, then, in the centre of the room, illuminated by an imaginary moon, the iceberg that photography cannot contain, the sheet of glass (an ancient memory of photography itself, perhaps) that multiplies to contain the block of ice in one piece, but that in doing so transforms it into an almost bodiless phantasmal vision (forced to carry the weight of glass – think of the difference with the lightness of paper, which is measured in grams), an apparition that resurrects a sense of wonder, the very moment our sight is captured by one of the principal aspects of climate change, melting glaciers. Expelled from the majesty of the world, humans return to the centre of the scene in a dual role, that of witnesses and respondents, in a short circuit that is resolved in the enchantment of a vision that gives meaning to all the others, since it sums up the extremes between knowledge and imagination, reality and dream, necessity and pleasure, uniqueness and multiplicity.

An Ostrich

However, to read this series of photos solely in terms of sublime would be limiting. It would prevent us from framing the project in its complexity, a project which goes beyond a certain attitude towards the wonders of nature. When we say that humans are the protagonists of many of these pictures, our intention is to emphasize that – besides the presence of the photographer – many of the photos on display have been made possible by man's action, and that this action, as we know, is far from being always in favour of the planet. The most dramatic images are undoubtedly those taken in Australia, but the ice and the uprooted trees in Trentino and Veneto are evidence of a situation that numerous studies have shown to be on the verge of collapse (if not beyond). With these landscapes, Pellegrin resorts to his original photoreporter background, further drying up his language, conceding very little to the fascination of destruction. He opts for black and white, and his line of action is similar to the one he adopts with the characters in his war reportages: these burnt, uprooted, battered trees and land are the silent but present witnesses of a man-inflicted violence – in this case, not on other humans, but on all humanity, metaphorically, since it is inflicted on the Earth and its non-human inhabitants. Here, it is no longer a question of incommensurability, but rather of damage calculation; it is the explicit acknowledgement –

and awareness – of one of the great issues of contemporary life, to which a thousand others are linked (consider, regarding the hidden presence of humans in these photographs, the inseparable link between global warming and migration), which is an integral part of the photographic ethics of Pellegrin, who is not and will never be just a landscape photographer. Moreover, it is not hard to see how plants and vegetation play a central role in this project: from Australia to Mexico, from Costa Rica to Namibia to Italy, plants are perhaps the most present subject, the one through which the greatest amount of information and reflections are channelled. Alone or united in forests, recognizable or part of a whole in which they merge, photographed at night or in broad daylight, plants become the common thread between the various territories, the recurring element in a journey into diversity. Particularly noteworthy are the plants intertwining into visual patterns recalling those of glaciers or volcanoes, where the skin element reappears, but combined with the new element of the threshold, the border to be crossed, as we clearly see in the Costa Rican Forest. And also, the verticality of the trees – although often wounded – recalling the verticality of anthropomorphic statues, in a dialogue with the all-over surfaces in front of which one is forced to wonder what is high and what is low, in a continuous play of opposites which in each photograph calls into question the foundations of vision and, above all, of reason, giving free rein to imagination.

This journey to Central America also contains several elements that characterize the entire series: the difficulty of photographing such a wealth of things, of details, of visual stimuli, which contrasts with the emptiness of the expanses of ice or volcanic concretions. The shift from total void to total fullness is extraordinary: there are some images of Costa Rican forests that leave almost no space for the eye to wonder, one cannot see beyond, but at the same time one cannot even fix one's gaze on a precise point of the surface in the foreground, because the eyes are attracted by its countless elements, like in a gigantic spider's web as those one would find in those areas. Once again, the problem of excess arises, but when applied to this subject it does not generate the "delightful horror" of the sublime, but rather the *horror vacui* of extreme decoration, which once again the human dimension of photography struggles to contain.

There are then two images that serve as a link between this subject and the no less important, though less conspicuous, subject of fauna: the first picture is a photograph of an elephant with its trunk resting on a tree, in which the particular point of view from which the photograph is taken makes the animal and the plant merge and become one; the elephant's skin and bark form a single structure, which in turn naturally ends up referring to all the skins of the world that make up this series, and which not by chance constantly return in this catalogue in the most diverse forms.

The protagonist of the second photograph is instead a gorilla lying in the midst of glowing bright vegetation. Looking at pictures like these we could give in, paraphrasing Barthes, to "the pleasure of the subject": the crashing waves, the incredibly orange lava flow, the flight of the birds, the sinuous quality of the dunes are in fact beauty at its finest, a beauty that the photographer and ourselves could indulge in. Beauty may not save the world, but it certainly makes it a more pleasant place to live in, besides being in any case part of the world itself. But apart from their fascination, what attracts our attention once more in these photos is the level of transformation a forest may experience: the site of a fairytale-like event or, better said, of a timeless event, which seems so remote but also so plausible within this sequence of images. Because therein lies another of the central elements of this series, namely the relationship with time. Pellegrin deliberately eliminates from these photographs any possible reference to a definite and recognizable time: this world is beyond time, it is before and after, which is another way of expressing the incommensurability of places: the endangered forest is the forest of today but it is also that of the Garden of Eden; the Etna rock is there now in that point of the mountain, but it is also an equivalent of the monolith in *2001: A Space Odyssey*; there are animals running in the desert today, but they have done so since time immemorial (the question is whether they will continue to do so), the *saguaros* in the desert have no time, just like their environment.

Therefore, Pellegrin changes scale not only from a spatial but also from a temporal point of view, reaching a dimension balancing between evocation, mythology, and metaphysics that does not prevent him from remaining firmly linked to the present day. An ostrich looks into the camera, surrounded by other animals who are unaware (or at least uninterested) in the photographer's presence; some birds are flying elsewhere, in a desert landscape that the sand makes misty – yet another apparition, this time not sublime but alienated, surreal, like a still from one of Lanthimos' films.

Side Note
(but not too on the side)

"To represent is to aestheticize: that is, to transform. It presents a vast field of choices but it does not include the choice *not* to transform, not to change or alter whatever is being represented. It cannot be a pure process, in practice. This goes for photography as much as for any other means of representation. But this is no reason to back away from the process. The aesthetic is not objective and is not reducible to quantitative scientific terms. Quantity can only measure physical phenomena, and is misapplied in aesthetics, which often deals with what is not there, imagining things into existence. To become legible to others, these imaginings must be socially and culturally encoded. That is aestheticization." (David Levi Strauss, *Between the Eyes: Essays on Photography and Politics*)

Epilogue

The much talked about book *Hyperobjects* by Timothy Morton was on the shelf next to the work table of Sergio Bianchi, the architect with whom Pellegrin gives life and three-dimensional form to his exhibitions of two-dimensional objects, now also accompanied by moving images. A complex, often quoted book, that probably most people did not read in its entirety, but which sheds light on a facet of Pellegrin's attitude towards this commission, in addition to the previously explored aspects of his search for a mythical and primordial dimension of the natural. Morton's book is about acceptance of the otherness of nature and of what follows in terms of approach to the environmental issue, no longer interpreted from a human-centred standpoint (the good old Anthropocene, which in the age of internet has already become obsolete, *sic transit gloria mundi*), but precisely from the hyper-objects that lie beyond and outside the human sphere. In any case, as a tribute to the meeting that initiated the complex adventure that led to the realization of this project in its entirety, I would like to end this essay with a quotation from another volume by the same author, which can undoubtedly serve as a further, significant key towards interpreting the images that follow and the reasons why they came into existence: "Being interested means I am in charge. Being fascinated means that something else is. The fascination of beauty is what some philosophy tries to ward off at all costs. When you experience beauty, you experience evidence in your inner space that at least one thing that isn't you exists. An evanescent footprint in your inner space – you don't need to prove that things are real by hitting them or eating them. A nonviolent coexisting without coercion". These images by Pellegrin are not just fascinating, they are captivated by the Earth's fragile wonder.

Walter Guadagnini
Director
Camera – Centro Italiano per la Fotografia

A few months after reporting on the battle of Mosul between Kurdish peshmerga and ISIS militiamen, Paolo Pellegrin boarded an old P-3 Orion military plane, a Cold War relic, a submarine fighter that can fly very low and has a maximal time range of over fifteen hours. Pellegrin took off from Punta Arenas, at the southern tip of Chile, heading towards something he had never seen.

Towards the absence of noise, towards spaces with no fighting, explosions, fire, soldiers, dust, and blood. "That day, flying over the ice of Antarctica, I found myself faced with absolute beauty, with something that spoke to me of eternity." For days, he repeated the same ritual, spending the entire day in the air with the NASA mission there to monitor the extent of the polar ice and its thickness. Paolo flew over endless expanses with no people to be seen, but his gaze, glued to the porthole, was searching for the consequences of human impact. That late 2017 was the beginning of a new season for Paolo Pellegrin: a photographer that for over thirty years had documented wars, revolutions, earthquakes, tsunamis was entering a phase of his life that would lead him to go searching every corner of our planet for traces of "the greatest conflict of our time: climate change". A journey that took him from Australia to Iceland, from Costa Rica to the Svalbard islands, crossing Namibia, Denmark, Mexico, Congo, and Italy.

Many photographers, at a certain point in their lives, exhausted by the harshness of bearing witness, by the toll taken by the awful facts unfolding before their lens, take refuge in nature as an antidote to horror, as the only way to recover faith in the world. This was not the case for Paolo Pellegrin.

His was not an escape, but on the contrary "a journey looking into an emergency that has no boundaries, that does not concern someone, but everyone". His work is impelled by his passion as a father wondering about the future of his daughters, as a citizen who understands that the countdown has begun. "I was moved by the awareness that time is fleeting. Climate change is also a conflict, one of which we must be fully conscious, and one that we need to work out how to solve."

His voice is clear yet tired, coming from Kharkiv, one of the Ukrainian cities where the Russian invasion has been most devastating. Over the last month Pellegrin's camera has gone back to documenting a war: "I'm back into the fire. Here everything is random, the Russians make no distinction between civilians and military, they target everything, so there is no relying on logic, we are at the mercy of circumstances beyond any understanding".

I had got in touch with Pellegrin in order to pick up the threads of the work and reflections he had developed over the last five years, between two very distant wars, one in Iraq and one on the eastern border of Europe. We had decided to meet in Chernobyl, the last stop of his journey into the resilient and evolving environment, to talk about how nature can take back and reconquer spaces deserted by humans. But then came the war, the soldiers surrounded what was left of the nuclear plant and Paolo's mission changed. News about the current events required his attention, but in the background there remained the epochal challenge of climate change, which he chose to recount in this major exhibition for the Gallerie d'Italia in Turin, not only showing the signs of what we are losing but above all focusing on the "fragile wonder" that is our planet Earth.

"I structured my research on the four basic elements of nature – air, water, earth, and fire – but I used these elements as archetypes, not in an obvious way. I wanted to find subjects that carried a broader message beyond mere representation. I had the opportunity to do this thanks to an enlightened commission that I received from the Gallerie d'Italia. They believe in the value of storytelling and gave me the chance to collect and put together all the necessary pieces of a precious mosaic."

There are three words written down on Paolo's notebook at the end of this journey around the world: beauty, sublime, and sacred.

These are the feelings that he tried to channel through his lens: "The climate and environmental changes have accelerated as never before. But what is fast for history can be very slow for a camera and hard to capture and represent. That's why I had to change my point of view and try to capture the mystery of beauty".

Paolo Pellegrin's work has always been characterized by a certain level of mystery. His photographs are like questions that do not require an immediate answer but must linger on, questioning our consciences. He explained this aspect to me the first time I met him, in October 2006: "There are two ways of communicating: there is a type of photography that reveals itself completely. Those are speaking images, that say things loud and clear. This type of picture is very readable, but also a concluded investigation, it is an image that corresponds to the photographer's version of the facts. The other way of communicating, the one that interests me the most, is an unfinished photograph, where the viewers have the chance to begin their own conversation. It's an invitation: I'll take you in one direction, but the rest of the journey is up to you". In his photographs, there is precisely that percentage of mystery, of indefinite, that may also be disturbing, but there is never morbidity, rather a decency that pushes one to take a step back: "I am displaying the question that I asked myself witnessing death, wars, sorrow. Then I leave space for everyone to question themselves, to develop their own idea".

However, when he found himself face to face with nature, Pellegrin had to update his point of view, also from a formal standpoint: "The question I asked myself when I got on that plane in Antarctica was: how am I to photograph this? Because the minute you remove human beings from the picture there is immediately a problem of scale, of how to represent the size of the landscape. I found a solution by flying over those endless expanses of ice and, to further confuse the observers, removing the only spatial parameter: the horizon. By doing so, these photographs could be read as metaphors, and the infinitely large and the infinitely small could coincide. Faced with that endless white space, made of cracks, marks, and ripples, I began to ask myself questions about beauty".

And on a boat in Greenland, during one of the hottest summers in history, he witnessed the dramatic sight of mountains of ice cracking deeper and deeper and then eventually breaking off, drift, and melt. "The amazing thing about these extreme places is their scale. We are not used to those dimensions and you're faced with something so much bigger than you that it leads you to transcendence."

How do we represent this emergency, how do we get the message across? This choice was not easy. When I first met Paolo, he was living in New York, in the Williamsburg neighbourhood of Brooklyn, in a world that today no longer exists: from his window he could see the East River with the pier where sand was still being loaded for construction. He had just received one of the most prestigious awards for a photojournalist: the W. Eugene Smith Memorial Fund. Smith was one of the fathers of modern photojournalism, a man obsessed with rigour and research, who didn't believe in the idea of a single image, of the perfect shot that encompassed everything. He believed in ample investigations that could decrypt complexity. He worked for *Life* magazine and was sent to Pittsburgh to photograph the great industrial city, the capital of work: he was supposed to stay there for ten days, but ended up living there for three years. Pellegrin shares Smith's idea "that we must document what happens, record facts and events in order to leave a trace and a testimony". For this reason, he defines himself "a cataloguer".

But, faithful to his idea of raising questions rather than imposing an answer, he immediately cast aside the idea of creating a large-scale, monumental, all-encompassing project and chose instead to focus on traces, clues, hints: "These aspects capture the viewer in order to build a conversation. What guides me is my wish to create an interaction with the viewers, I want to draw them in, make them participate".

After exploring the subject of water, documenting the melting of the ice in Antarctica and Greenland, it was time for Paolo to turn his lens to the air. He chose to travel to the coast of Denmark on the North Sea to observe the *sort sol*, the "black sun" phenomenon, the migration of a million starlings between Southern Europe and Scandinavia occurring every spring and early autumn: "There are so many birds flying at the same time that they cover the sun".

The subject of air eventually brought him back to Italy to photograph the trees that had been torn down by the Vaia storm, one of the most extreme weather events of the recent years: at the end of October 2018, an actual hurricane, one of those that normally occur only in tropical areas, formed by hot sirocco winds blowing up to two hundred kilometres per hour, destroyed over thirty million trees in the Dolomites and the Venetian Prealps. An eerie scenario of destruction and fallen trees, a wounded landscape that will take decades to heal completely.

The subject of fire presented Pellegrin with an even more extreme scenario with the consequences of the great Australian wildfires that burned thirteen million hectares of land during the same months that the virus that would change our lives was beginning to spread. "In mid-February 2020 I was in Australia, photographing the effects of the great fires, one of the worst attacks on biodiversity in modern history, another of the consequences of climate change. After ice, fire: the extremes of nature's uprising. I worked on traces and the ruins left by fire. Once the daily news coverage faded, I wanted to describe the devastation left by the fires, and the hardships of going back to a normal life. It was an exceptional situation: thirty-three people died and an unimaginable number of animals were killed or had to leave their habitat." When news arrived that the virus had reached Italy, Paolo stopped: "While I was immersed in those lunar landscapes, I learned that Covid-19 had begun to hit Italy and Europe. I immediately rushed to the airport; I was afraid I would remain stuck on the other side of the world. I wanted to get home before the borders started to close".

For the first time in his life, the strongest call was not that of work. He did not rush to get to the hospitals or ambulances in the most affected countries; he did not chase the great news stories but chose to remain in a private sphere. An inner voice made him choose a more intimate dimension, based on the relationship with his family and with nature. "I took my wife and daughters to a farm in the mountains. Faced with the unknown, I didn't want this time to become a trauma for the girls, I felt the need to be with them and I'm happy I made this choice." When the world started to reopen and breathe again, Paolo left once more to continue collecting the pieces for his great fresco. He flew to the Svalbard islands and then to Iceland: "In front of the Fagradalsfjall Volcano, which had been sleeping for eight hundred years but after weeks of earthquakes had resumed its activity, I understood how fire is at once destruction and source; after all, this is one of the ways lands came into existence. I picked up the philosophy books I used to love when I was a boy, to investigate the meaning of sublime. It seemed to me I was finally understanding Schopenhauer, the feeling he describes when you observe the power of a phenomenon that is able to change reality and destroy it".

As his research continued, the sublime gave way to mystery, those "perfect moments when things seem to align". "It would often happen to me just before dawn: a gust of wind, a sudden fog, moments when I had the feeling of grasping the mystery of this nature in transformation. Its beauty, its fragility, the perception of something beyond anything: the sacred."

Channelling these feelings with photography is very hard: "It is virtually impossible, it's a sixth-degree climb. The landscape doesn't look back at you, you can't look for its eyes to create a connection, so the challenge is finding a relationship with it in order to take its picture. Then there are these moments when you sense something that goes beyond what you can explain to yourself. One night in Namibia, in one of the world's oldest deserts, that has existed for eighty million years and has a small forest of dead trees, all black but still standing, I remained under the stars waiting for dawn. The hyenas were howling, it was foggy, and before the sun came up, at dusk, I felt something bigger than myself. I took a photo. Did photography capture that? I don't know, but I tried, and for me even giving back a small part of that mystery, of that sense of sacredness, would be enough to give meaning to this work of mine". There are phenomena that require us to grasp and follow the movement, the variable geometries, so Paolo also produced a series of videos: "One of the most amazing moments was in Denmark where I observed a huge group of starlings, an extraordinary spatial architecture. They moved as if they were one single organism". The action, the force, the power of an erupting volcano in the stormy Icelandic Sea – "it looked like a divinity creating the world" – or of recovering nature. "I wanted to conclude this work in Chernobyl, a synthesis of the clash between humans and the environment, one of the places where nature has taken back its space. Chernobyl is an example of how, when there are no human beings, nature is capable of regaining control over the things that we have built. But humans have returned and have done so with violence."

"In Latin America I was looking for a primeval, primitive forest, there are several. I wanted this project to encompass the idea of the Garden of Eden, of a space untouched by human presence. I finally found it in Costa Rica. It is about the existence of untouched places in the world that humans have not tampered with. My last day was the most beautiful: it started raining and a sudden fog appeared. I photographed it. It doesn't have that flavour but it contains a small trace of that mystery, that emotion and that beauty. The synthesis of what we must save, this fragile wonder."

Mario Calabresi
Journalist
CEO Chora Media

Index of places

30 Etosha National Park, Namibia, 2022

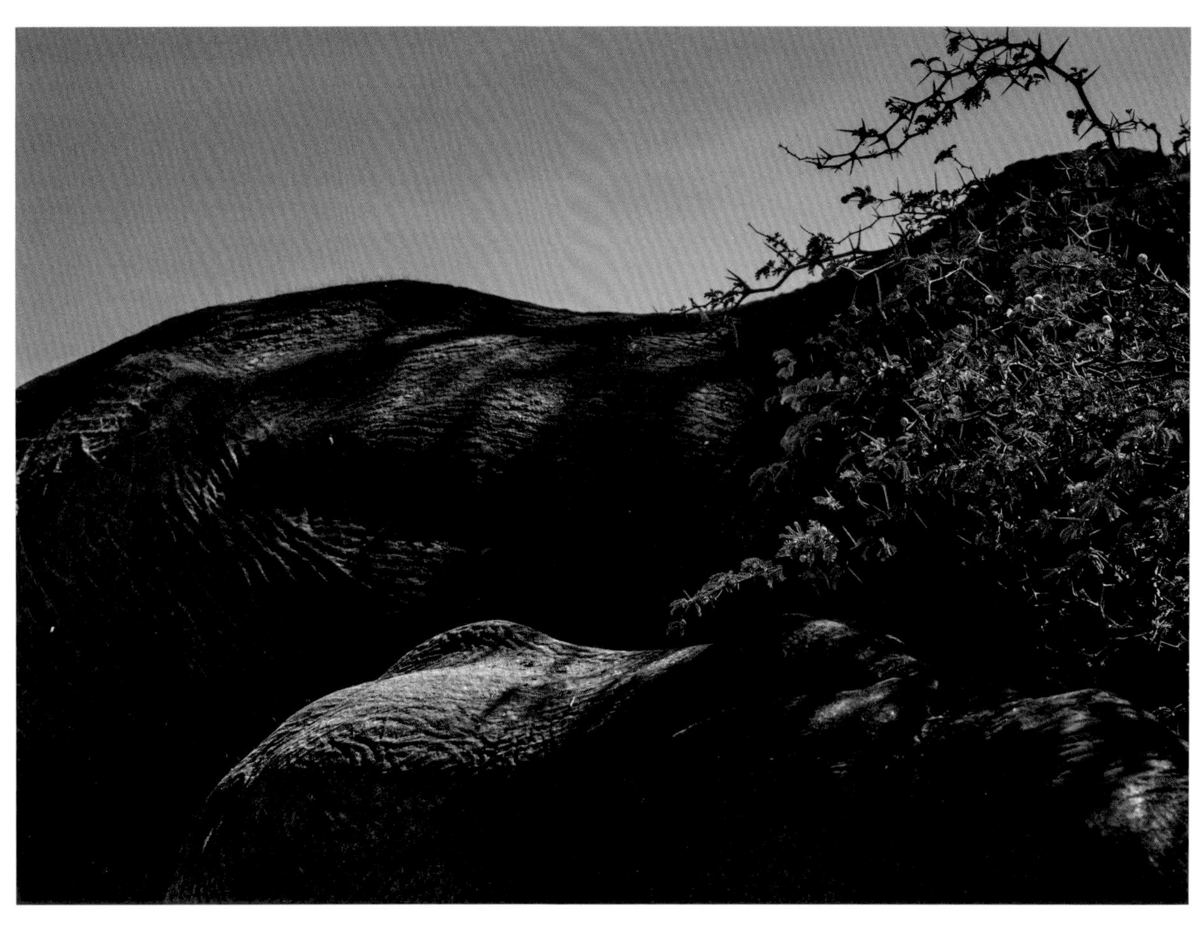

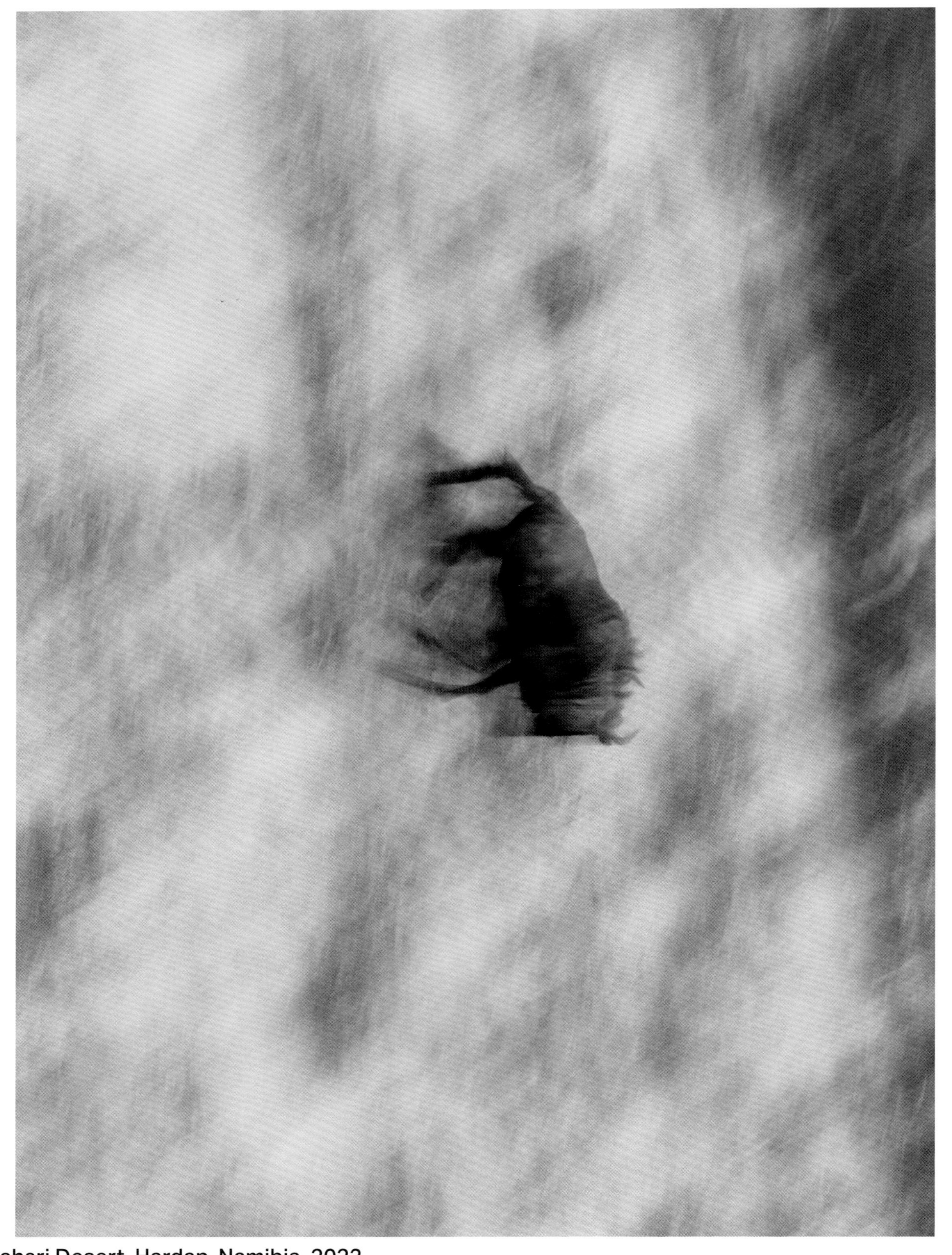

 Kalahari Desert, Hardap, Namibia, 2022

Namib-Naukluft National Park, Namibia, 2022

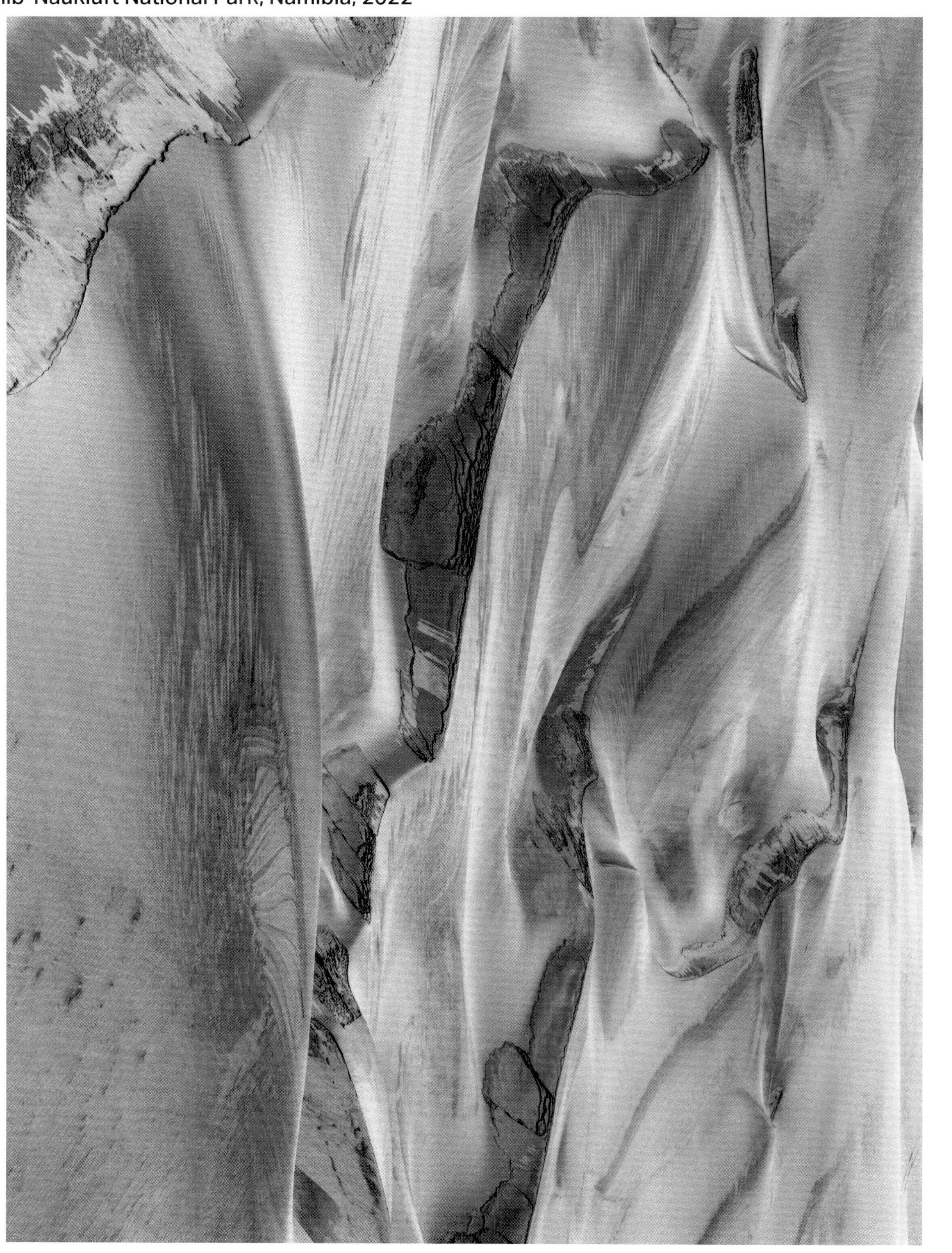

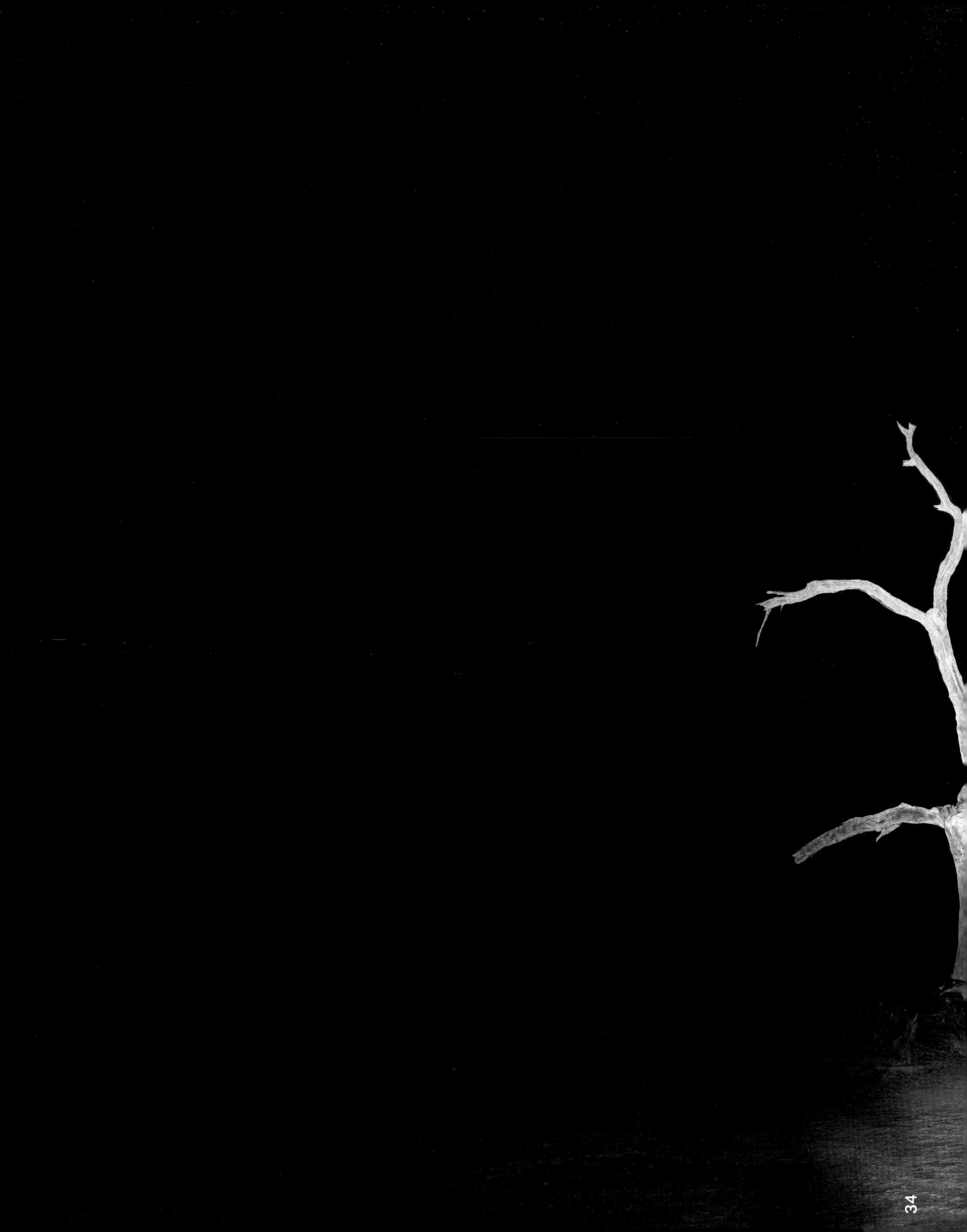

Sossusvlei, Namib-Naukluft National Park, Namibia, 2022 (frame video)

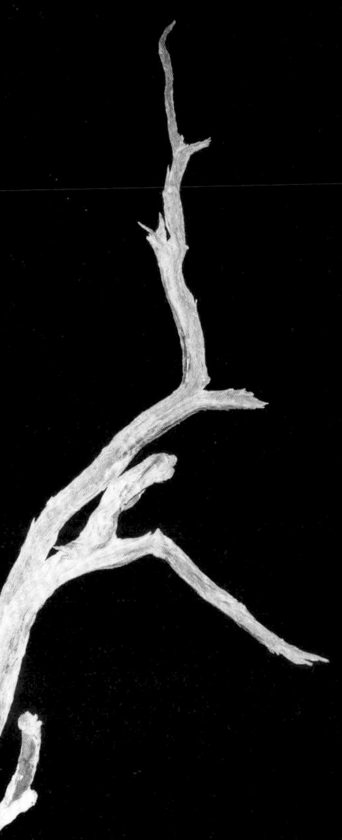

36 Namib-Naukluft National Park, Namibia, 2022

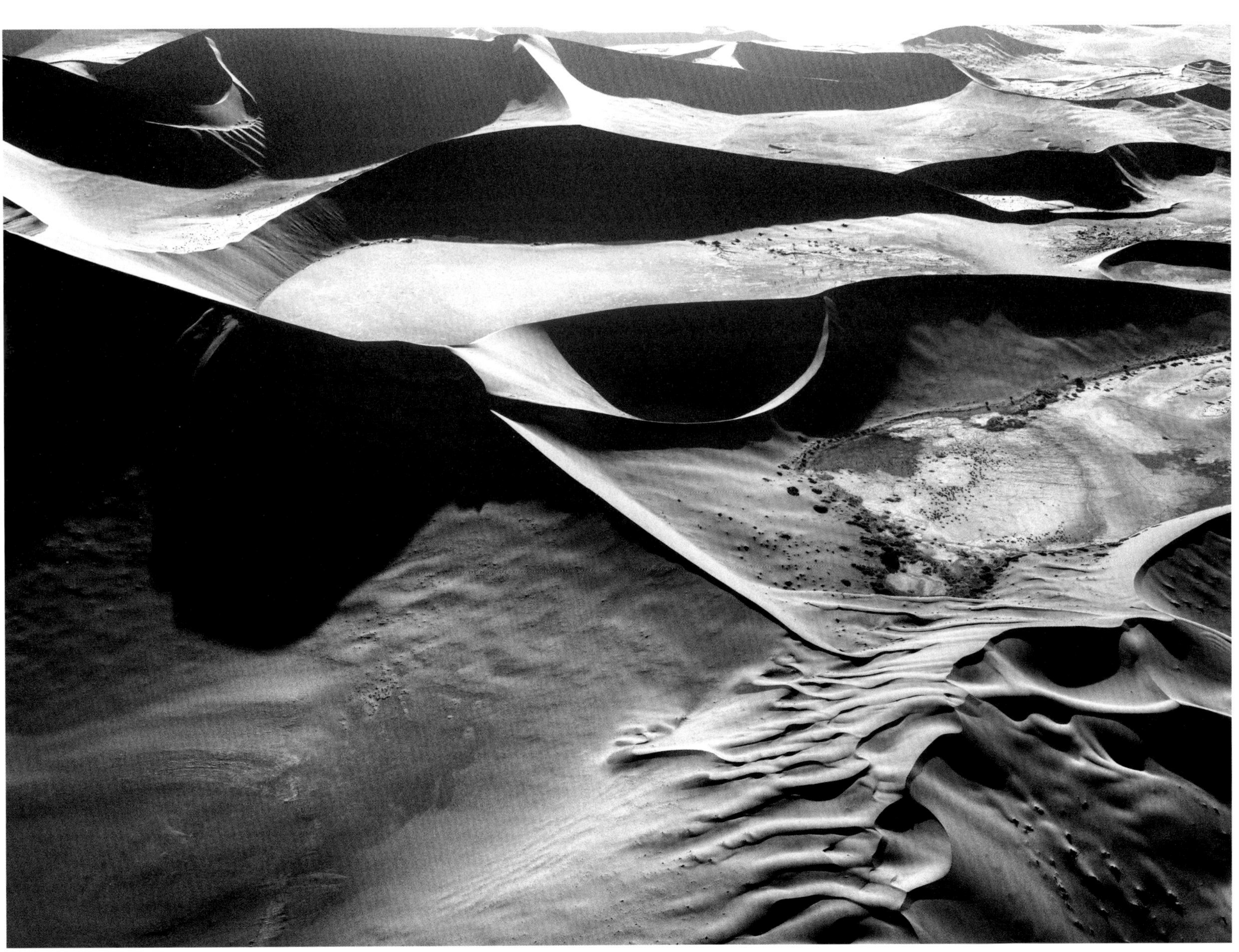

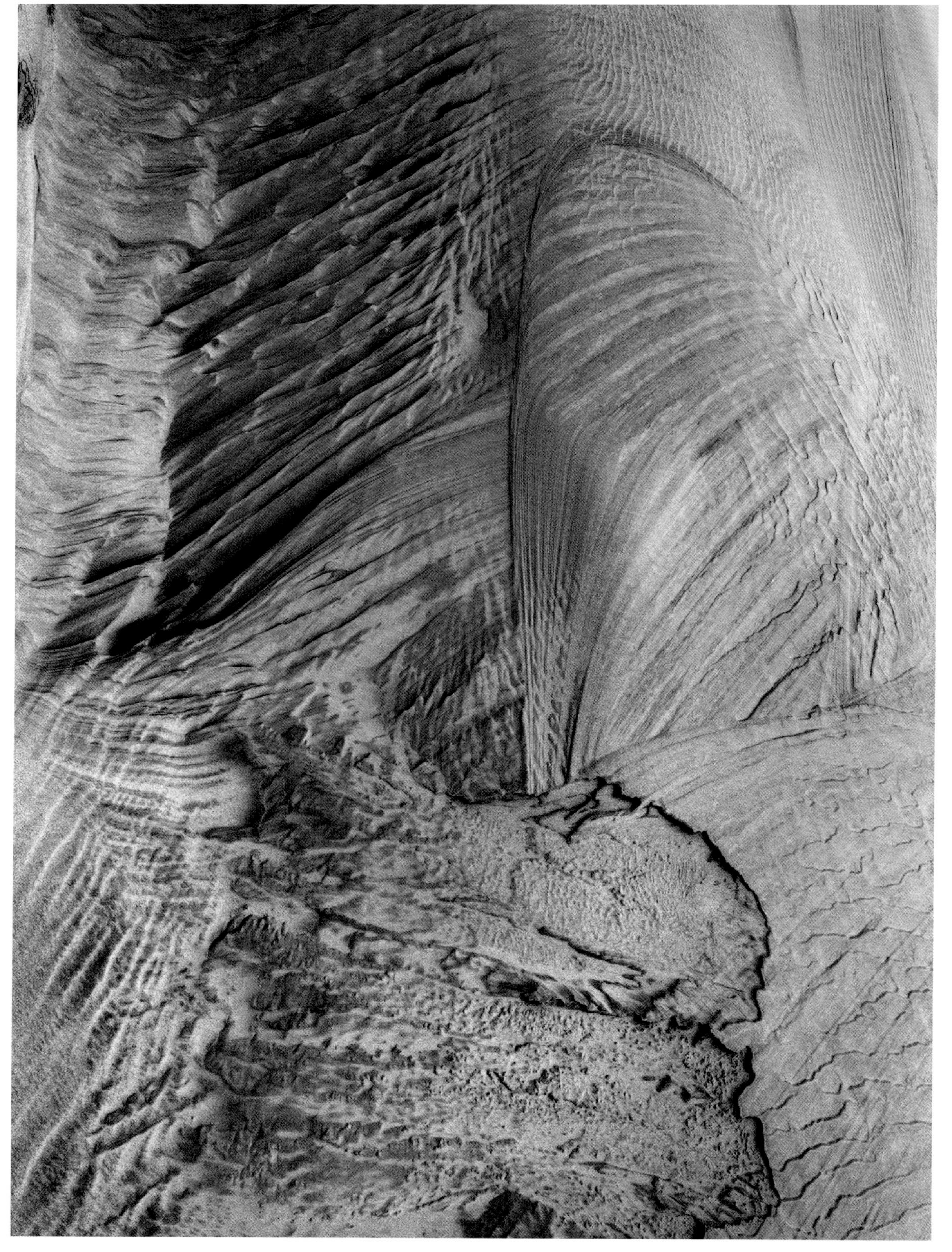

39 Namib-Naukluft National Park, Namibia, 2022

 Sonoyta, Sonoran Desert, Mexico, 2019

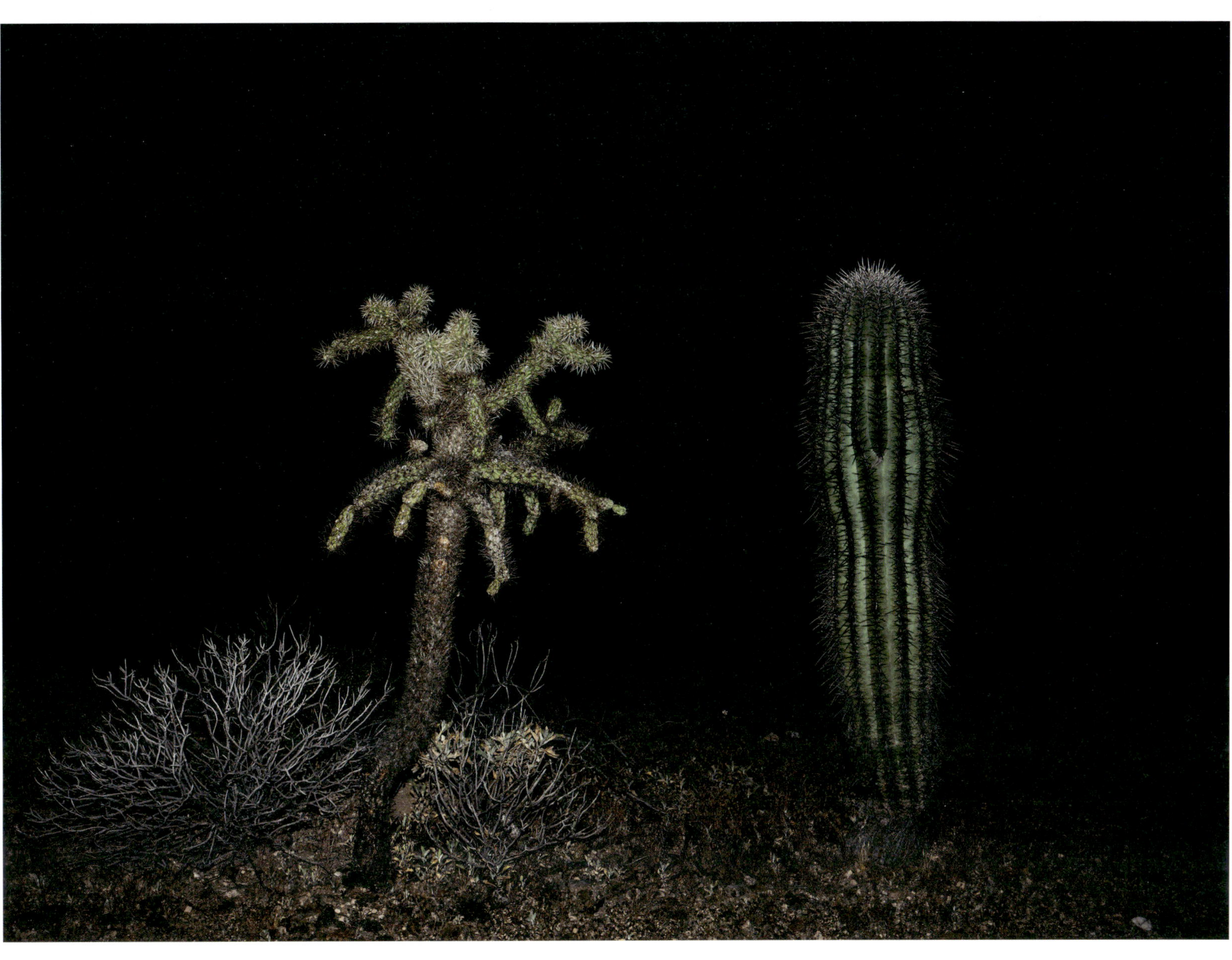

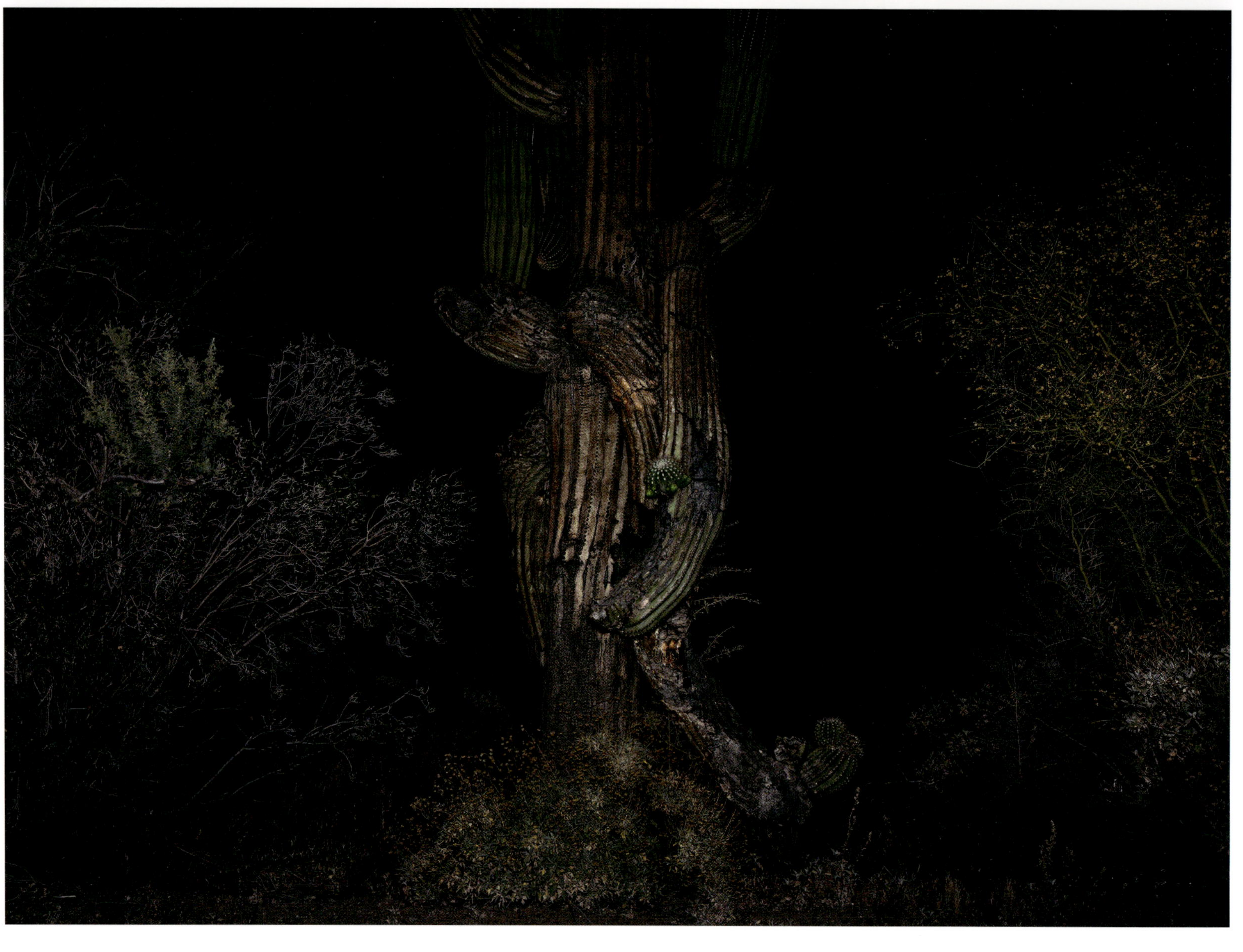

Sonoyta, Sonoran Desert, Mexico, 2019

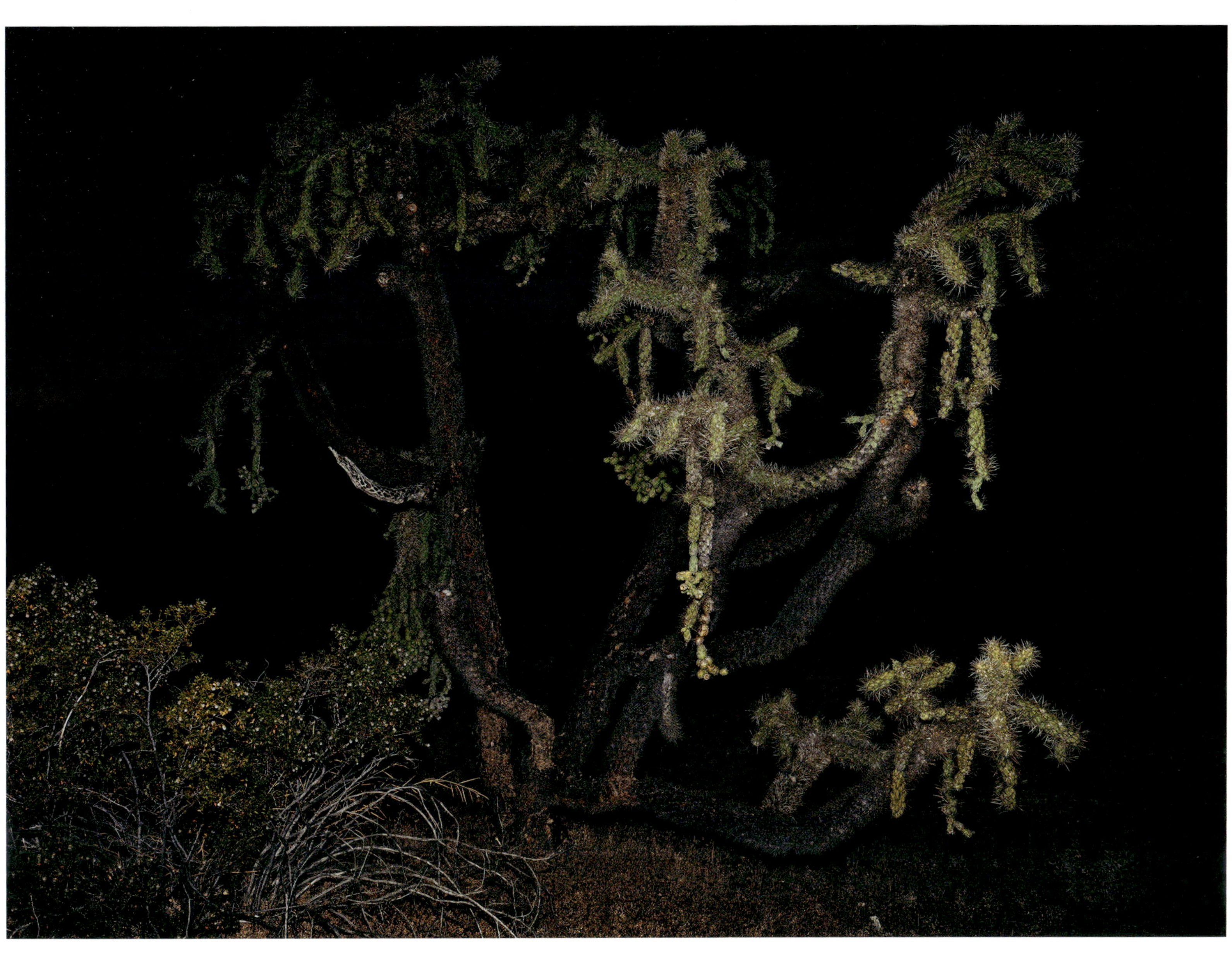

44 Tenorio Volcano National Park, Costa Rica, 2022

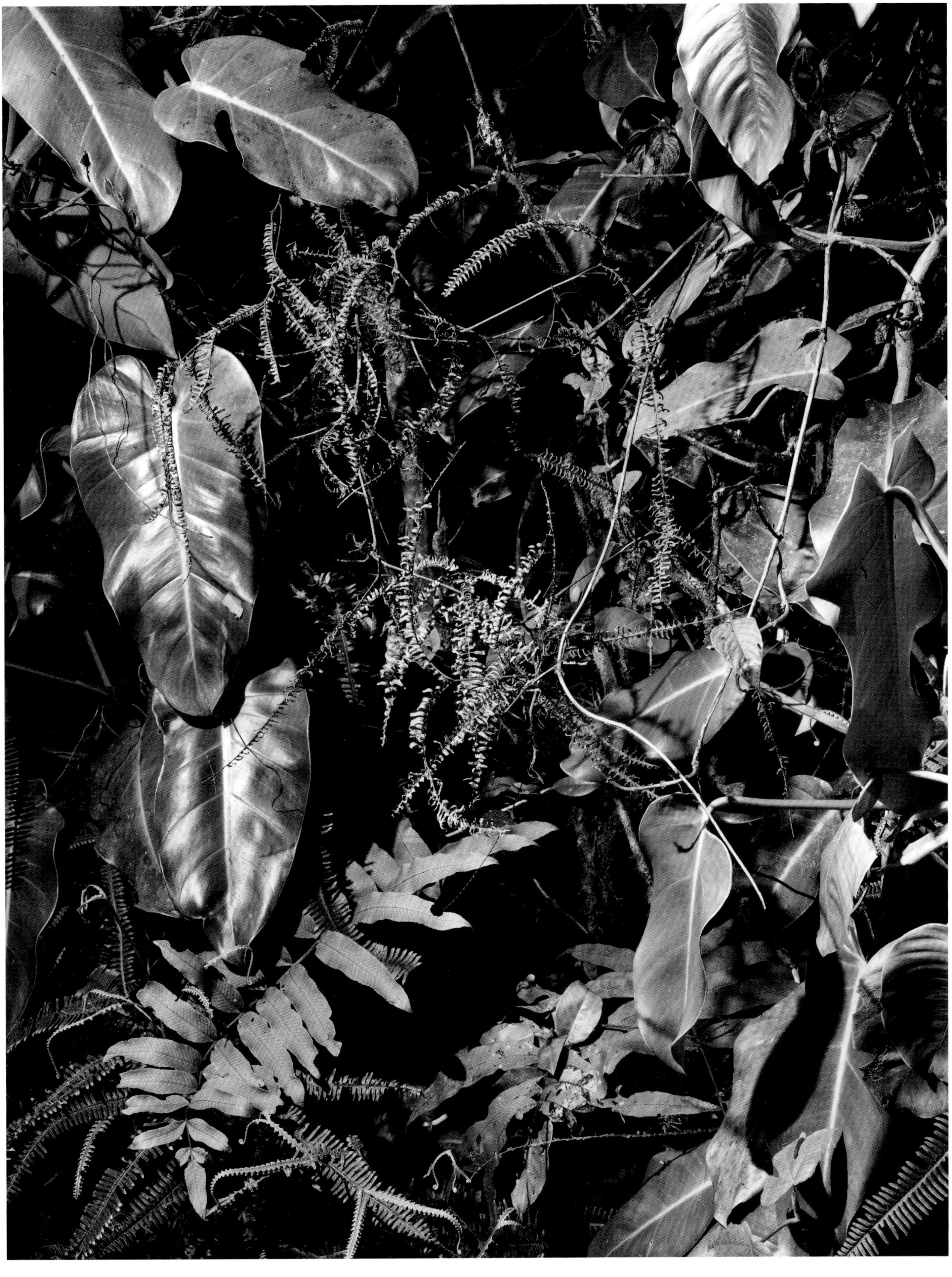

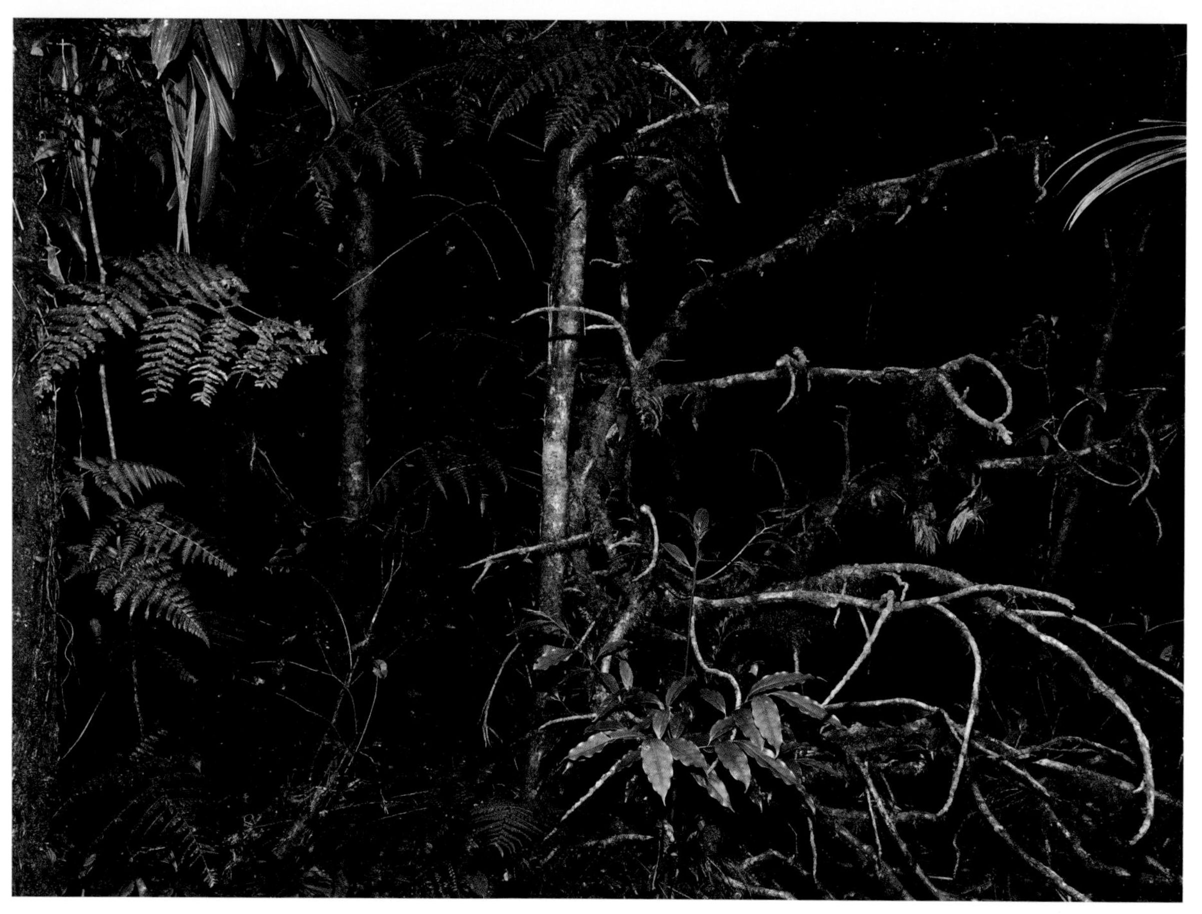

47 Monteverde Cloud Forest Biological Reserve, Costa Rica, 2022

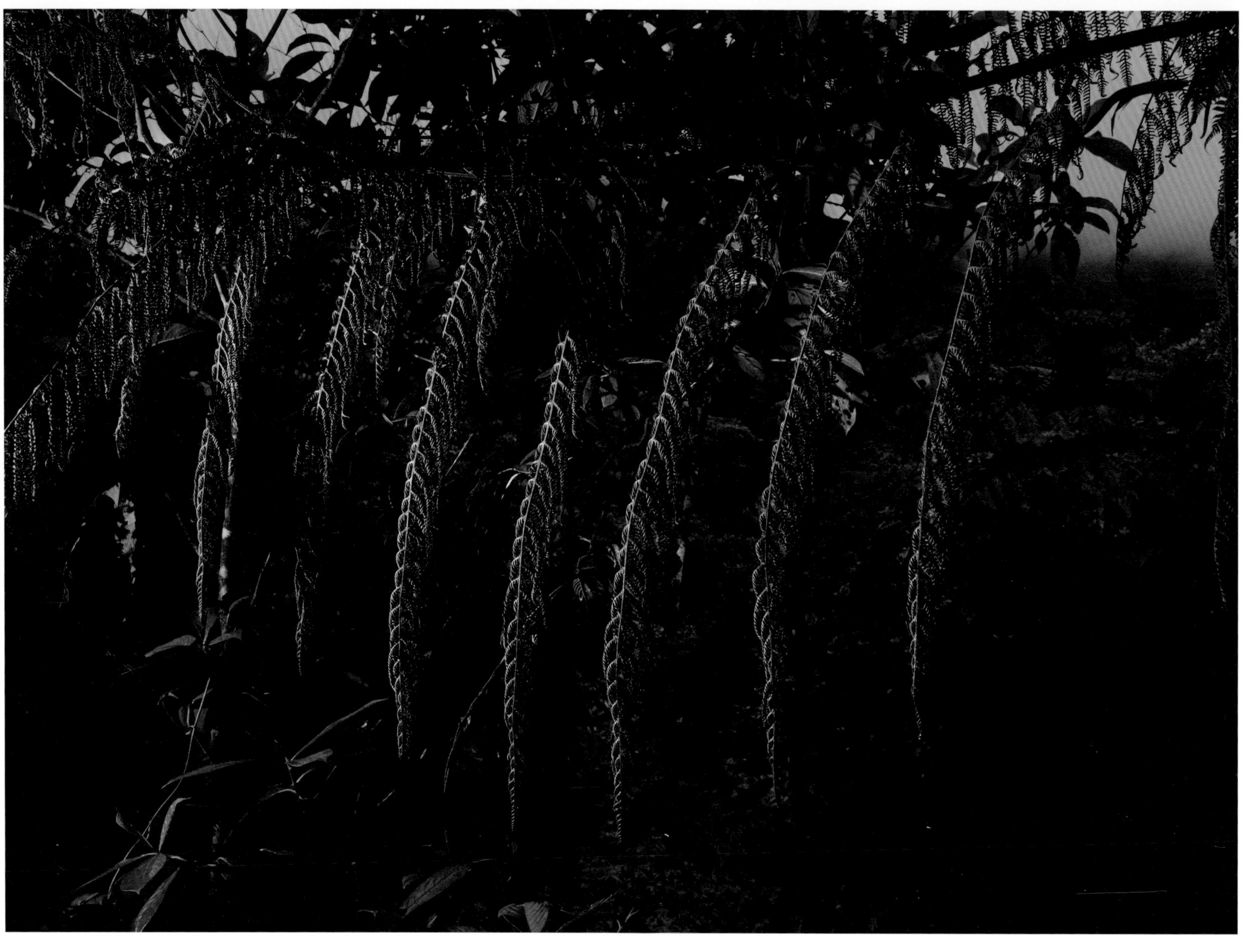

Tenorio Volcano National Park, Costa Rica, 2022

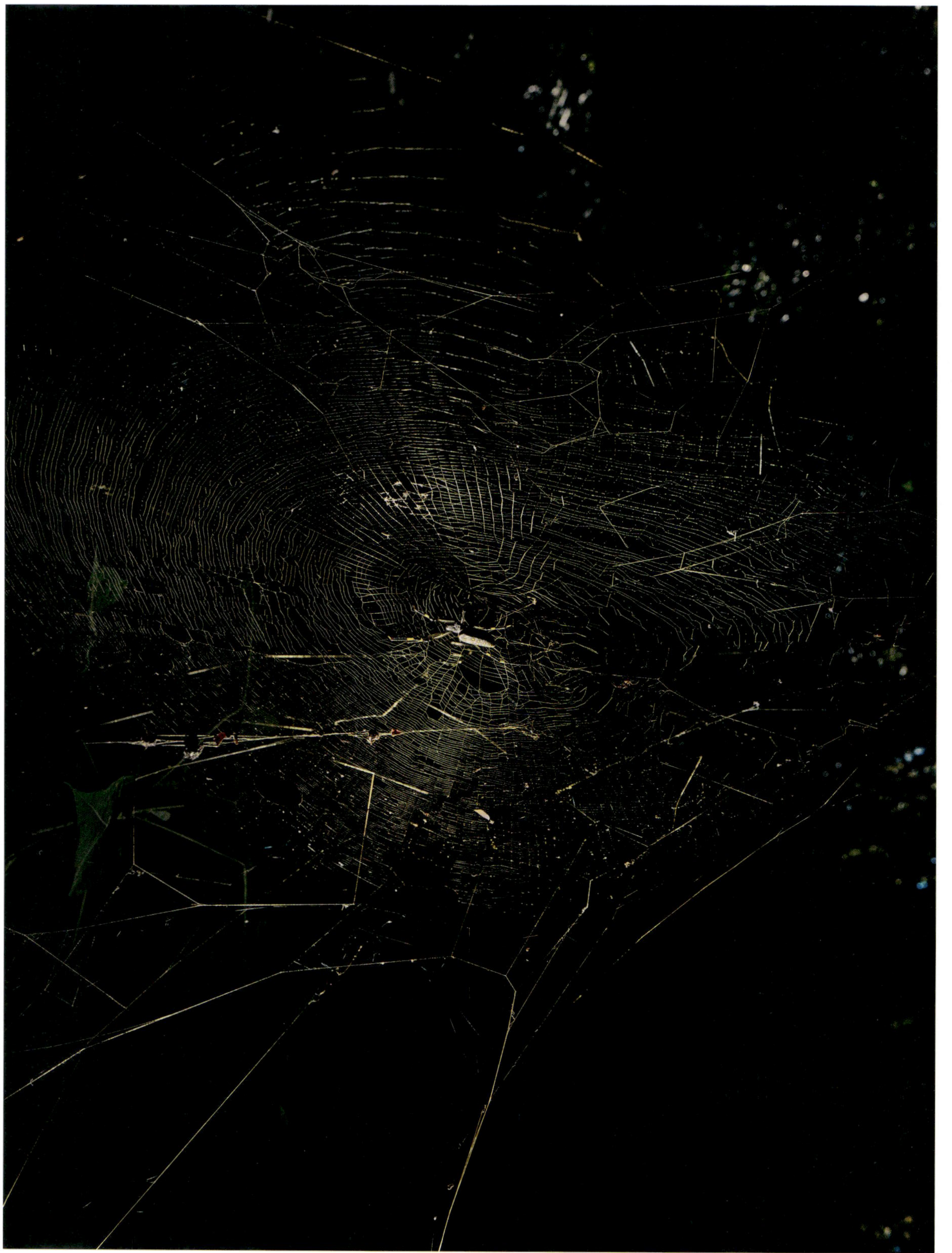

Karen Mogensen Nature Reserve, Nicoya Peninsula, Costa Rica, 2022

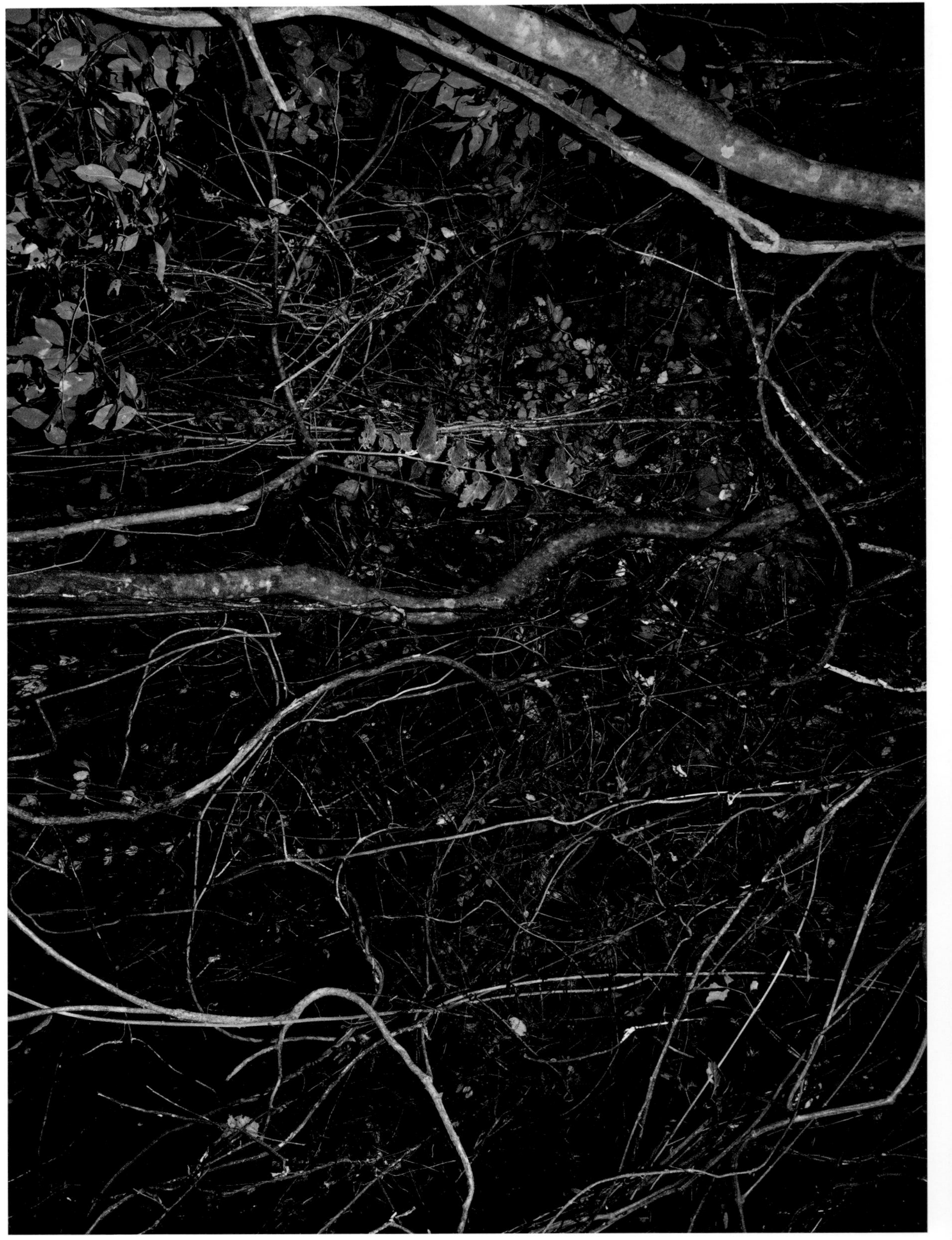

 Karen Mogensen Nature Reserve, Nicoya Peninsula, Costa Rica, 2022

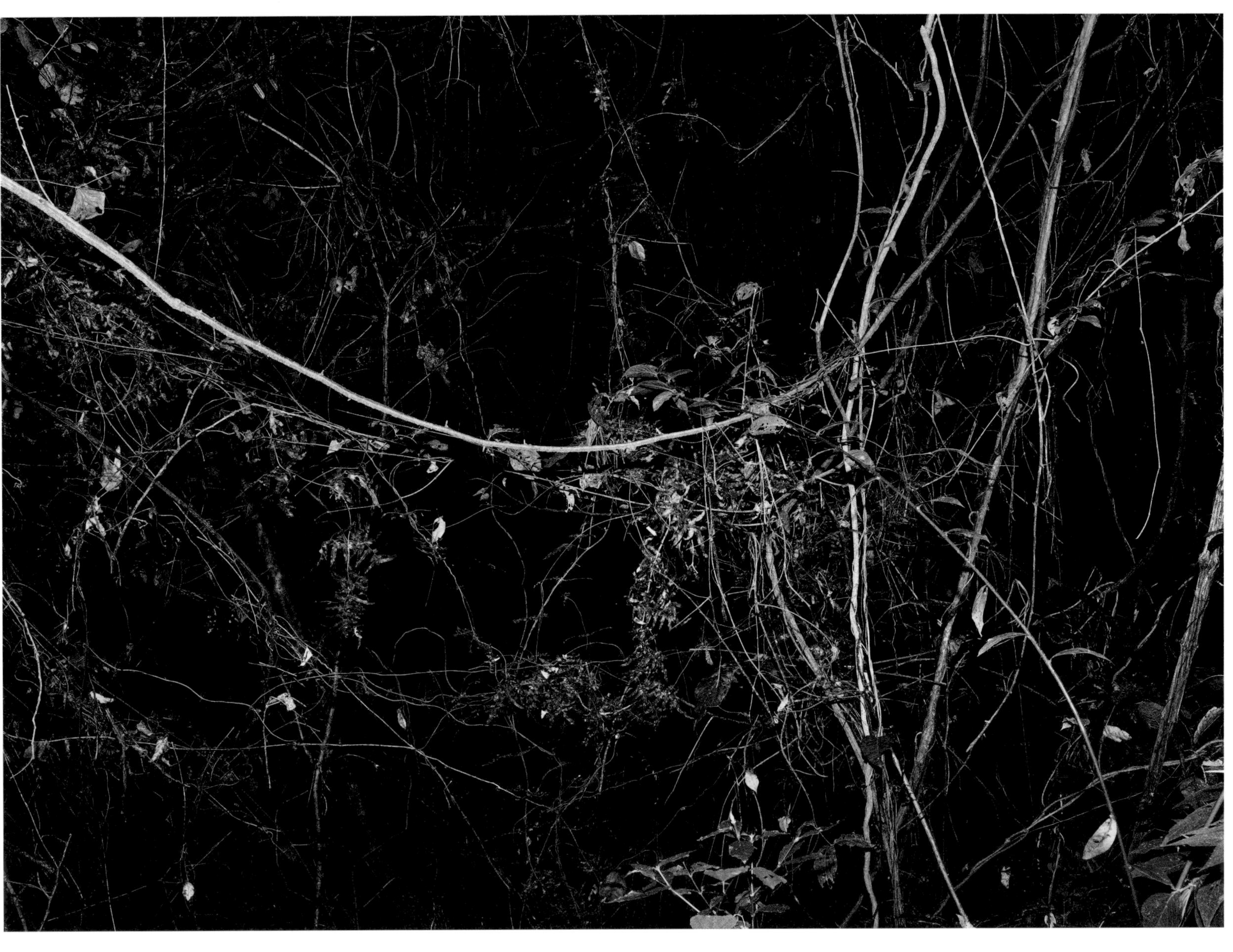

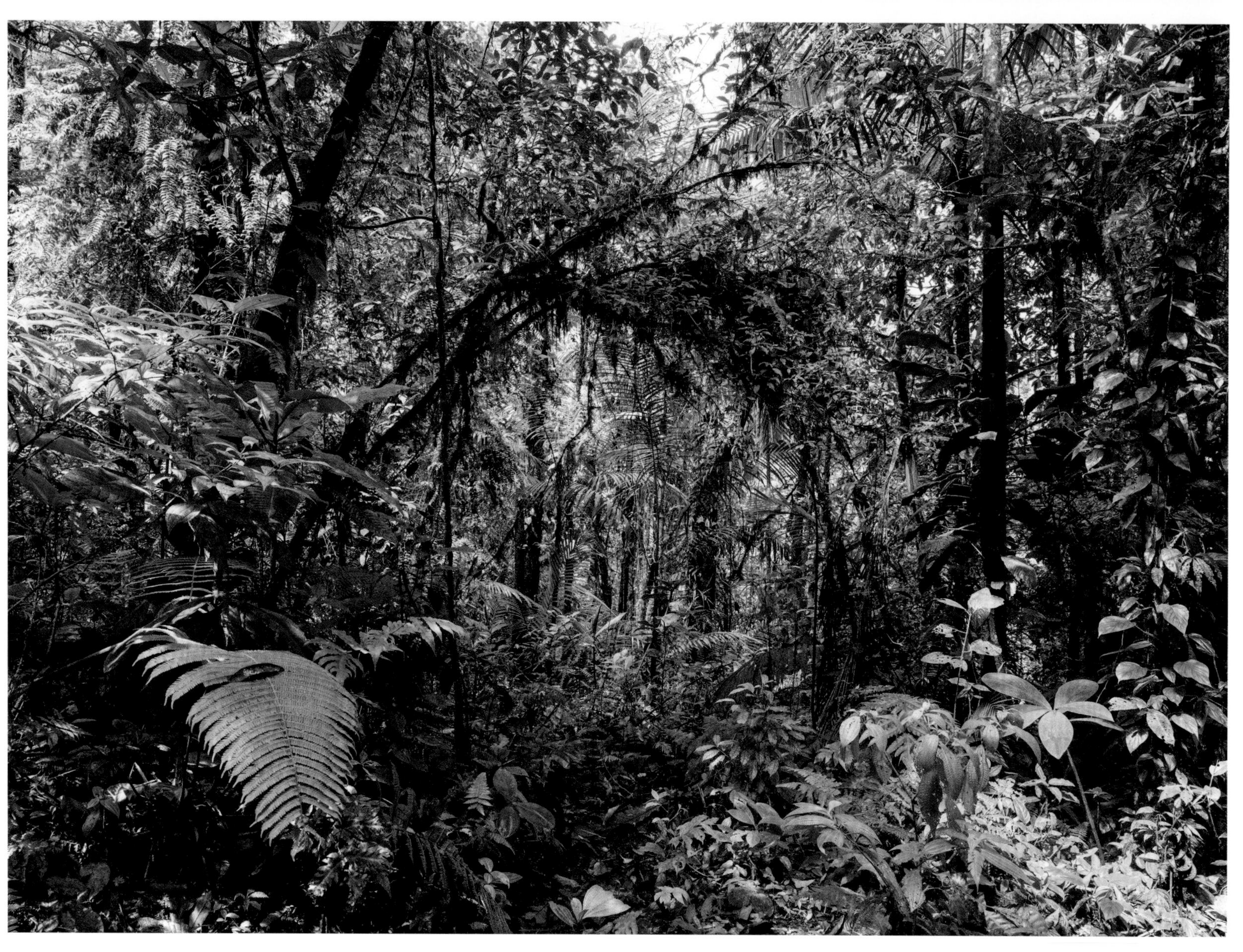

Monteverde Cloud Forest Biological Reserve, Costa Rica, 2022

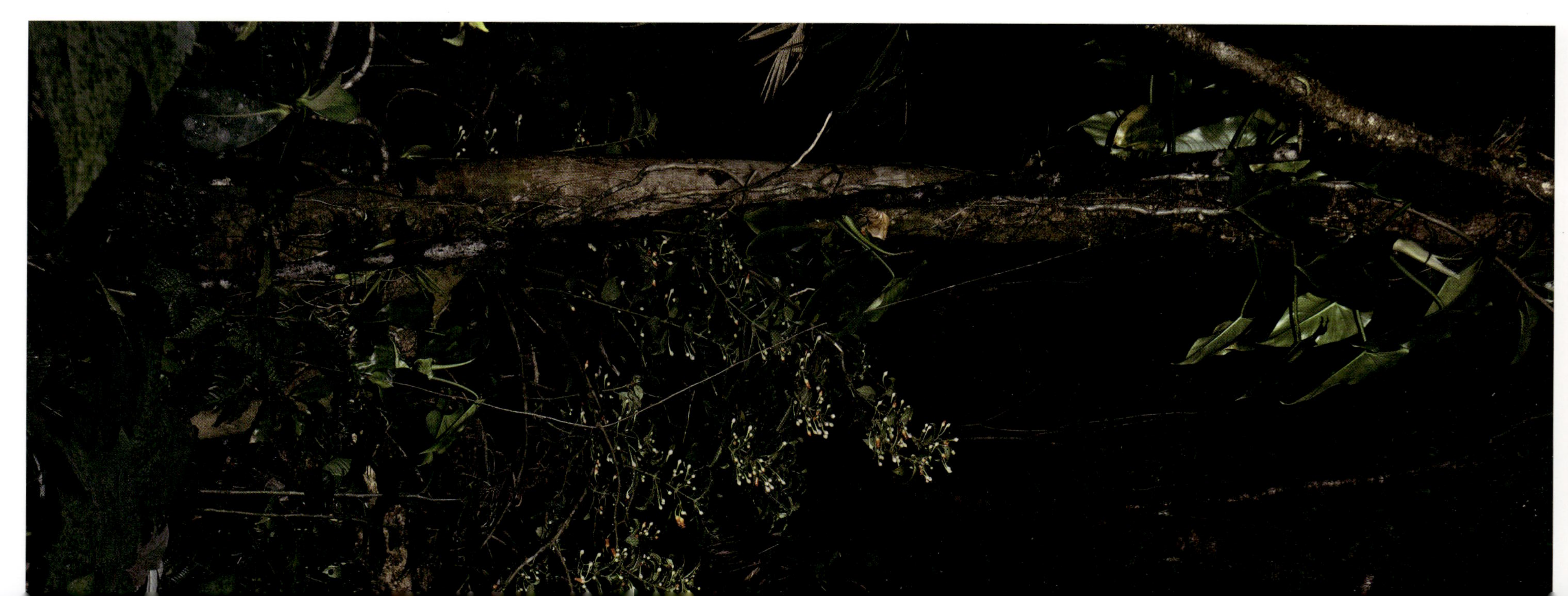

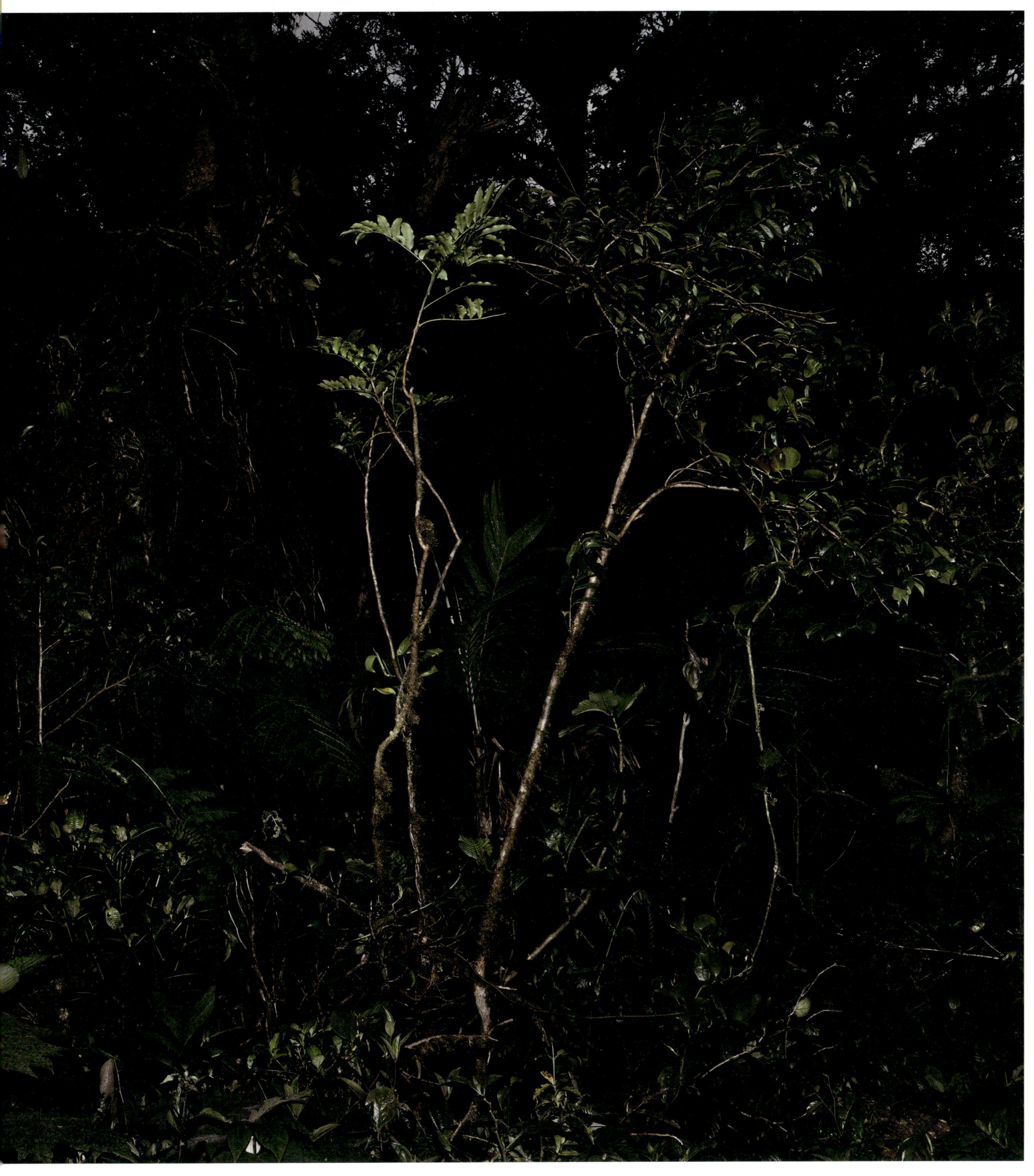

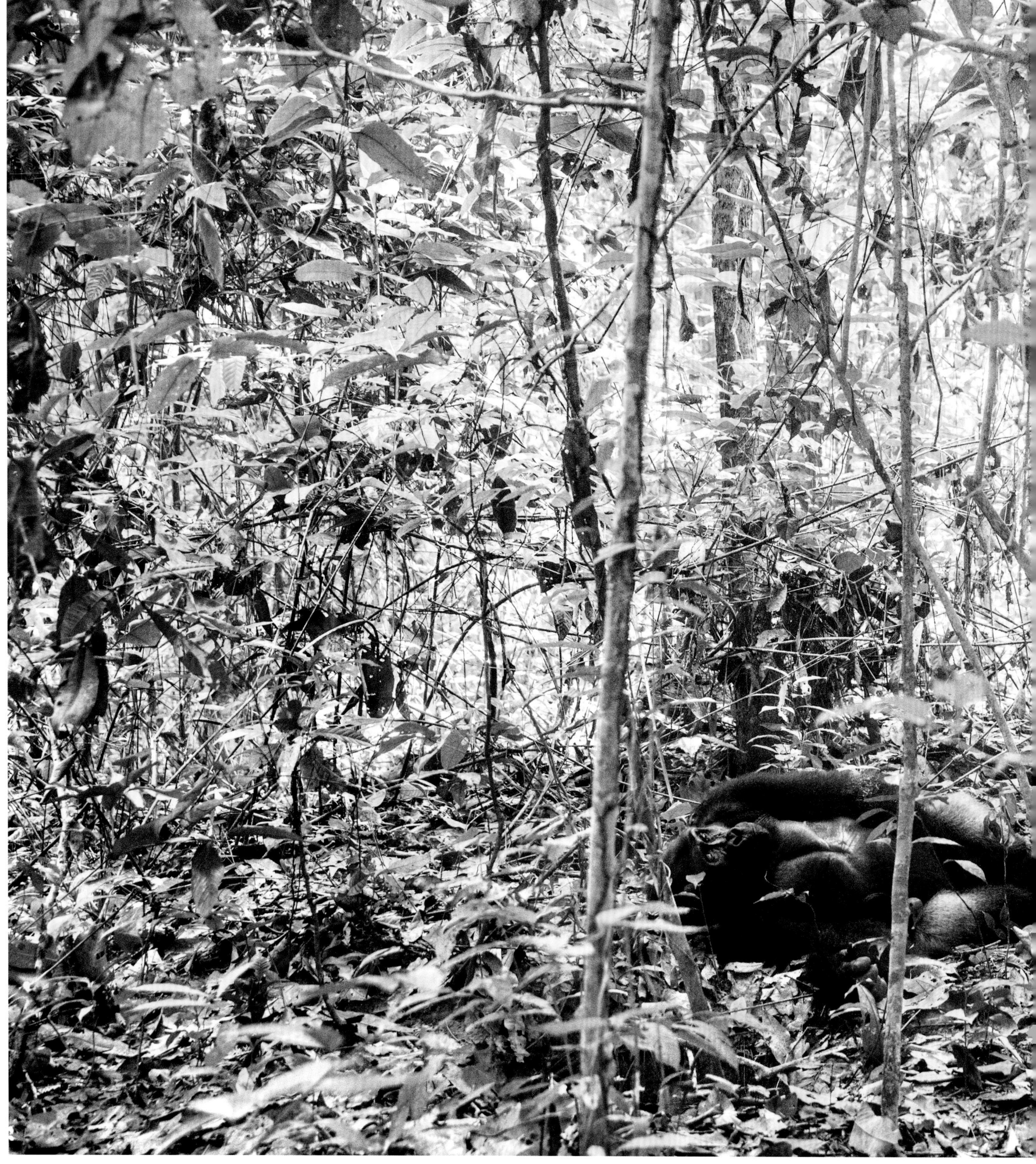

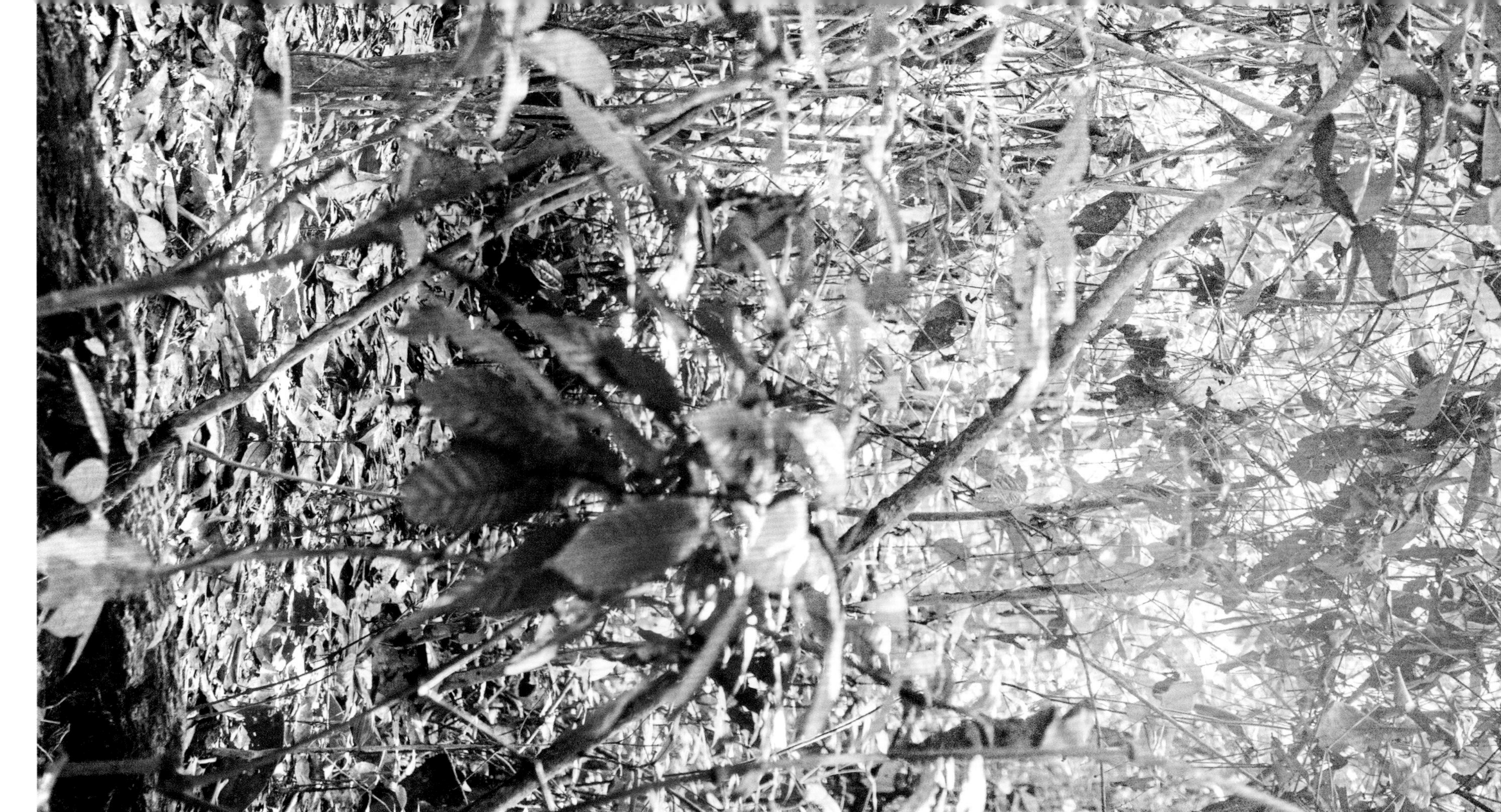

Congo-Brazzaville, 2013

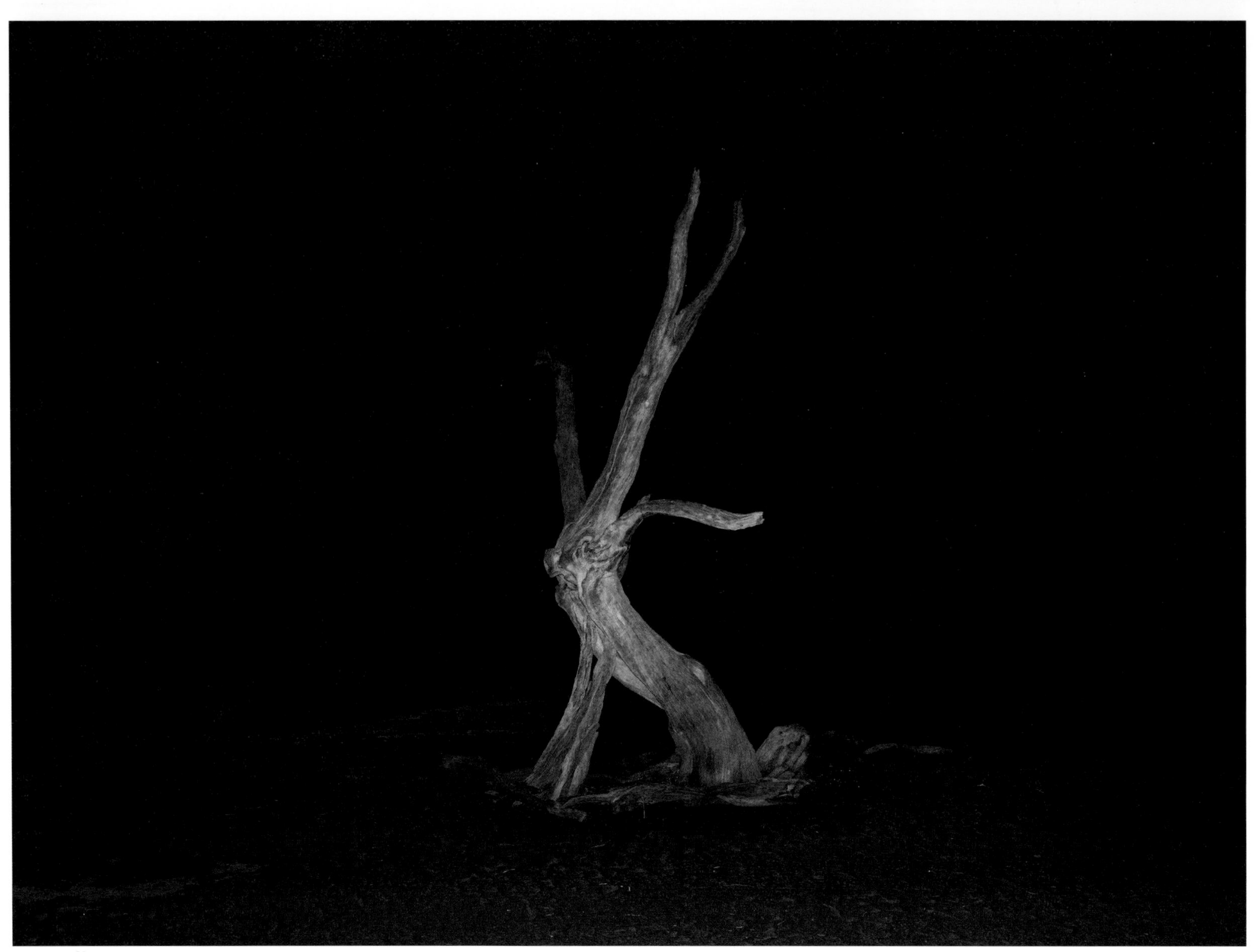

59 Sossusvlei, Namib-Naukluft National Park, Namibia, 2022

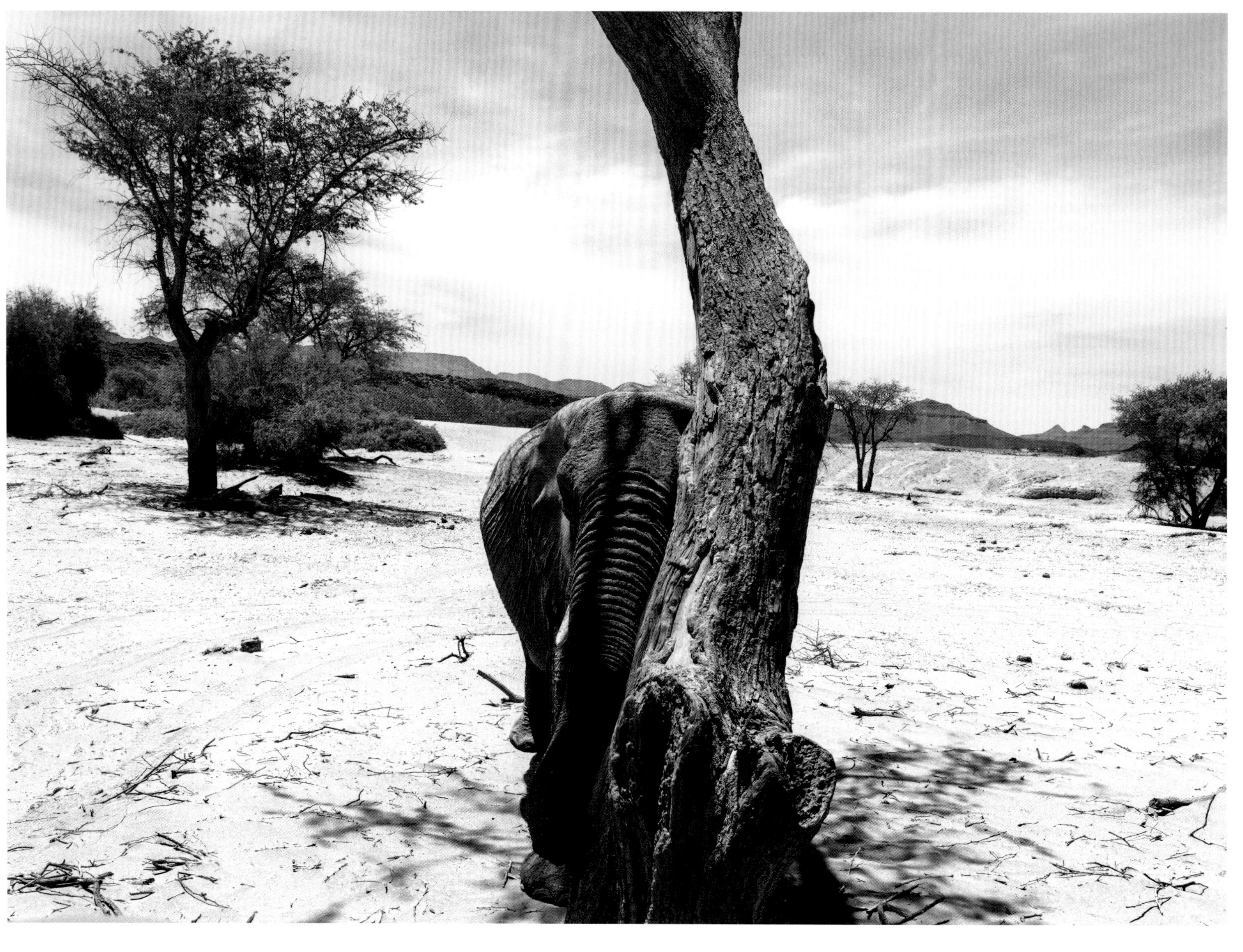

Etosha National Park, Namibia, 2022

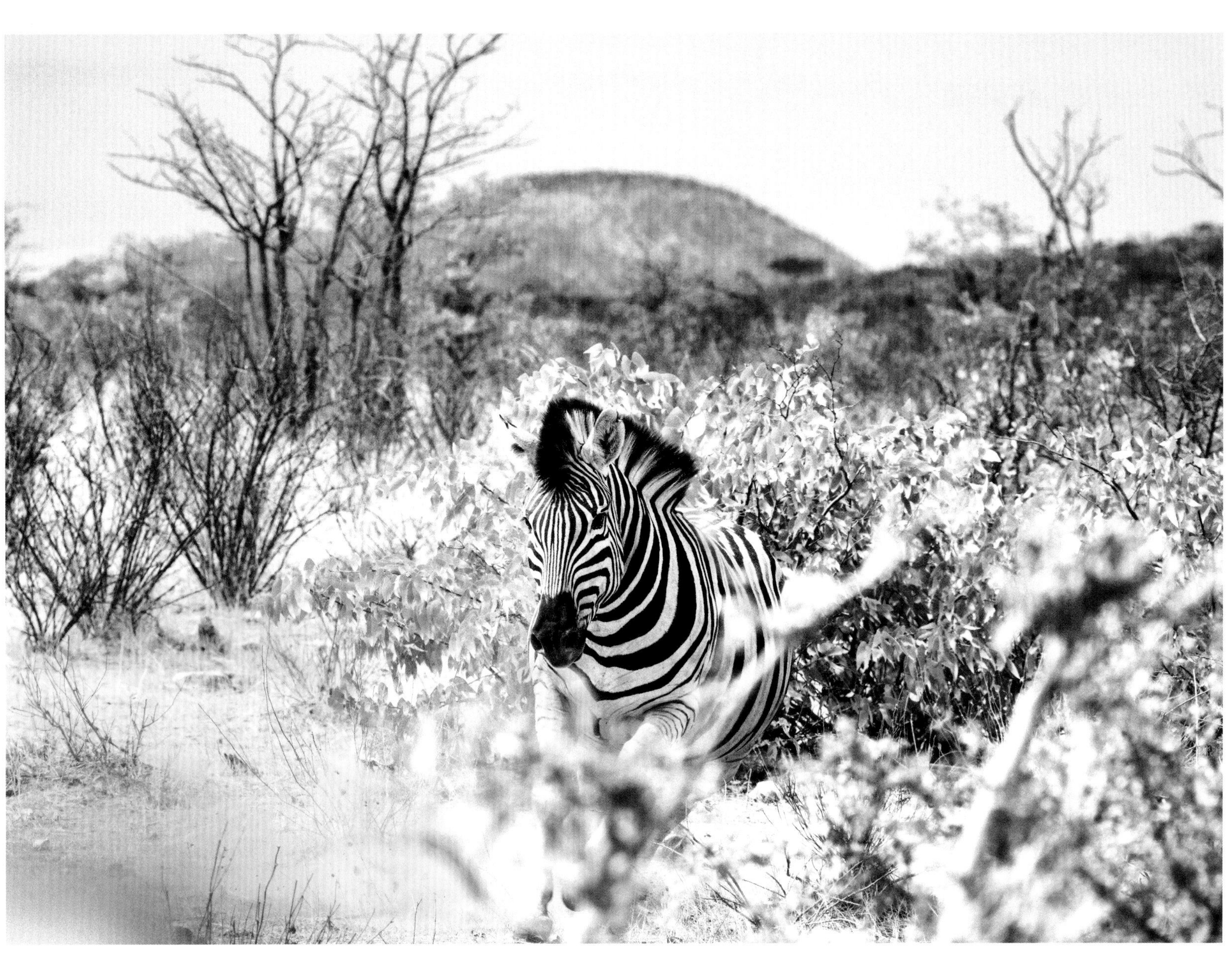

Sossusvlei, Namib-Naukluft National Park, Namibia, 2022

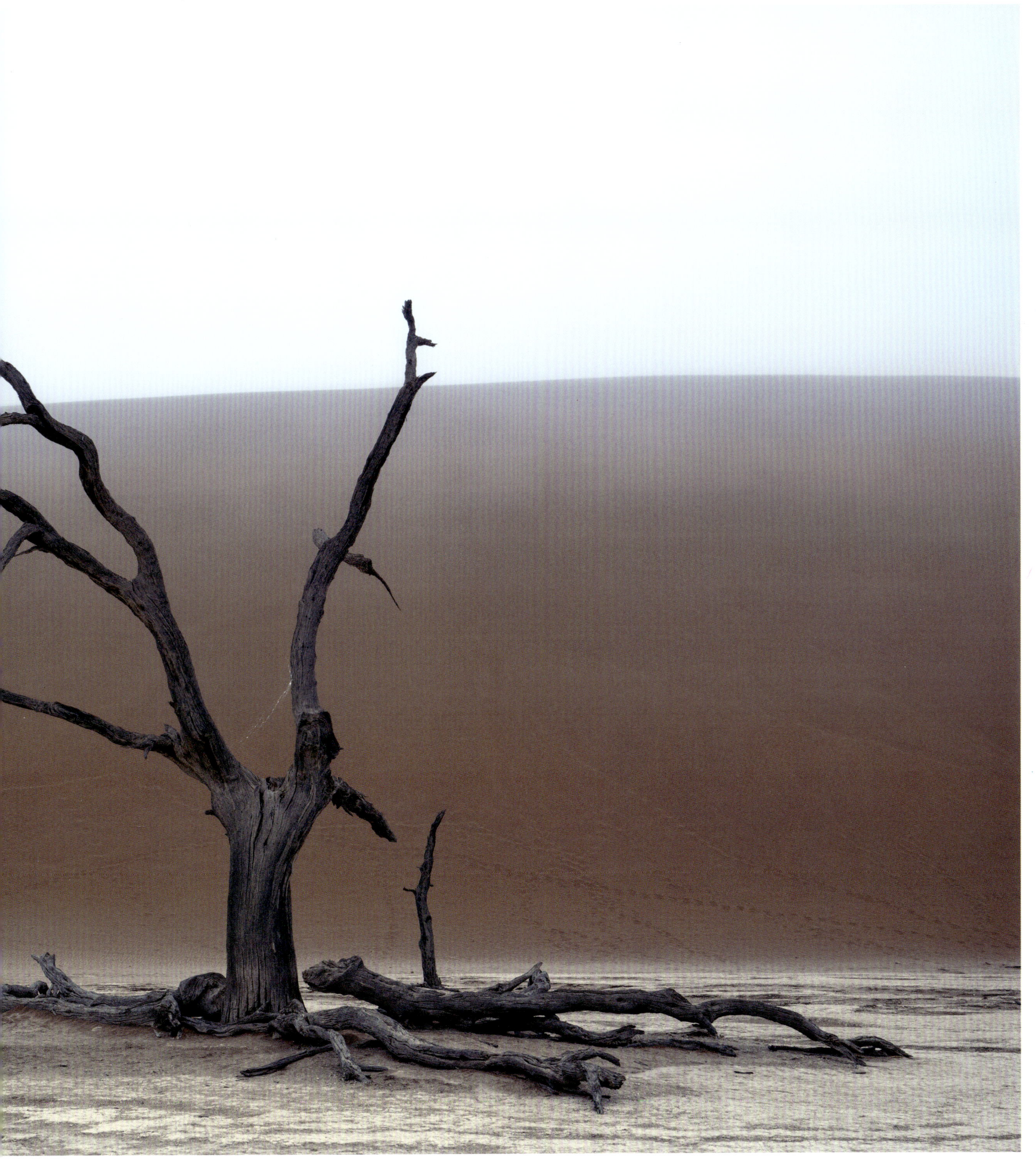

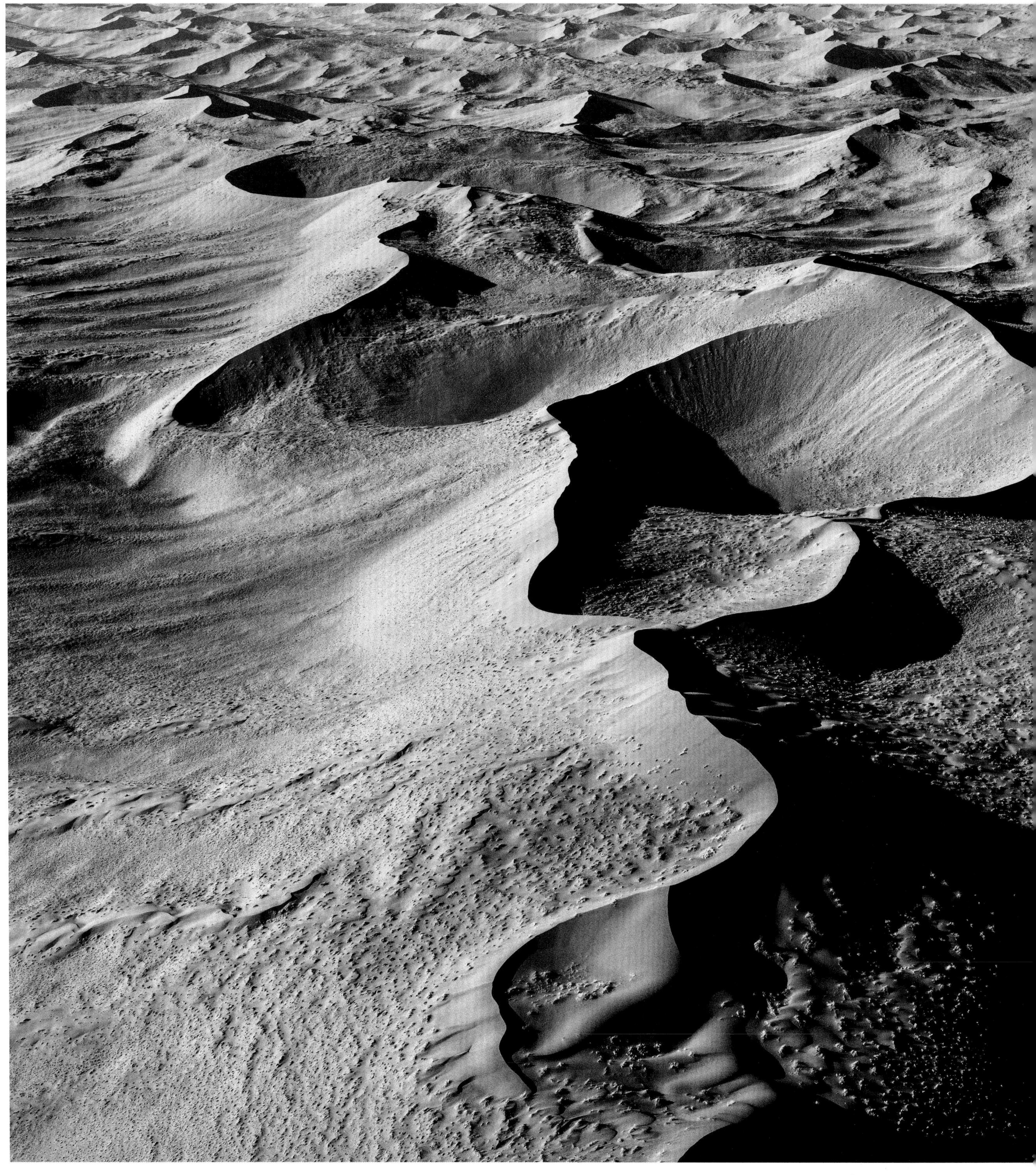

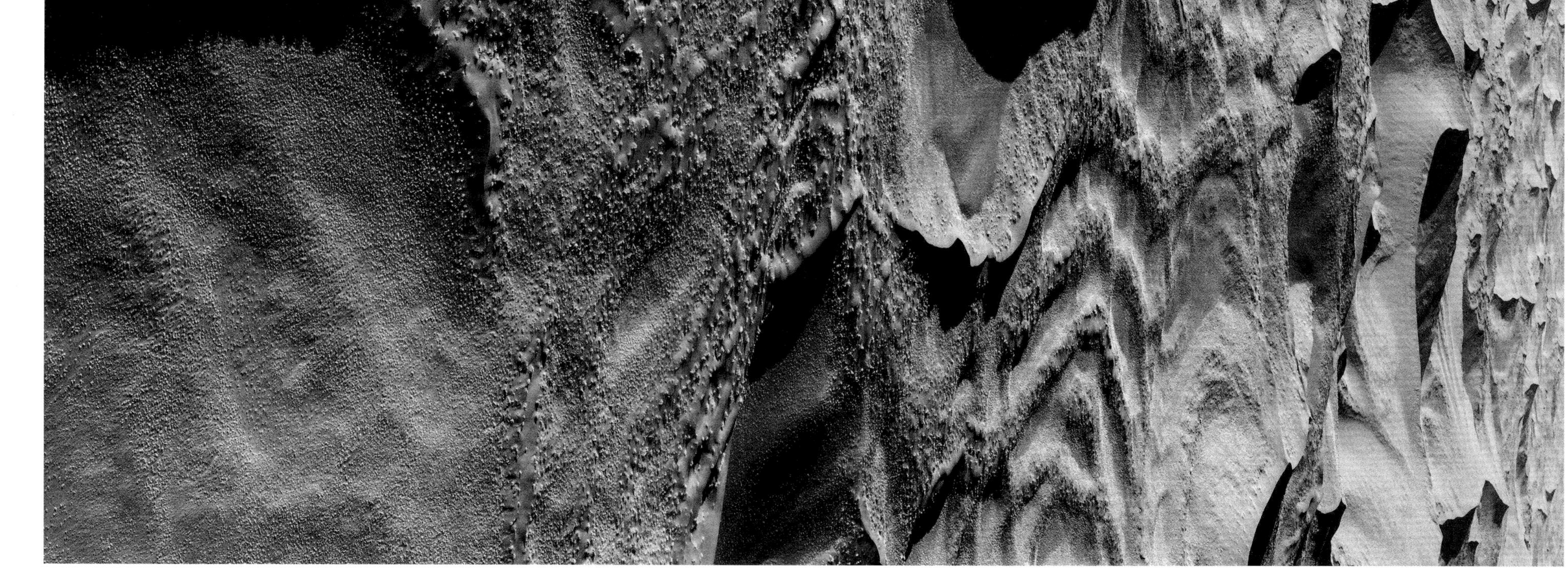

Namib-Naukluft National Park, Namibia, 2022

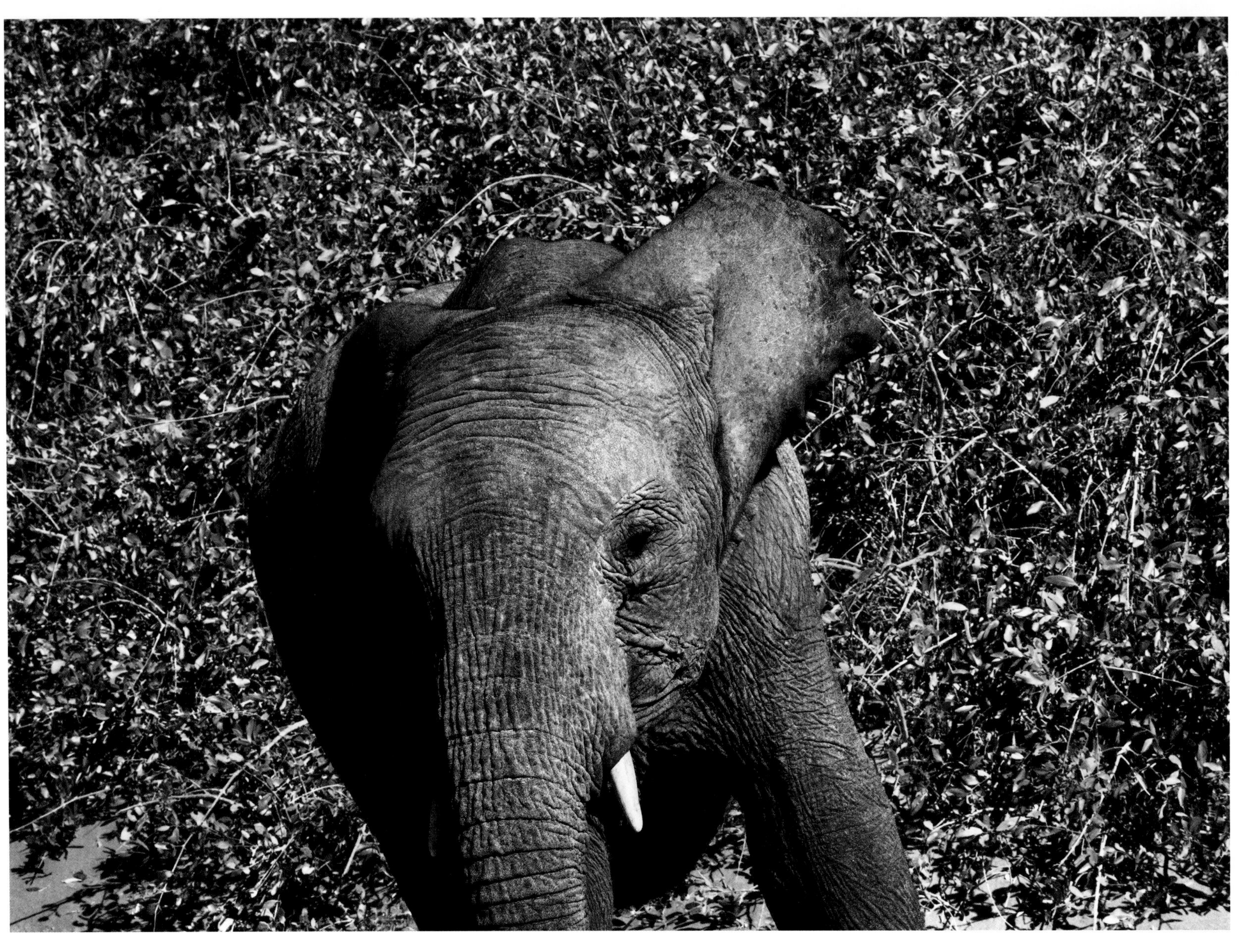

Etosha National Park, Namibia, 2022

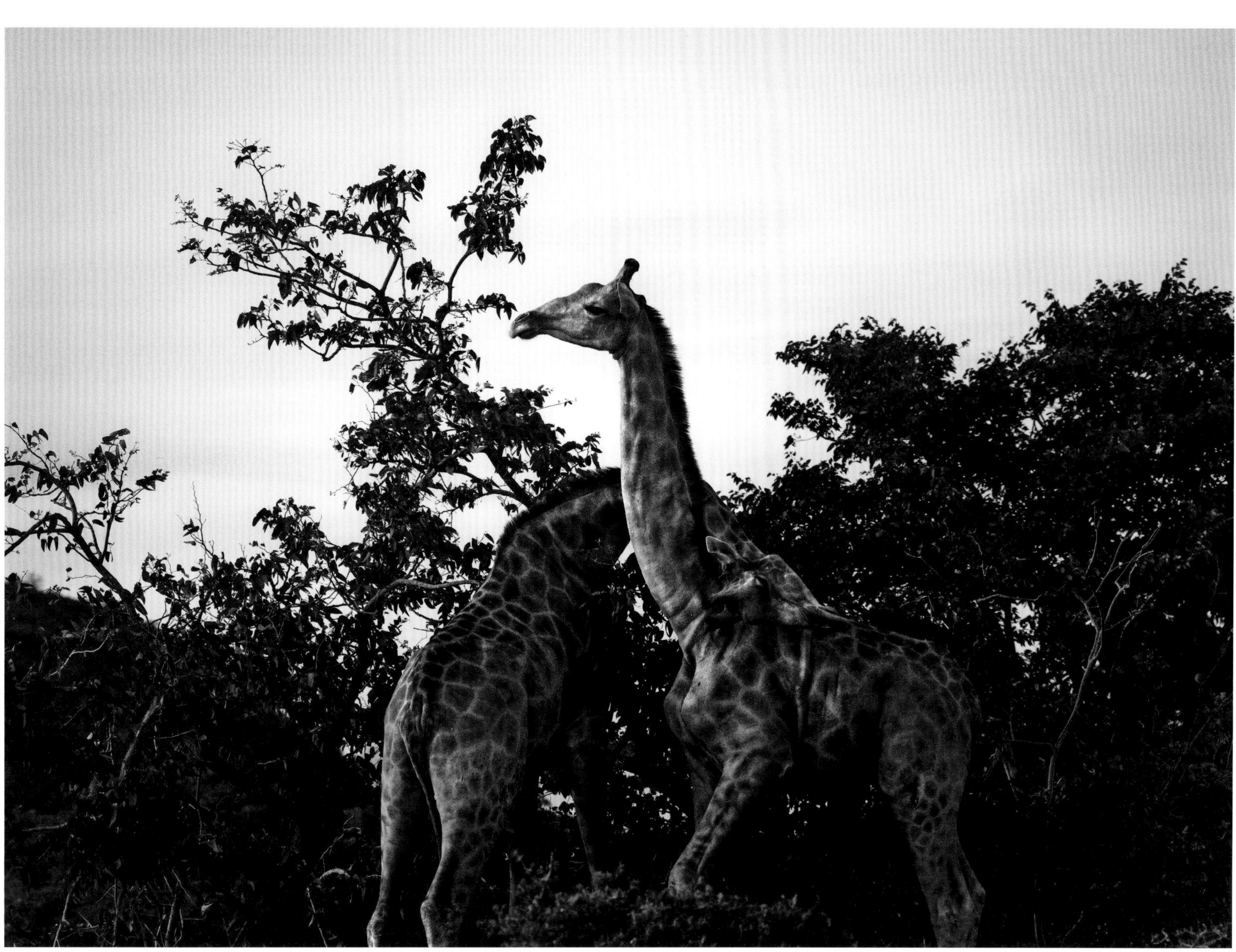

Palmwag Concession, Damaraland, Namibia, 2022

Namib-Naukluft National Park, Namibia, 2022

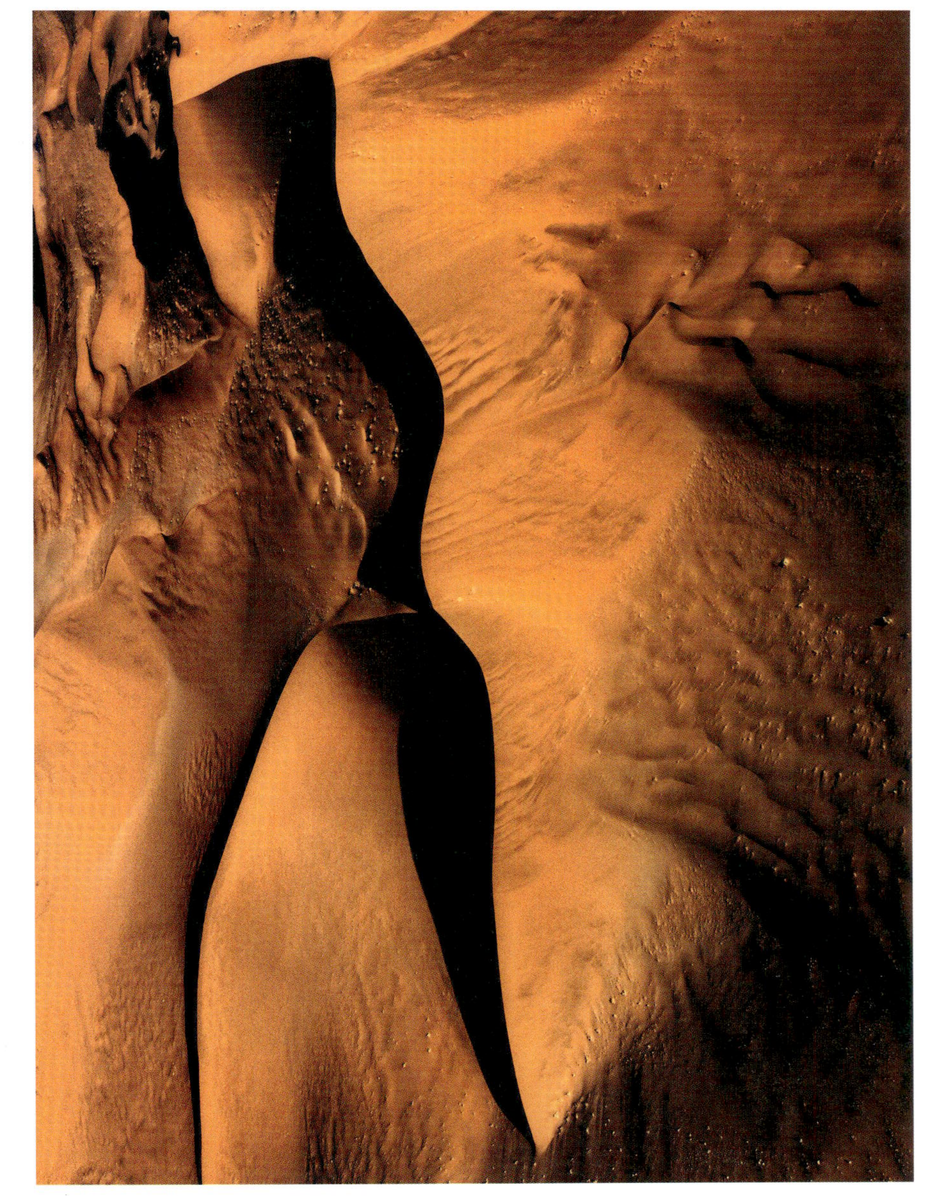

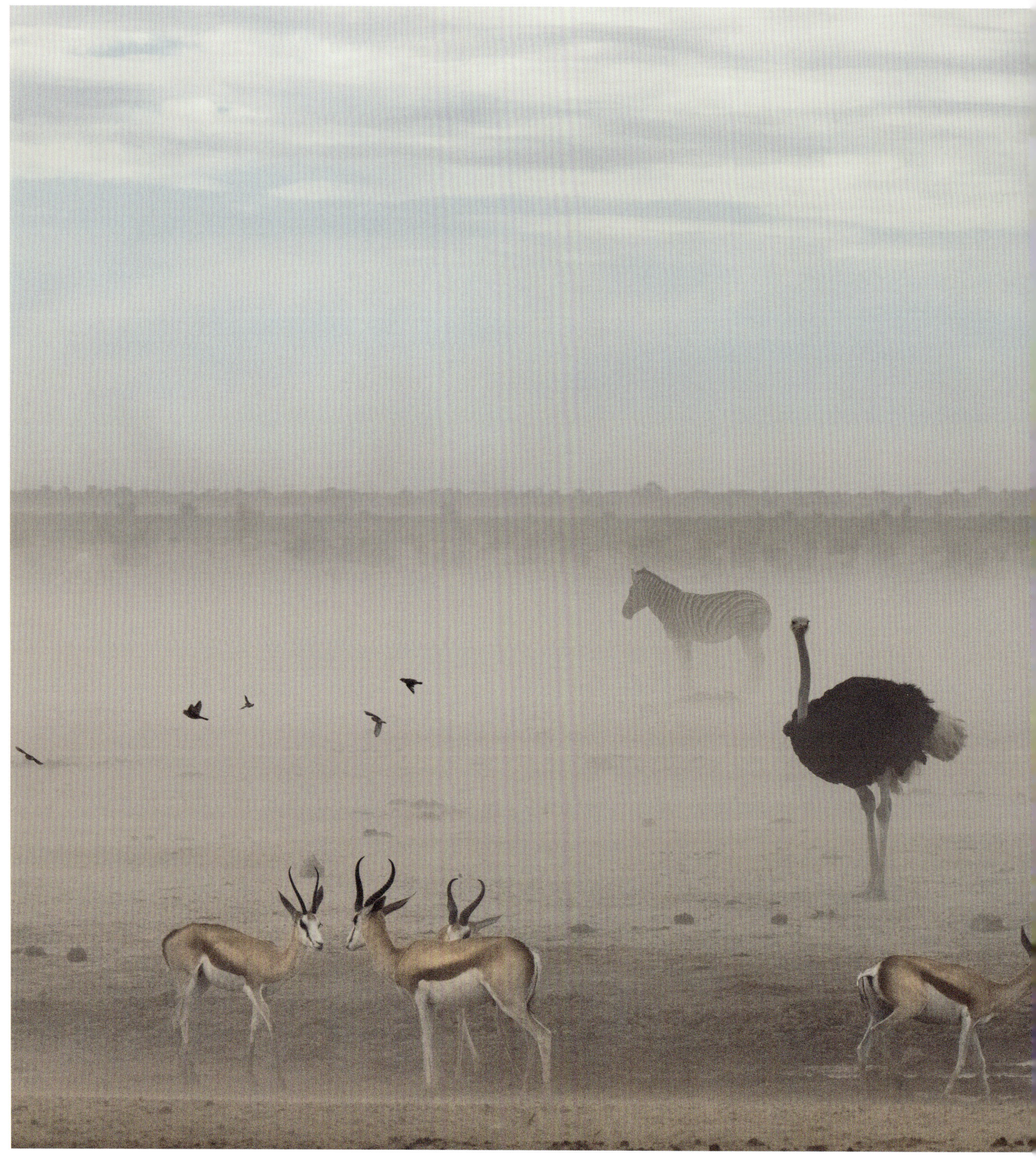

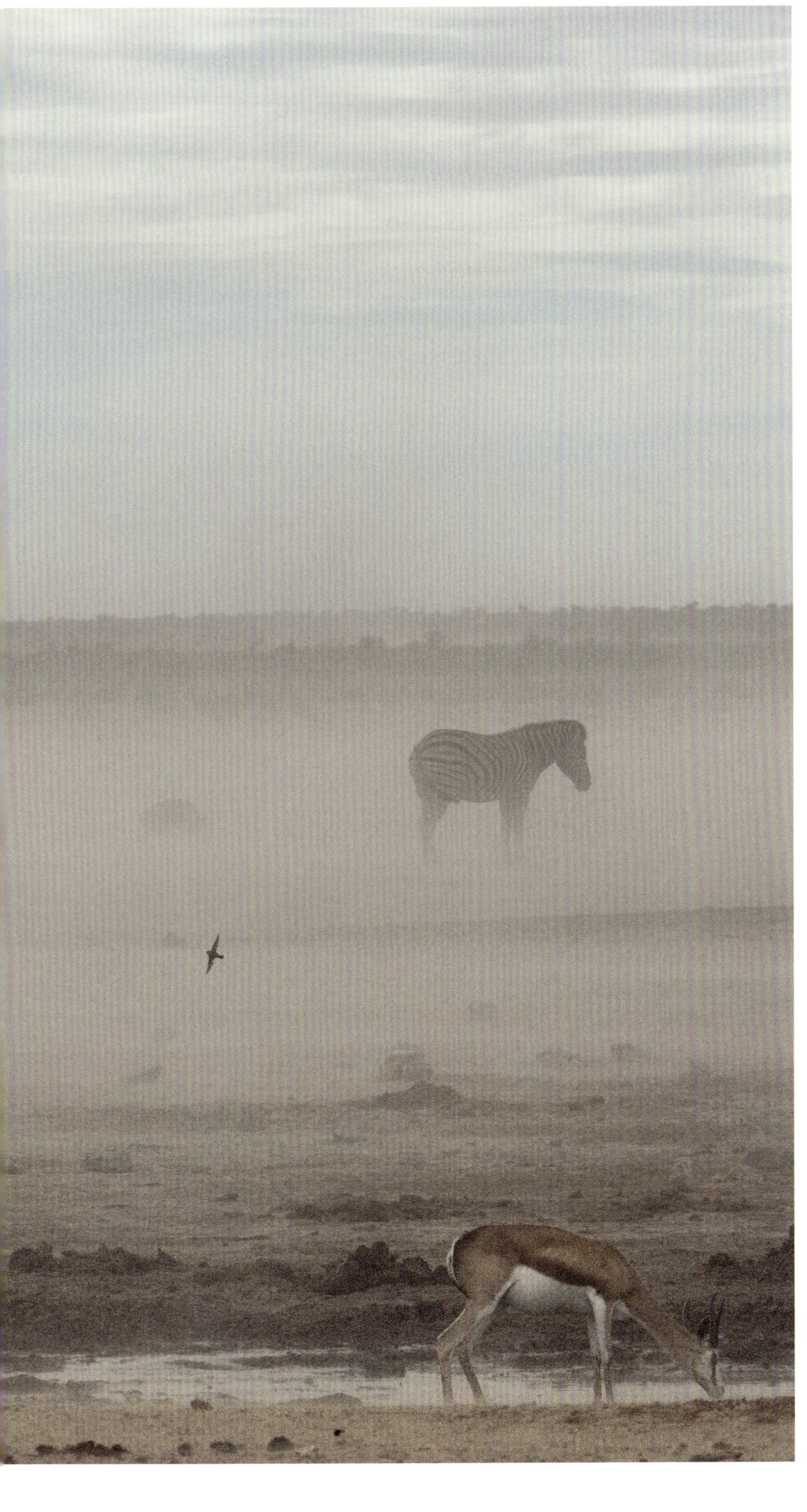

Etosha National Park, Namibia, 2022

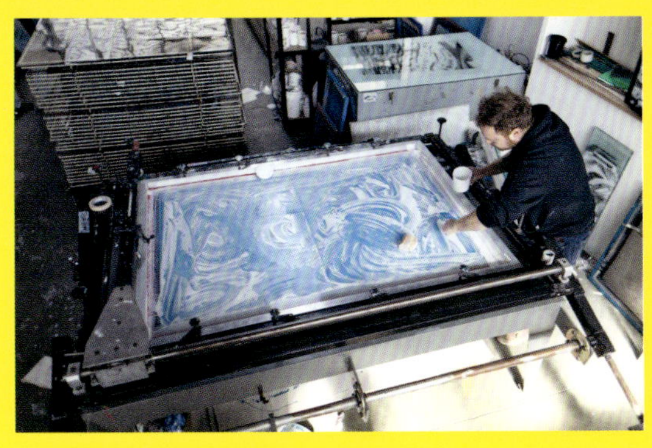

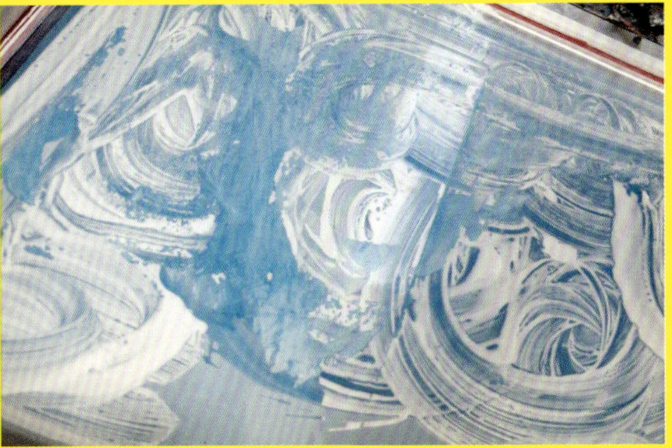

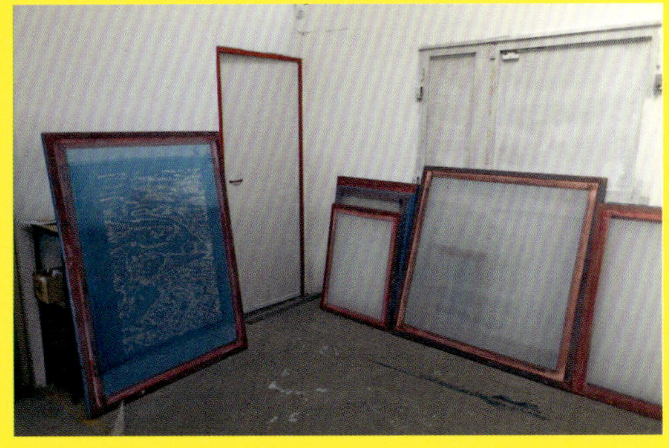

Making of

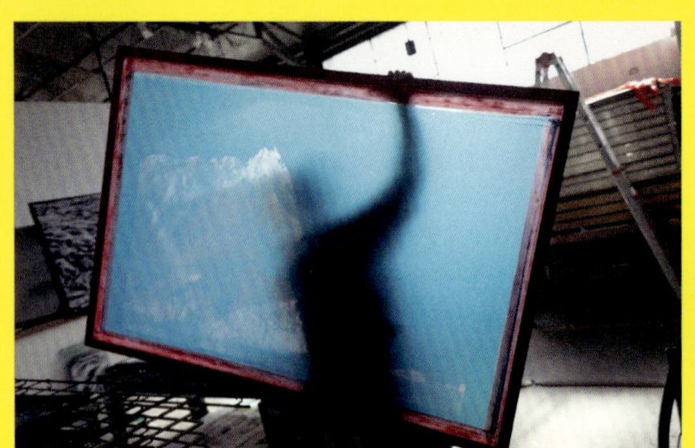
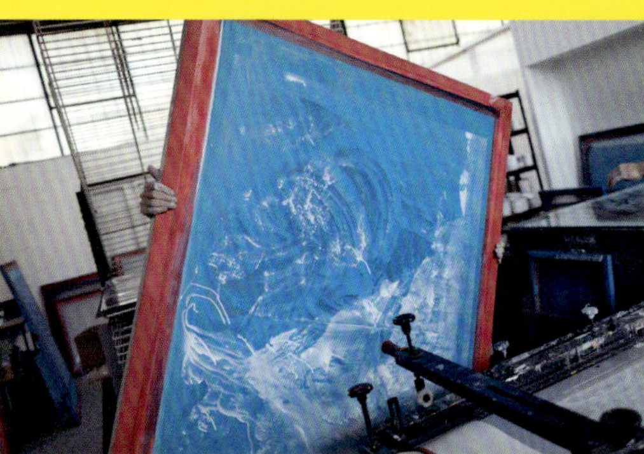

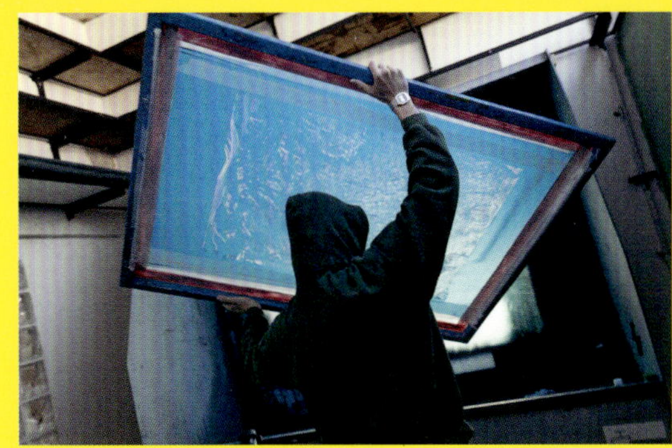
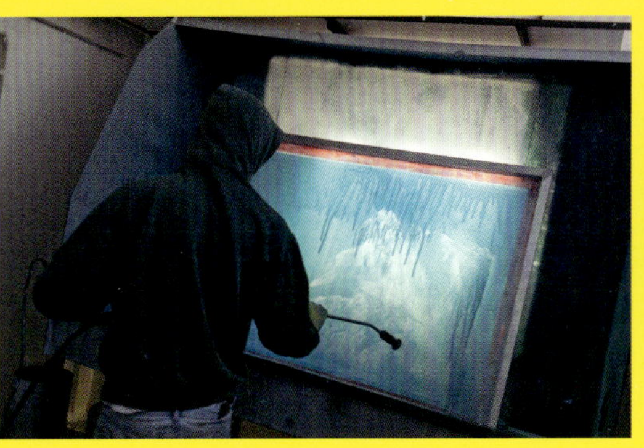
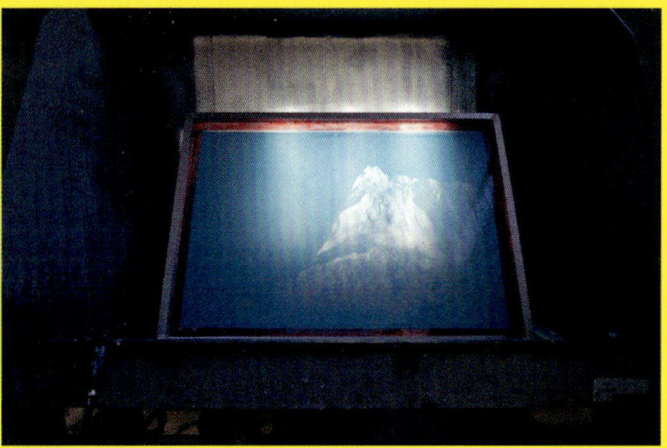

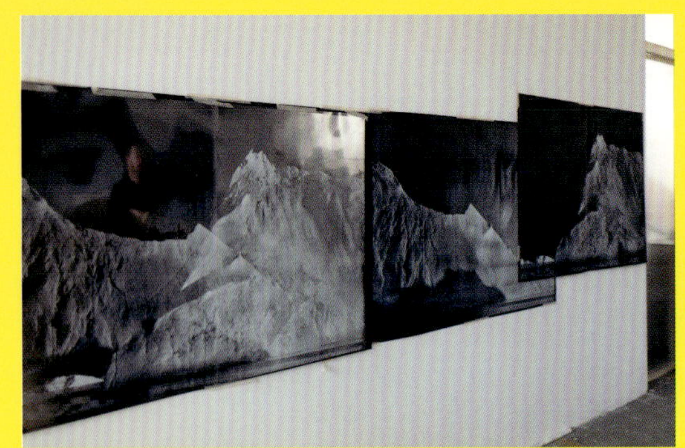

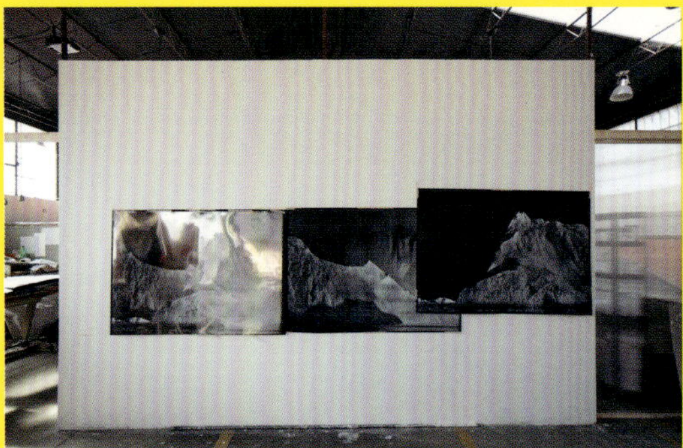

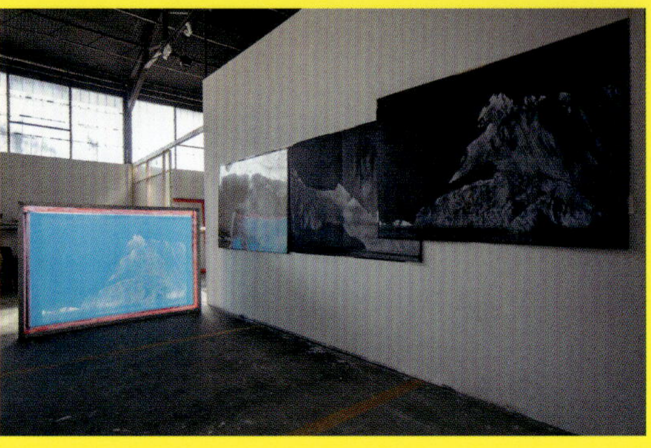

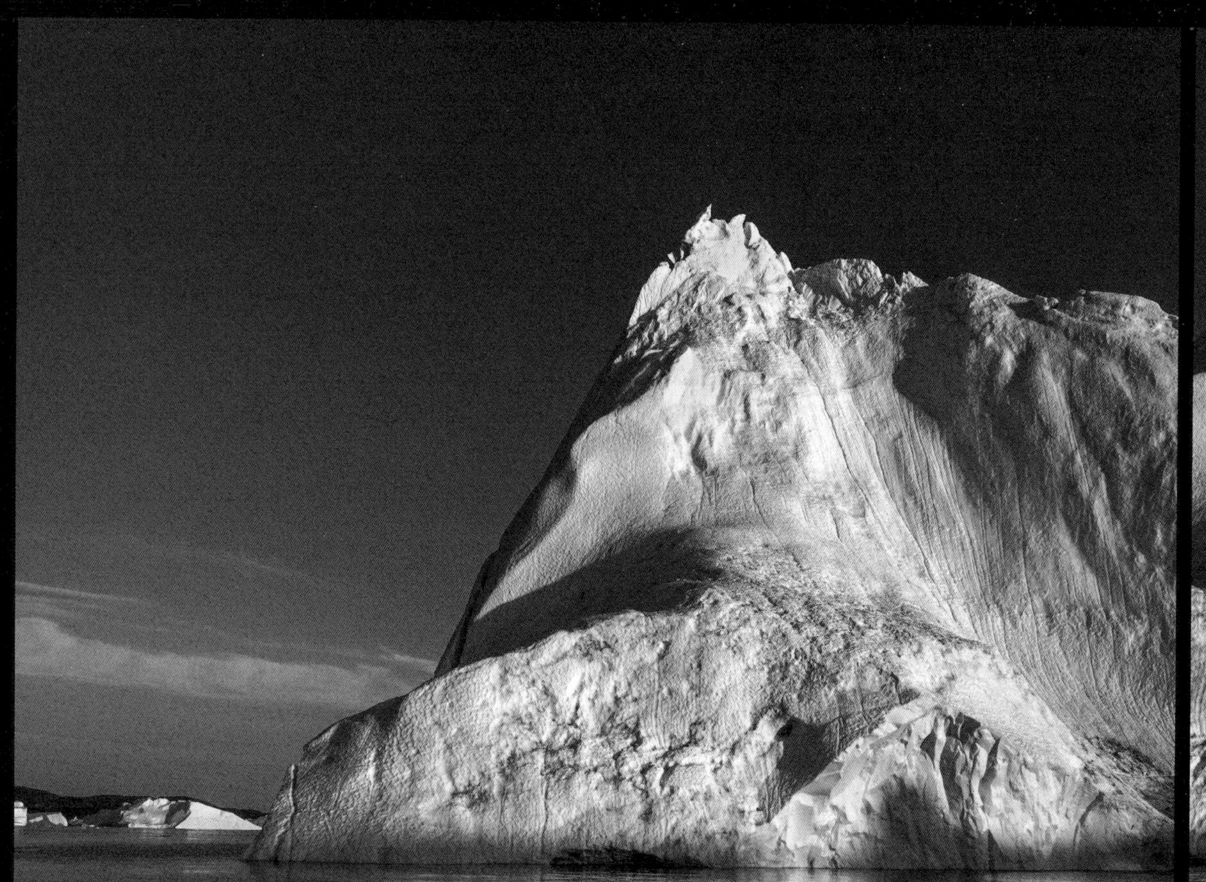

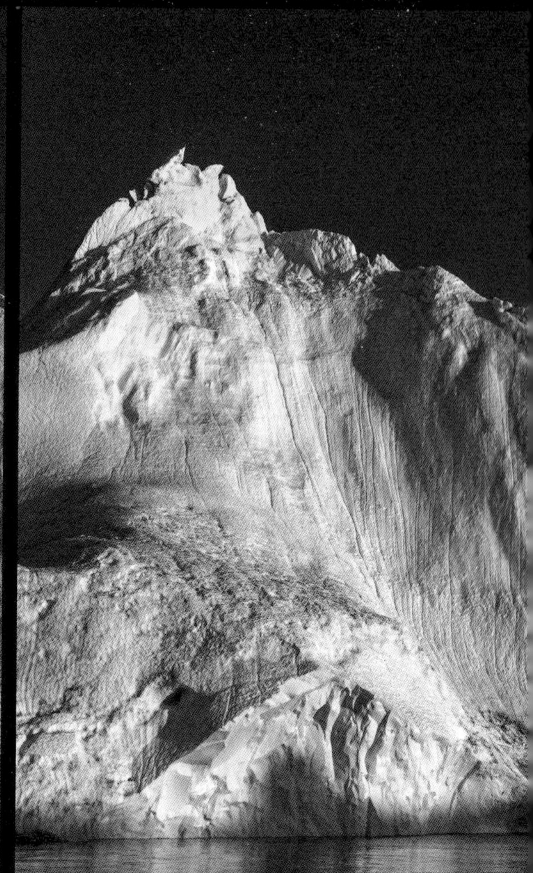

Disko Bay, Ilulissat, Greenland, 2021

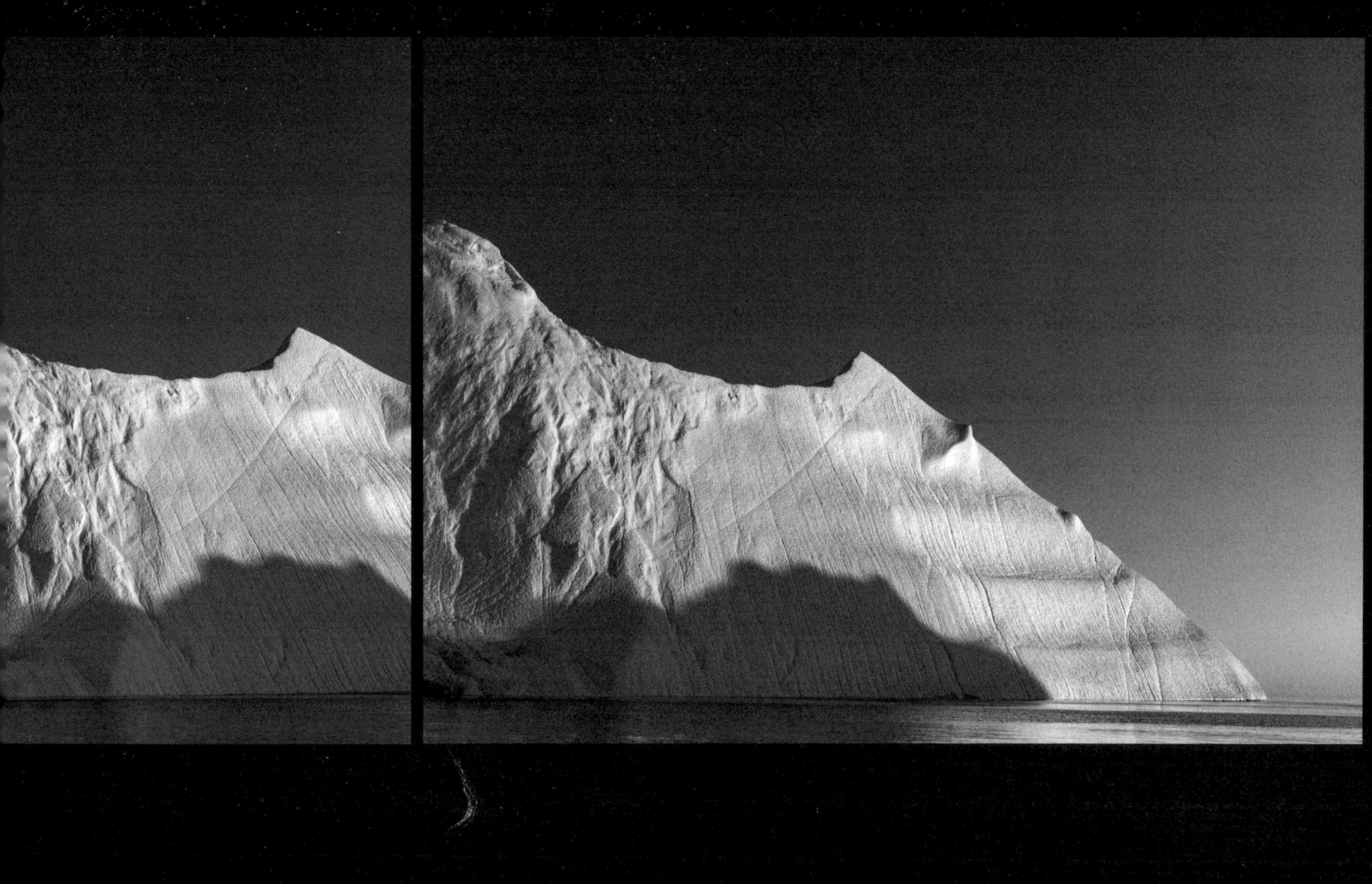

Ribe, Jutland, Denmark, 2021 (frame video)

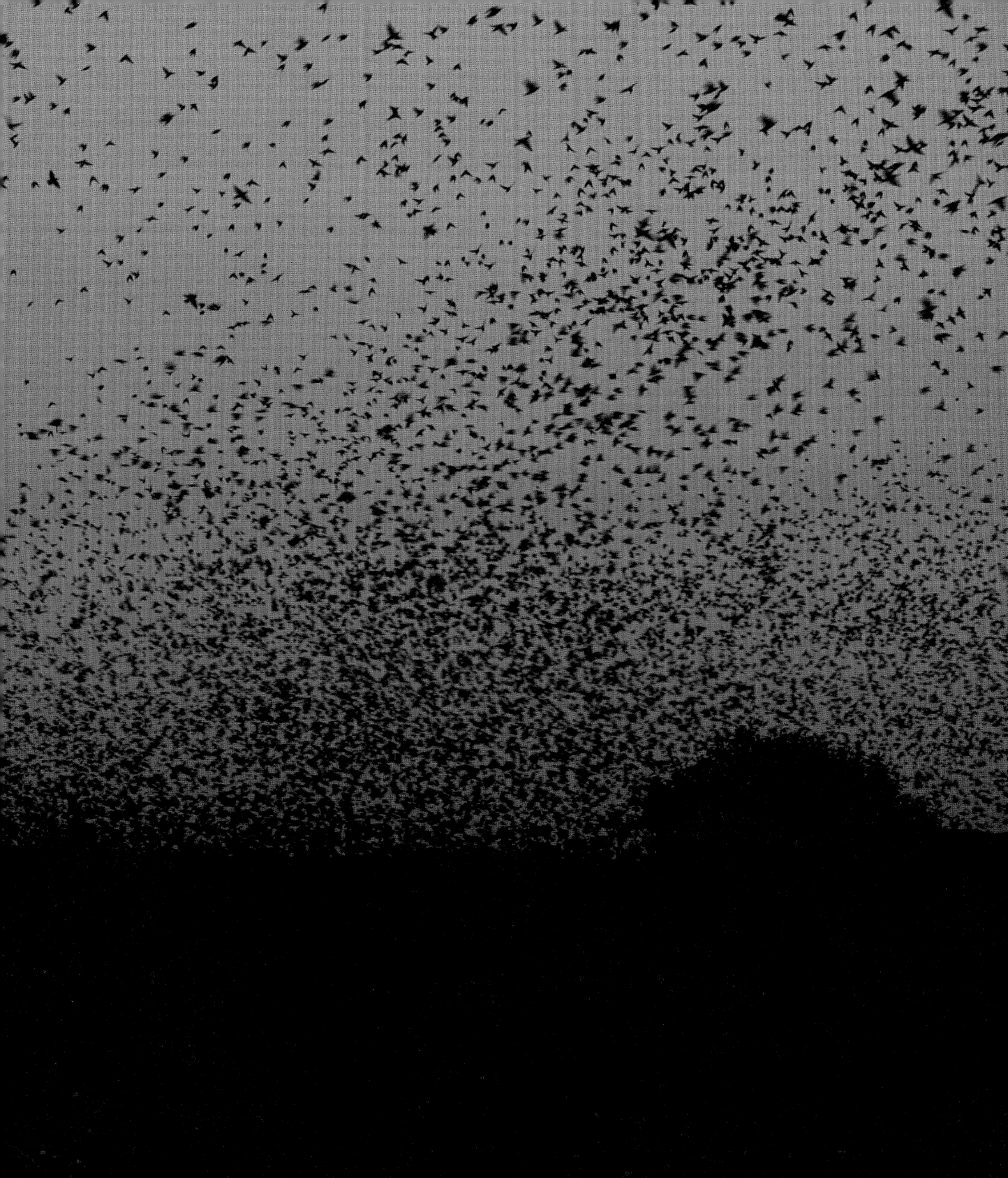

Fagradalsfjall Volcano, Reykjanes Peninsula, Iceland, 2021

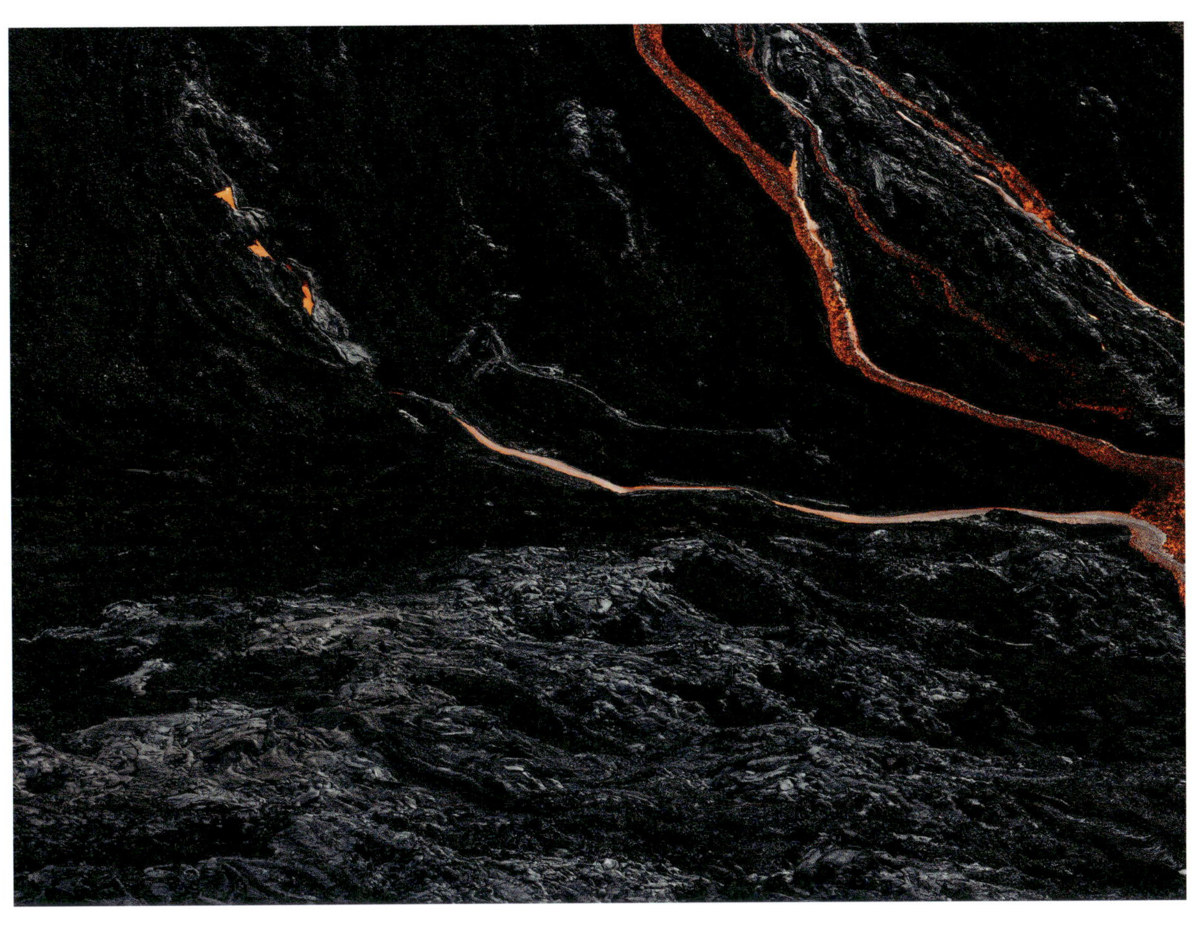

Vatnajökull Glacier Area, Iceland, 2021

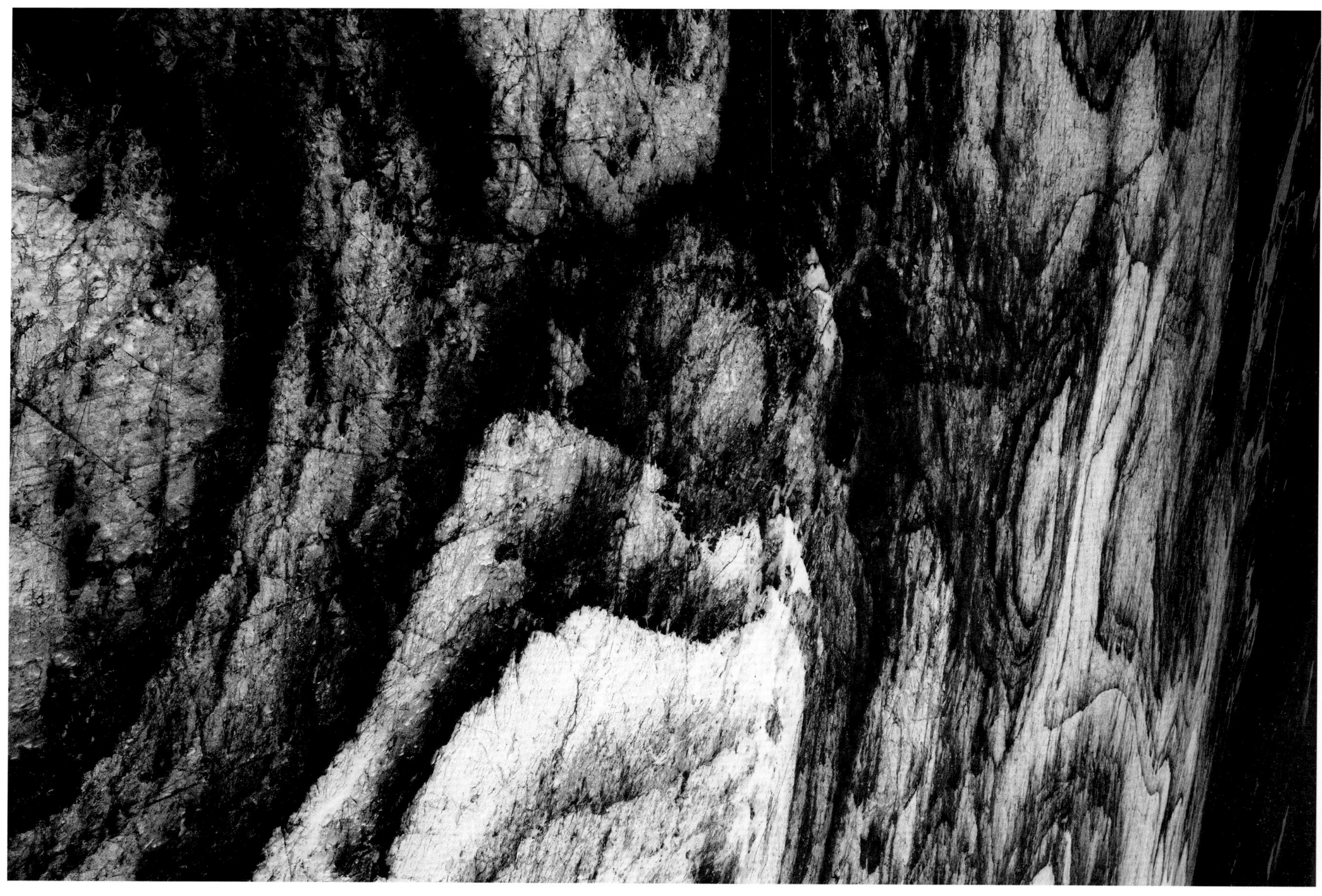

Bondi State Forest, New South Wales, Australia, 2020

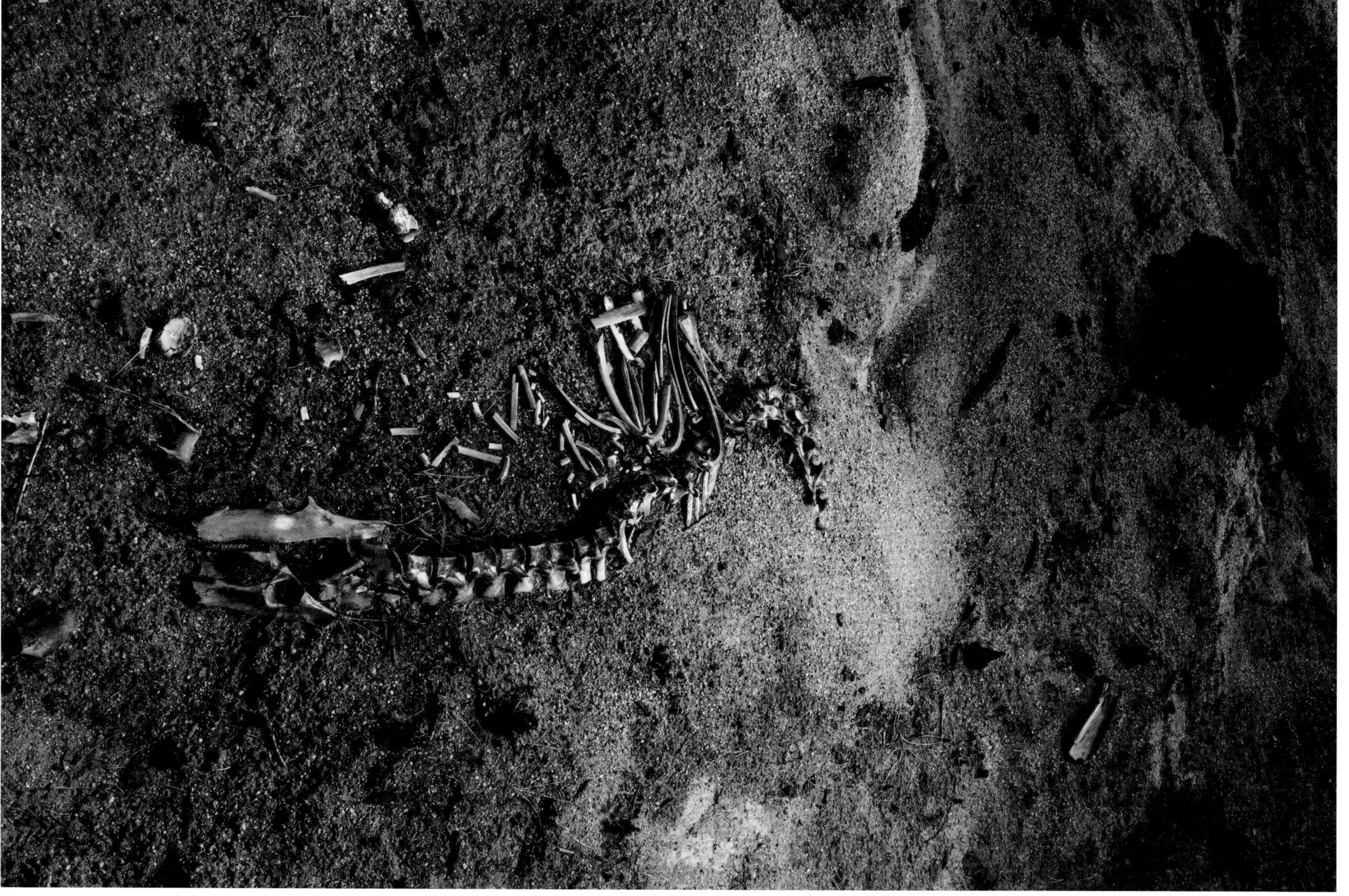

Fagradalsfjall Volcano, Reykjanes Peninsula, Iceland, 2021

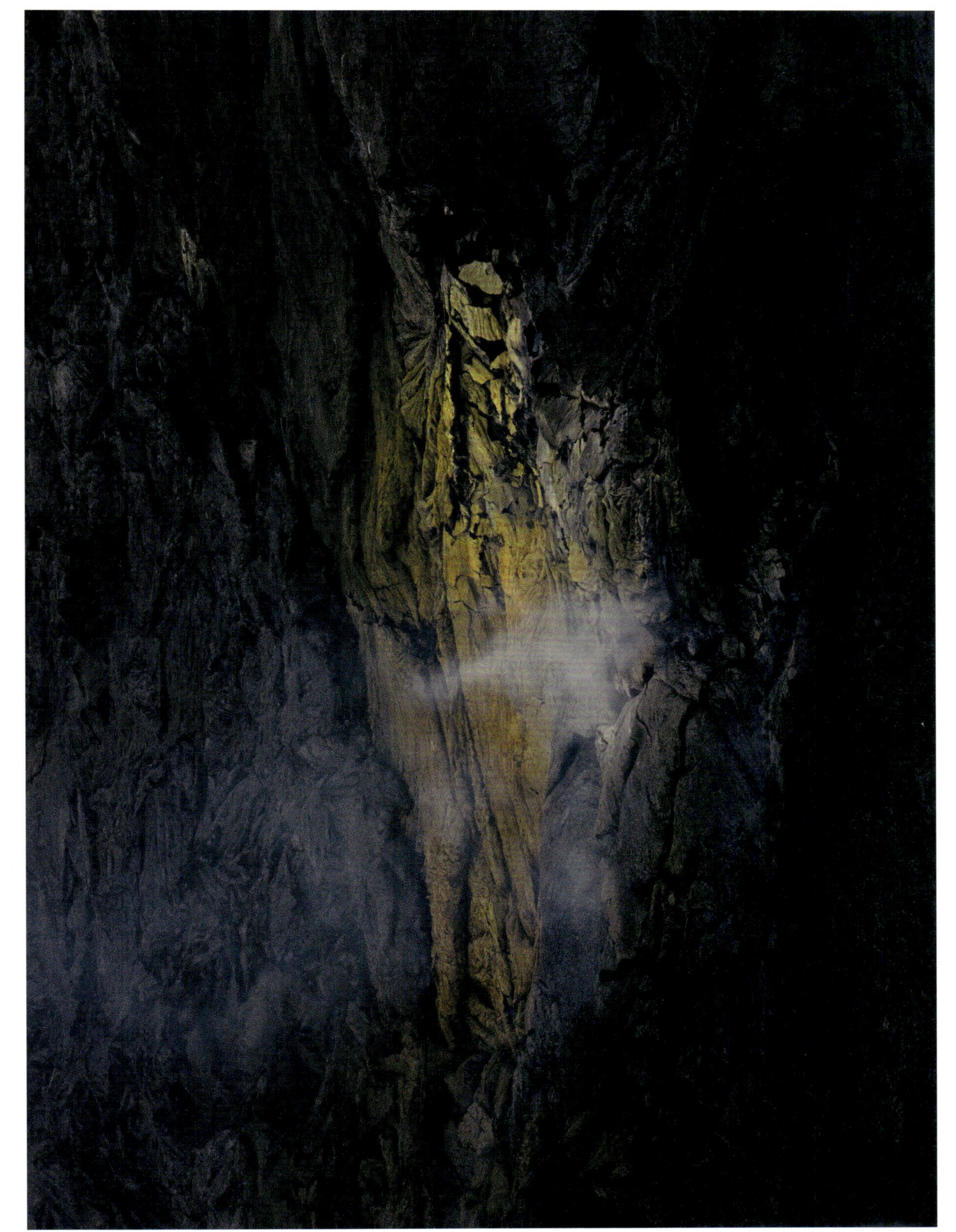

Fagradalsfjall Volcano, Reykjanes Peninsula, Iceland, 2021

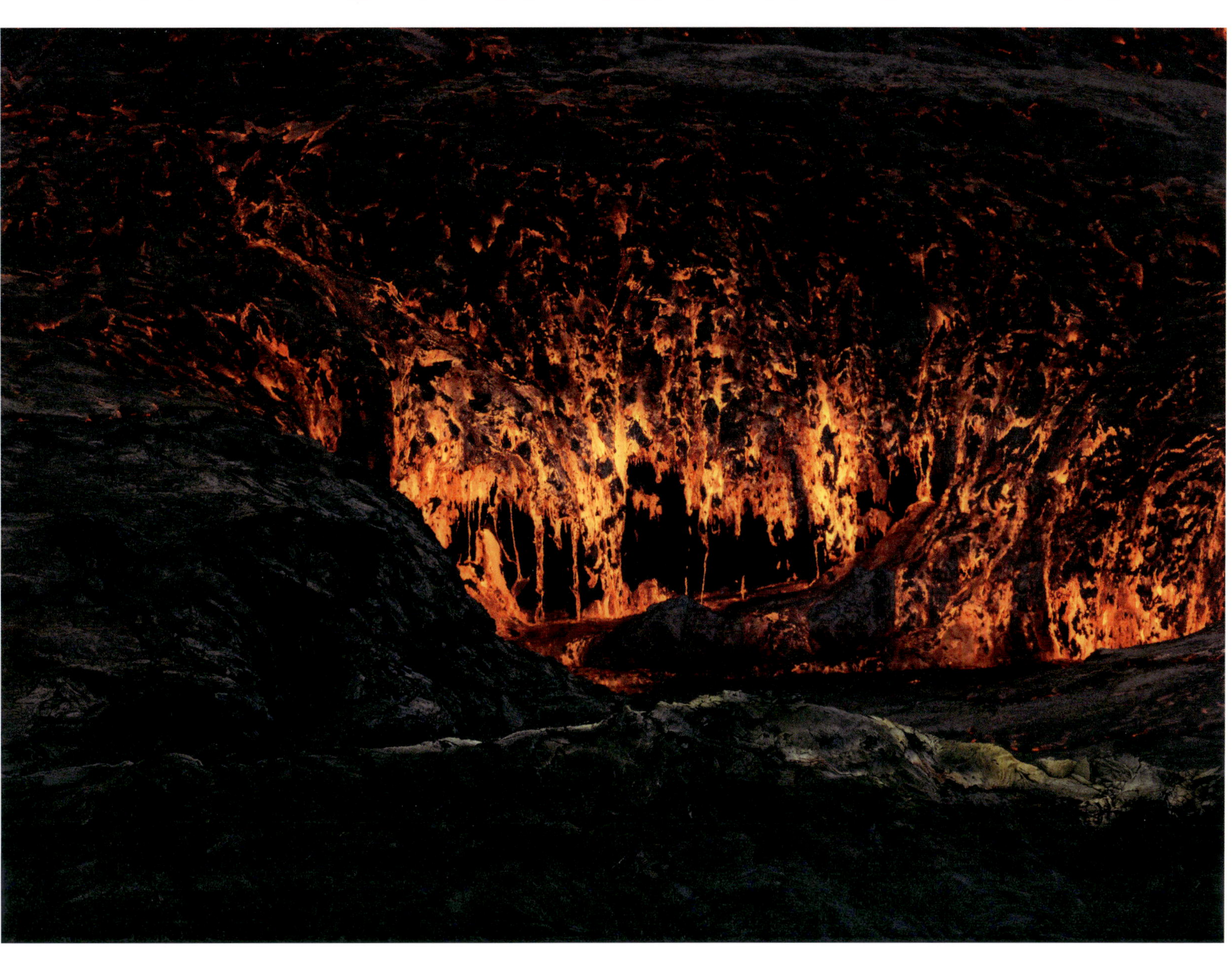

Raufarhólshellir, Reykjavík, Iceland, 2021

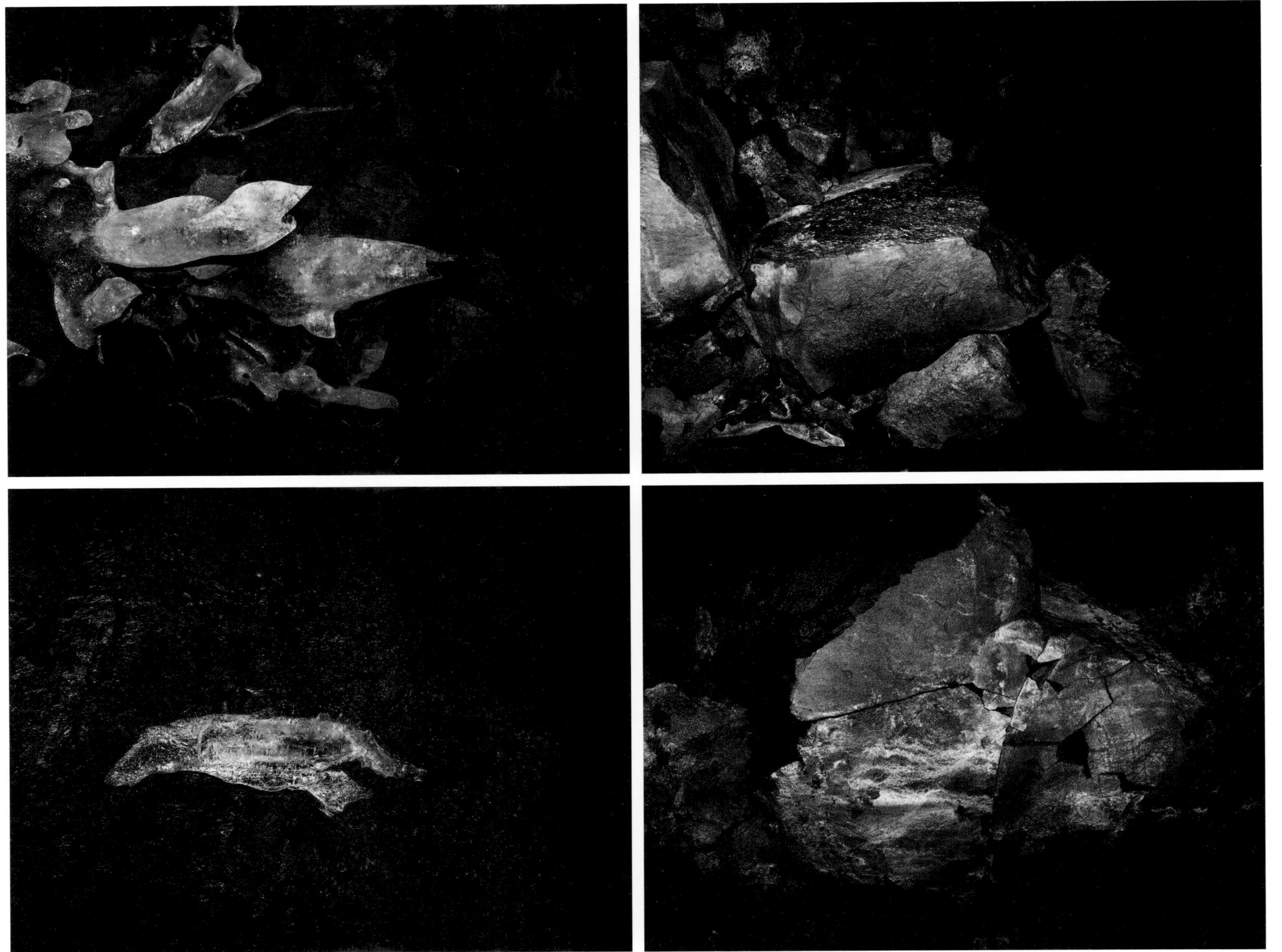

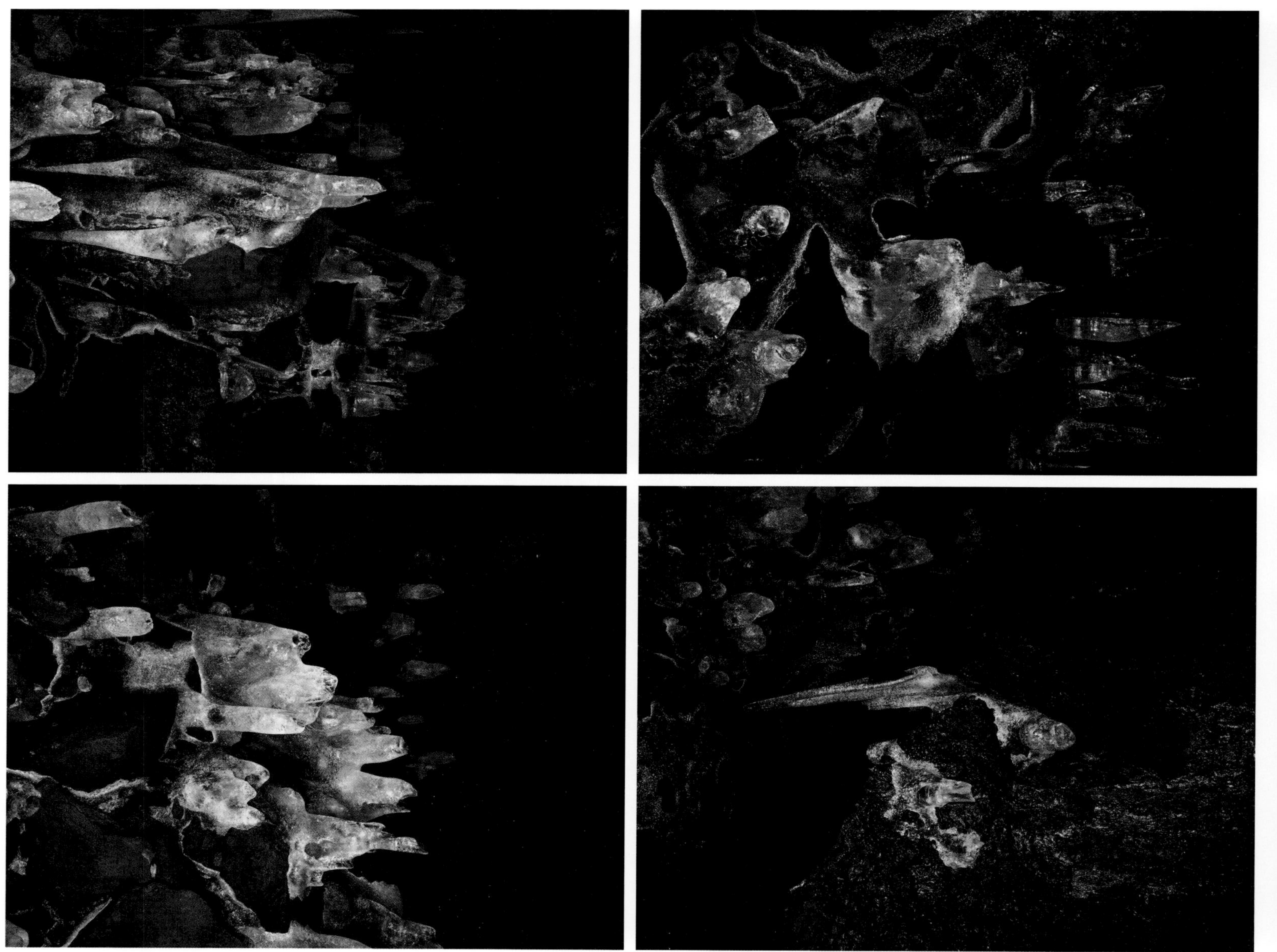

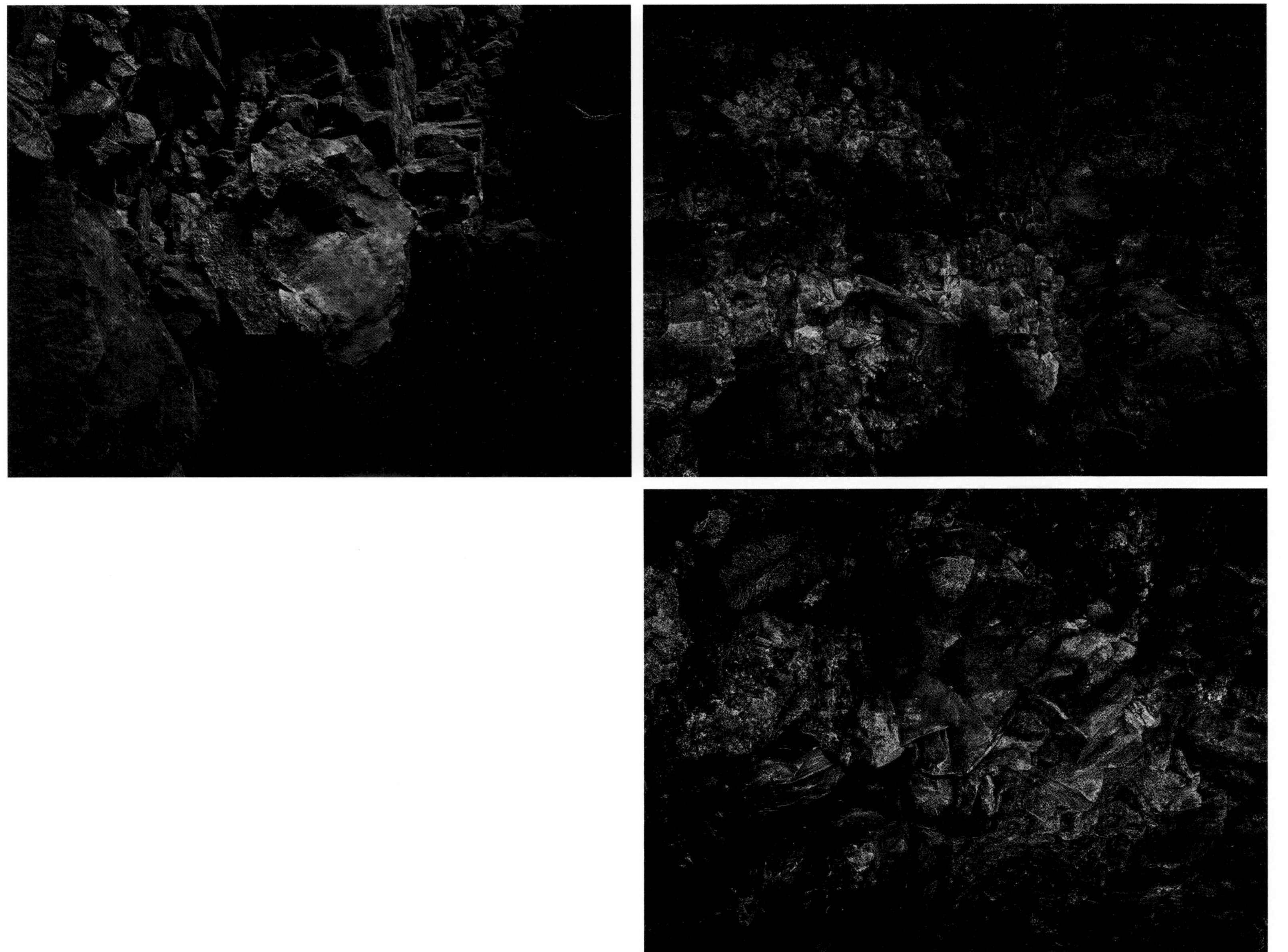

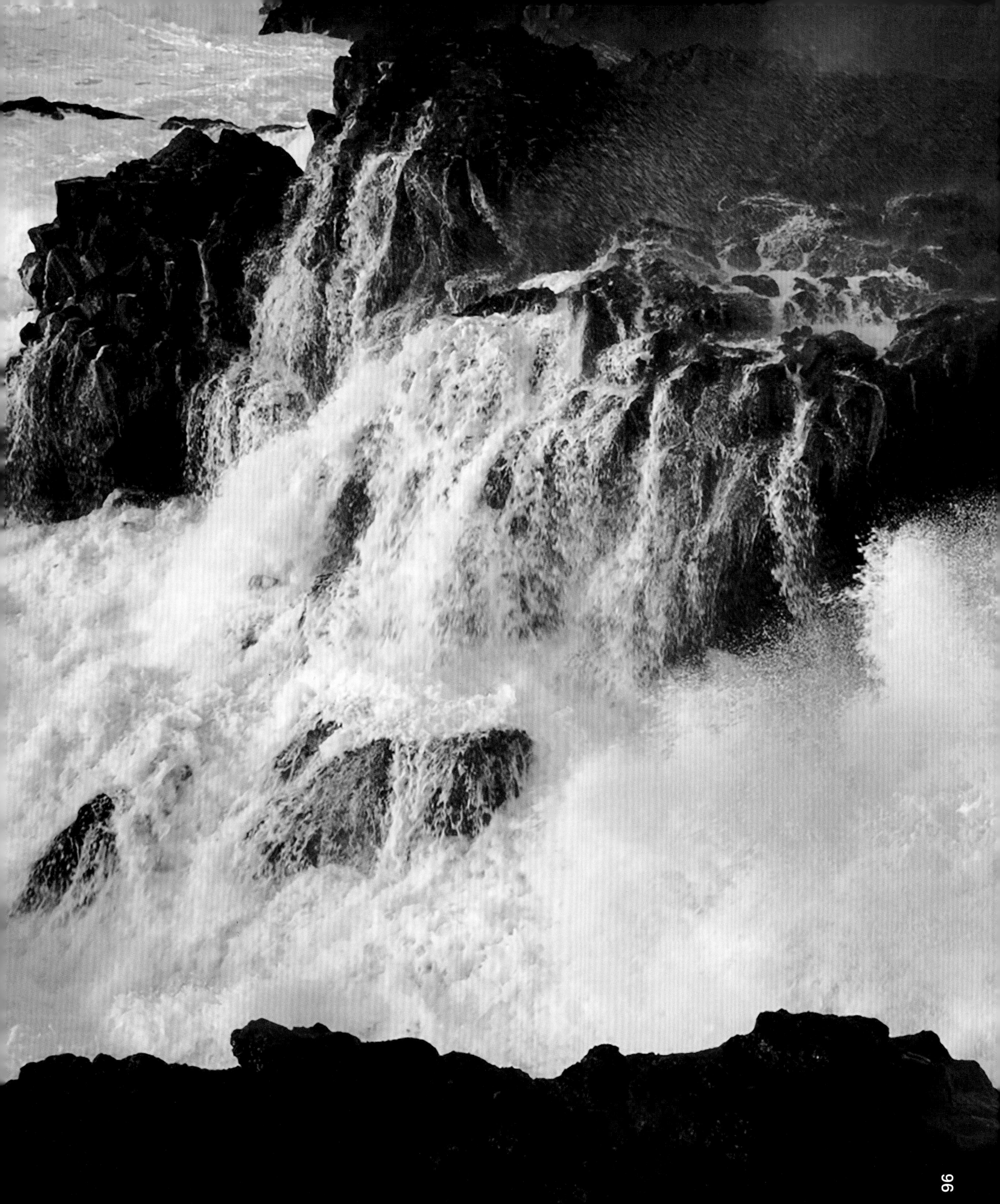

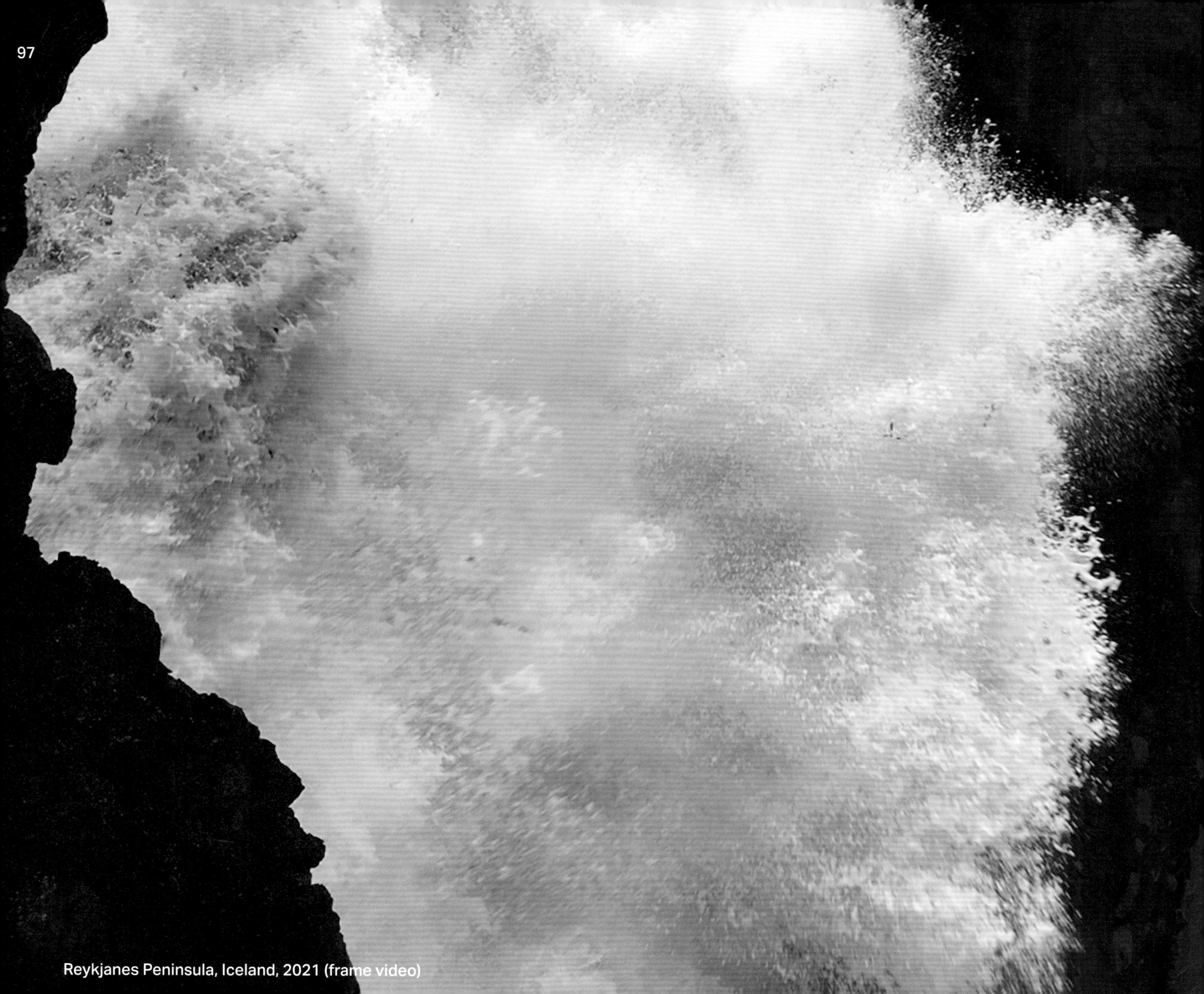

Reykjanes Peninsula, Iceland, 2021 (frame video)

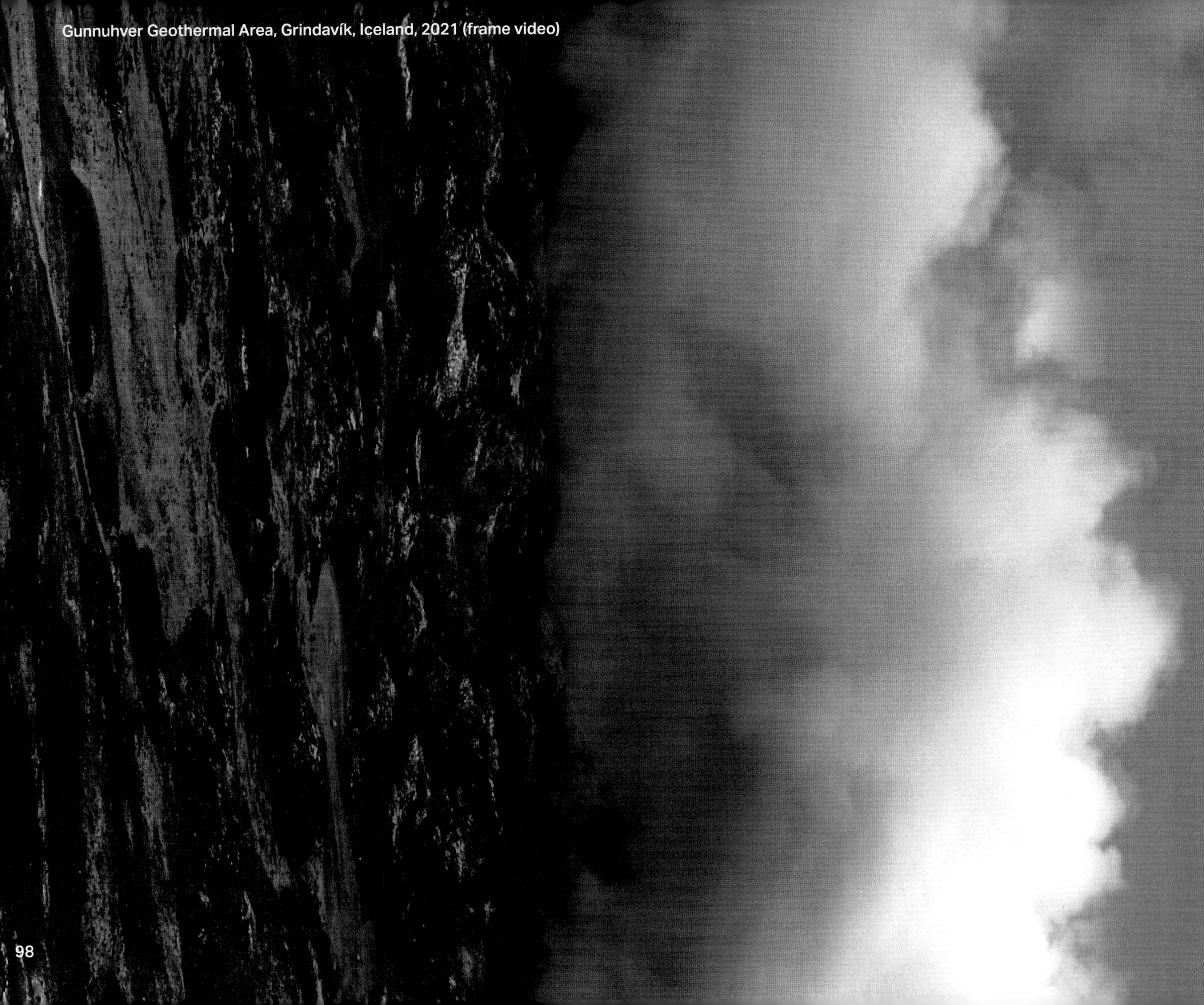

Gunnuhver Geothermal Area, Grindavík, Iceland, 2021 (frame video)

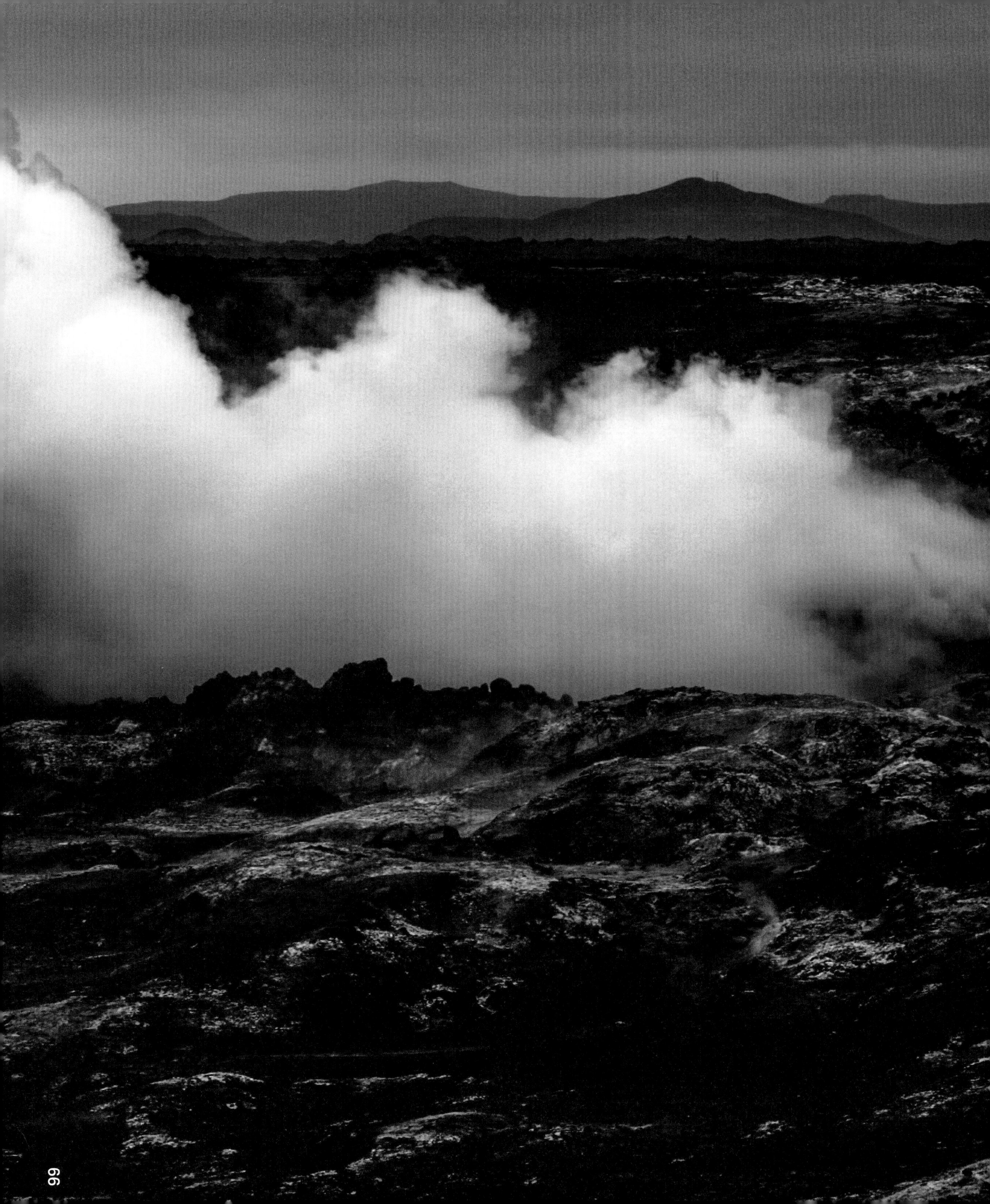

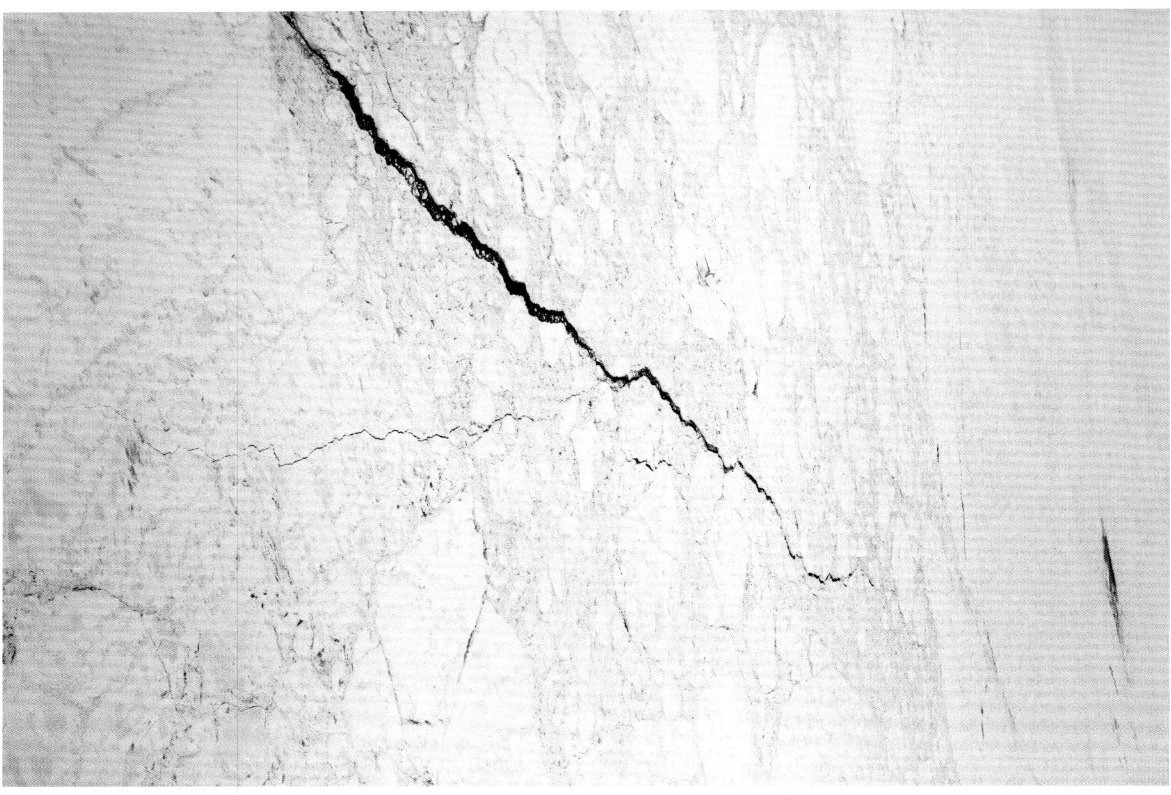

 Seelye Loop South, Venable 01A, South Peninsula A, Larsen C Gravity, TanDEM-X B, Antarctica, 2017

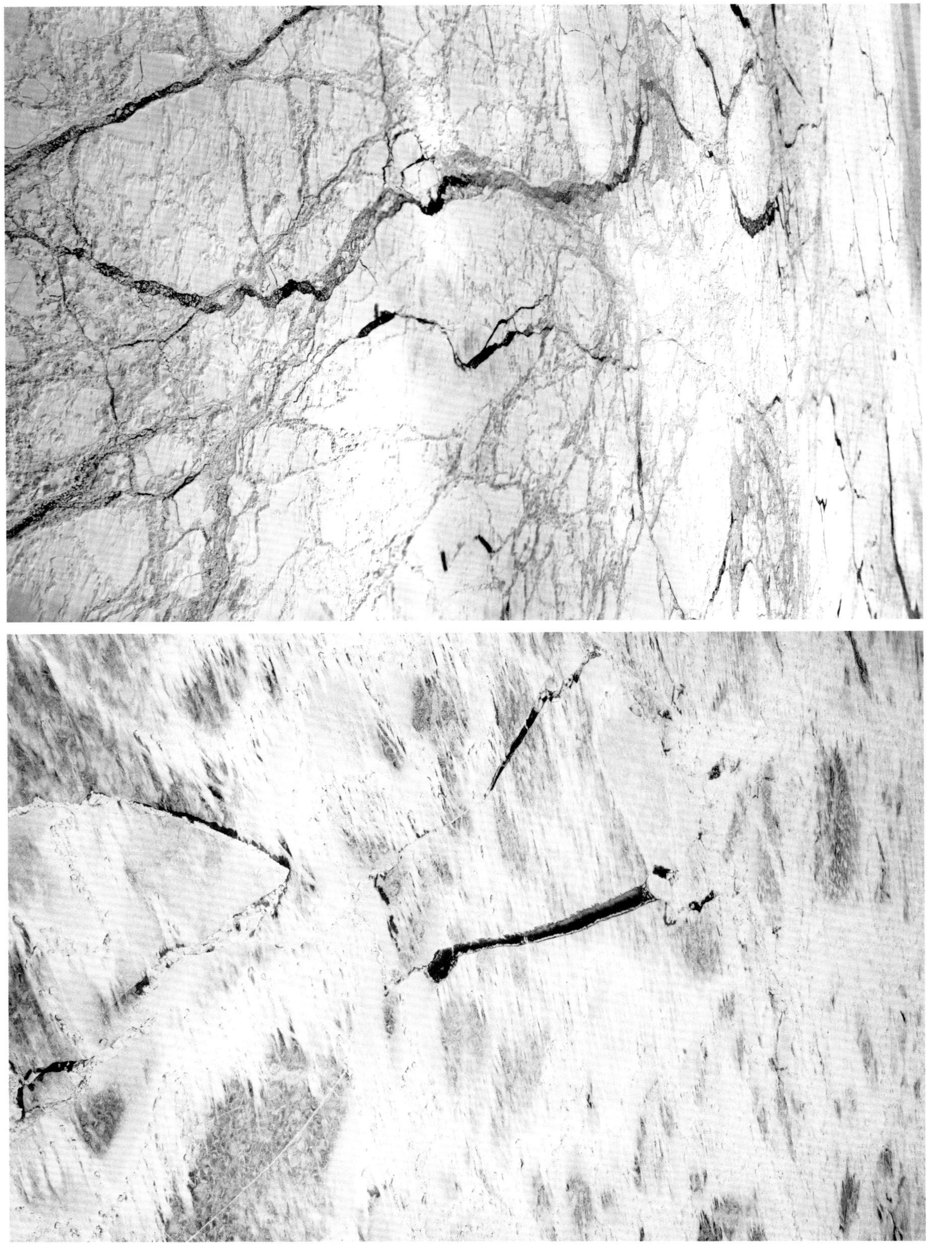

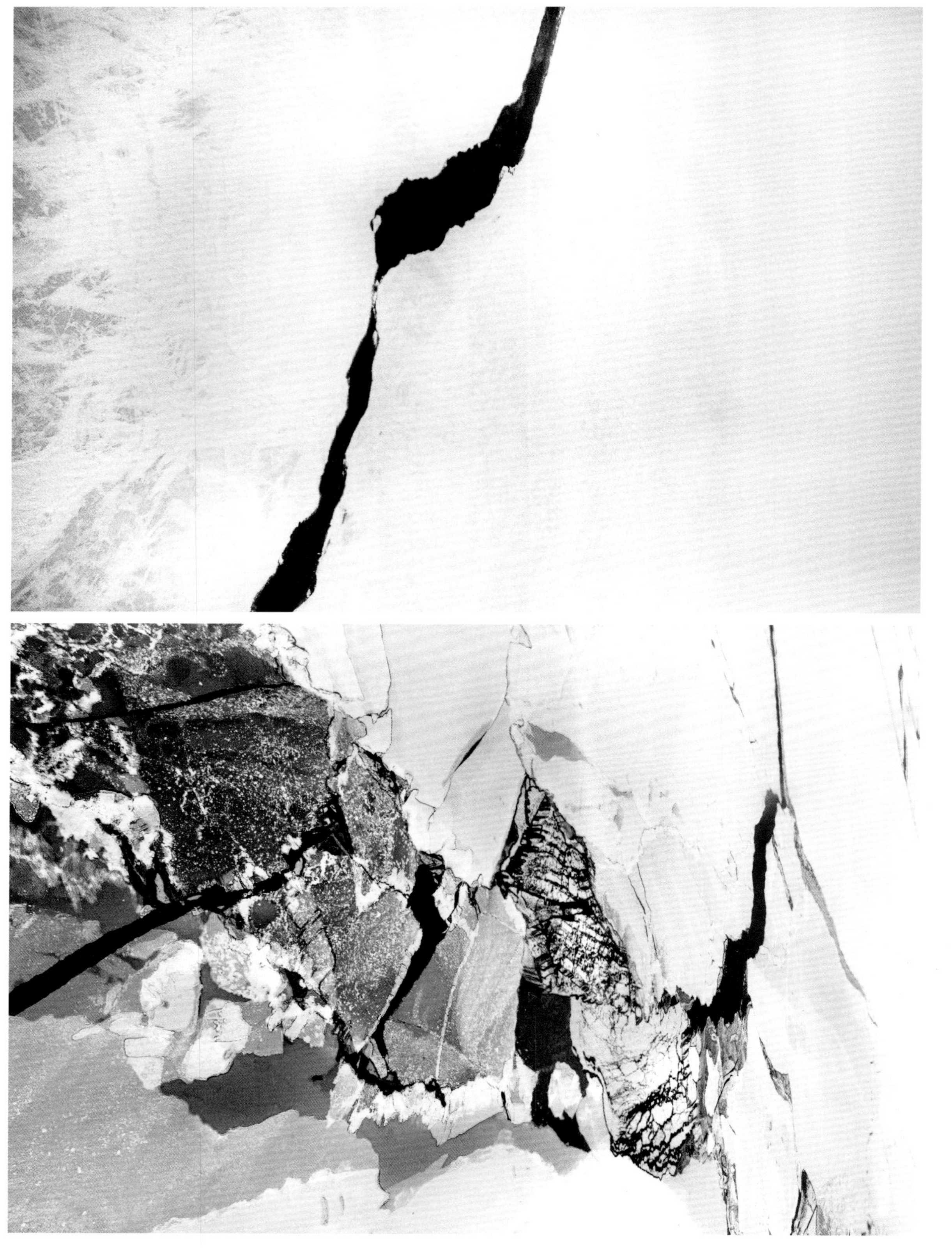

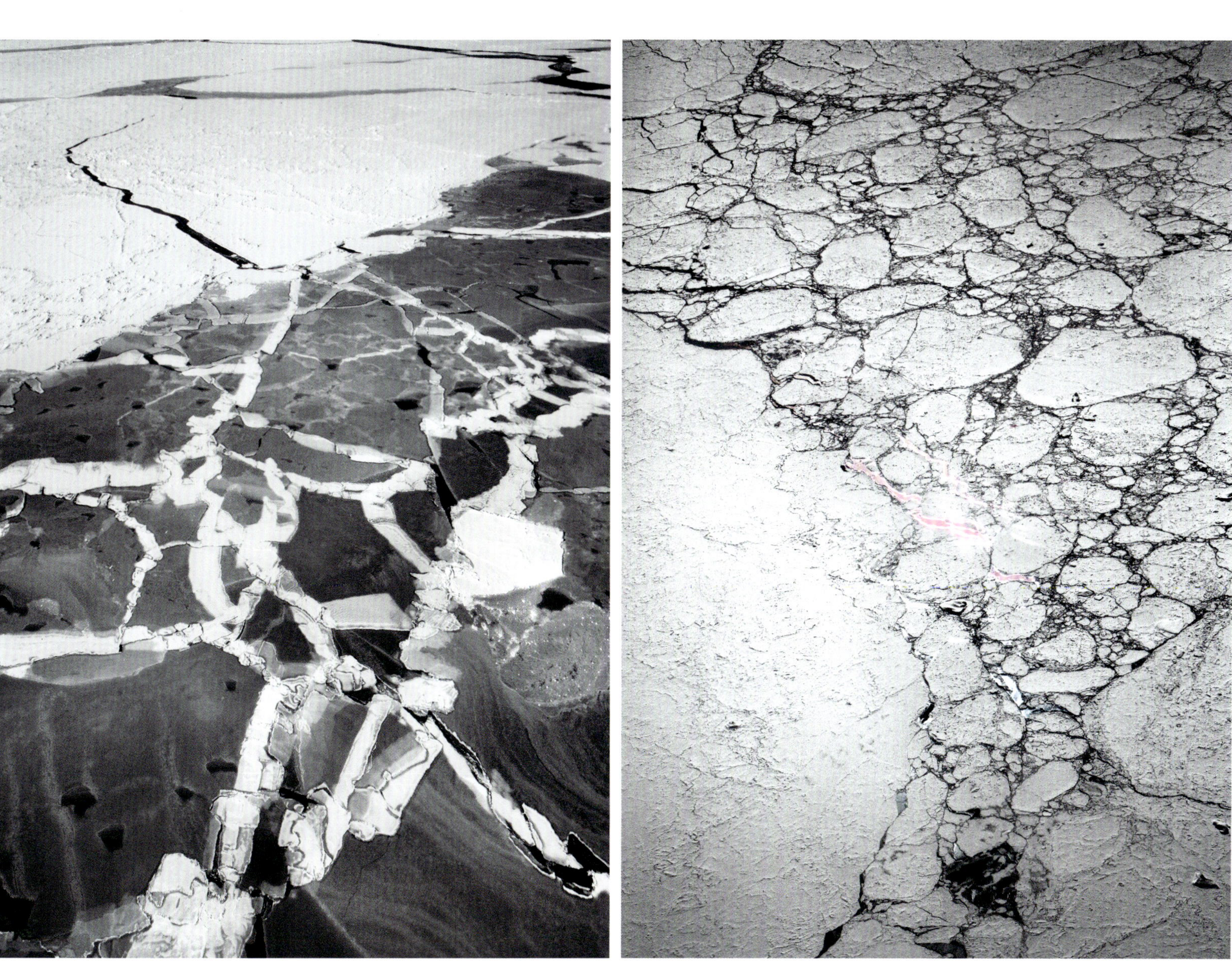

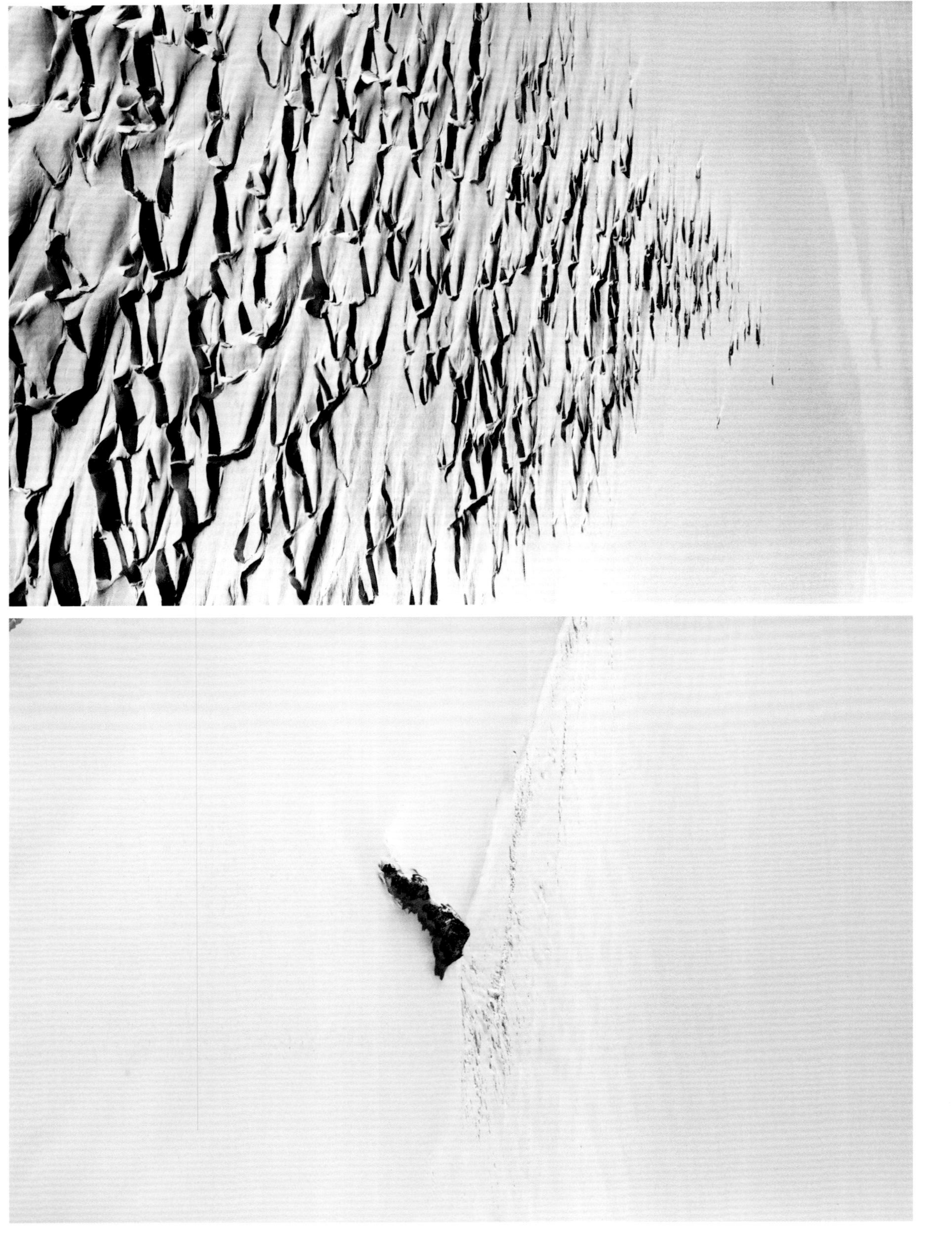

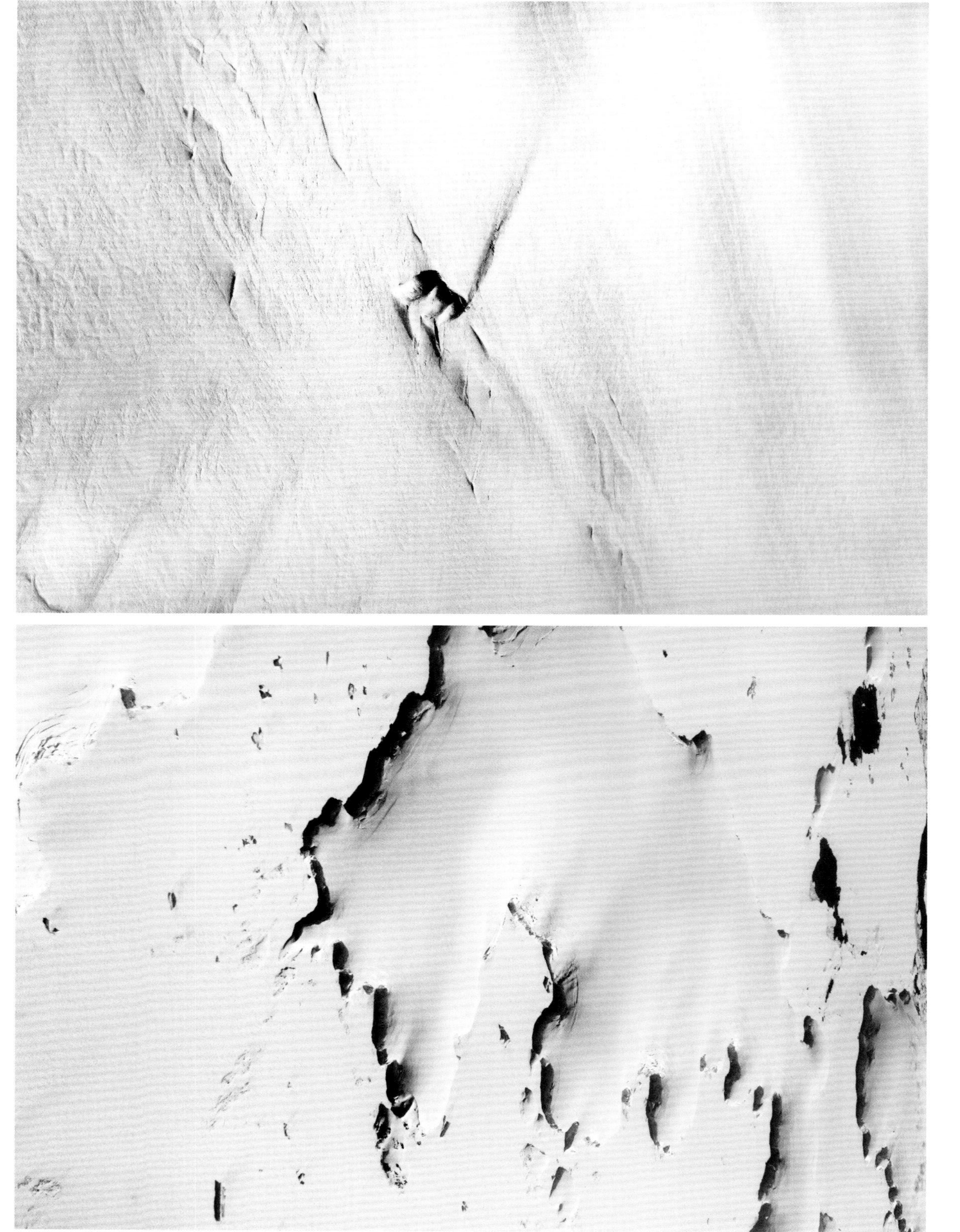

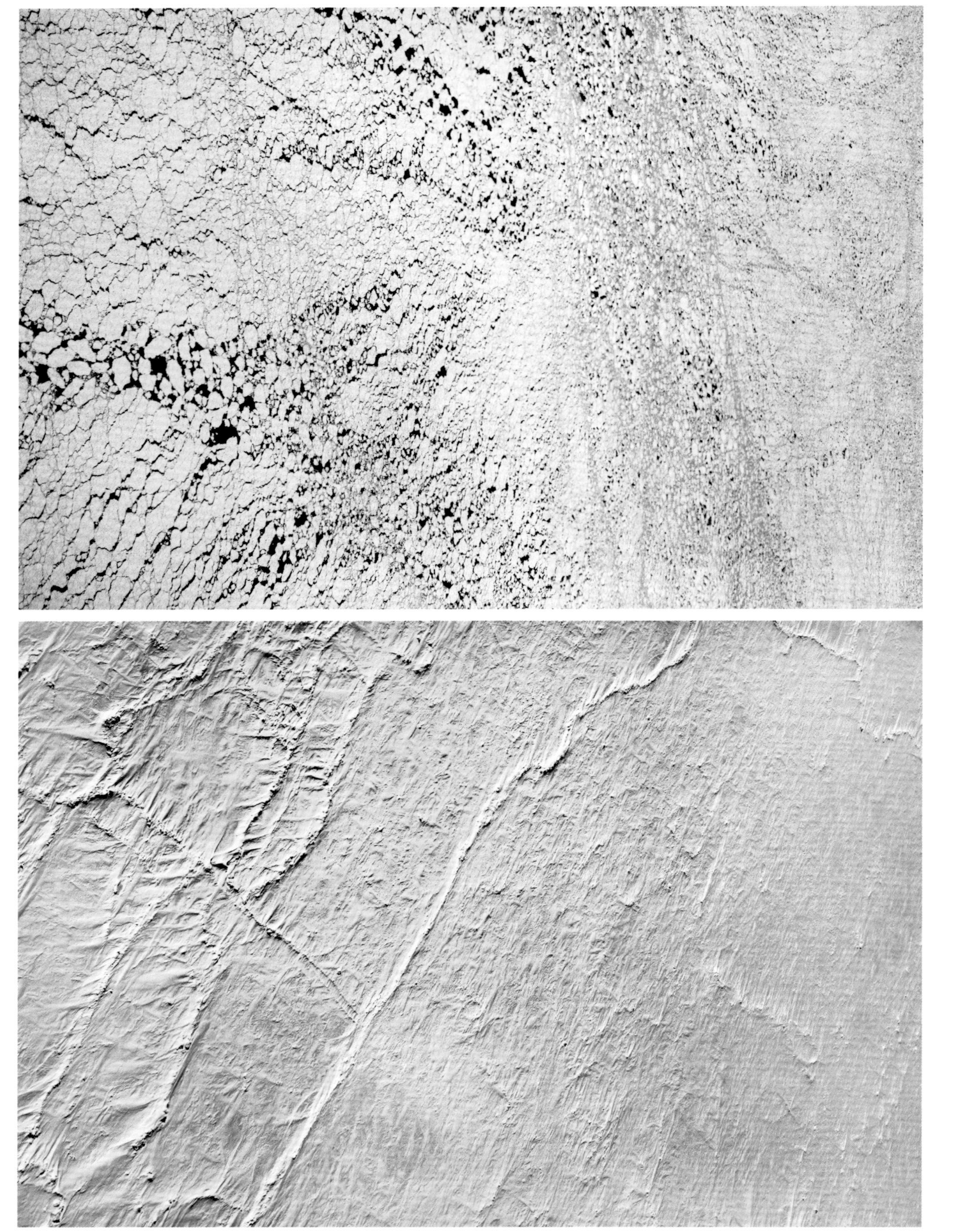

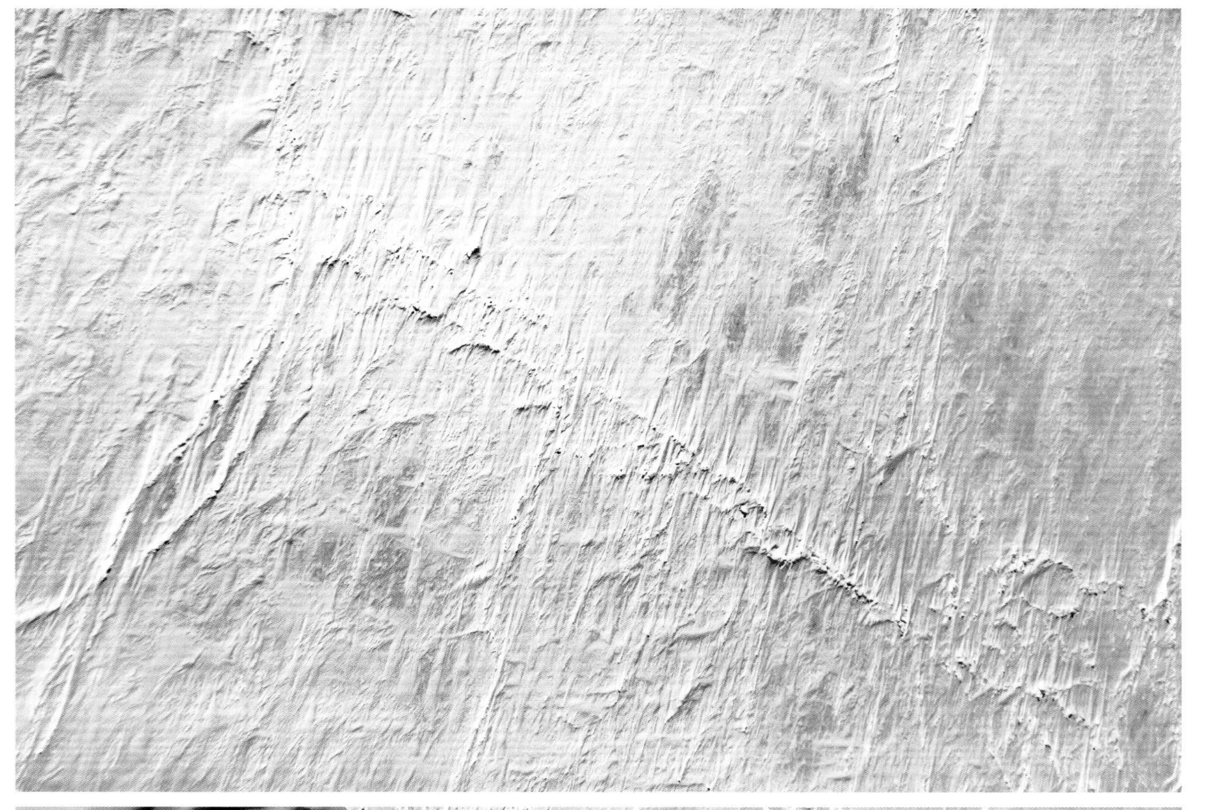

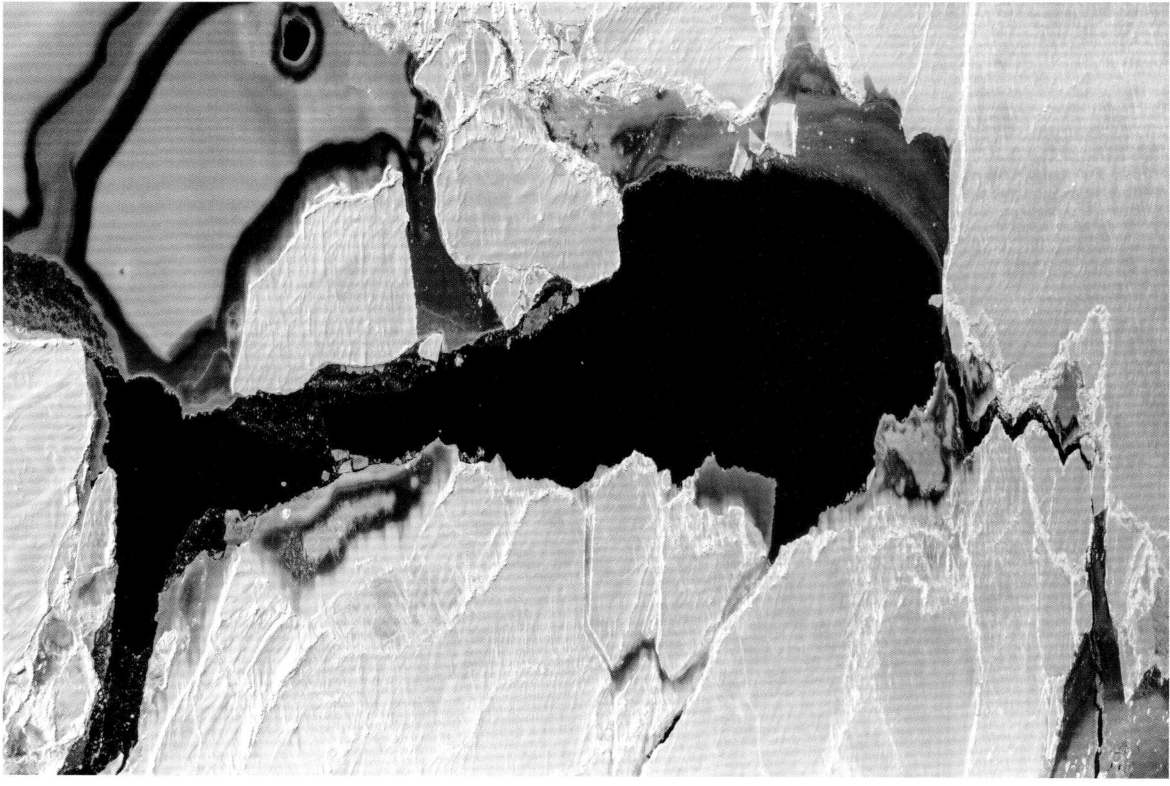

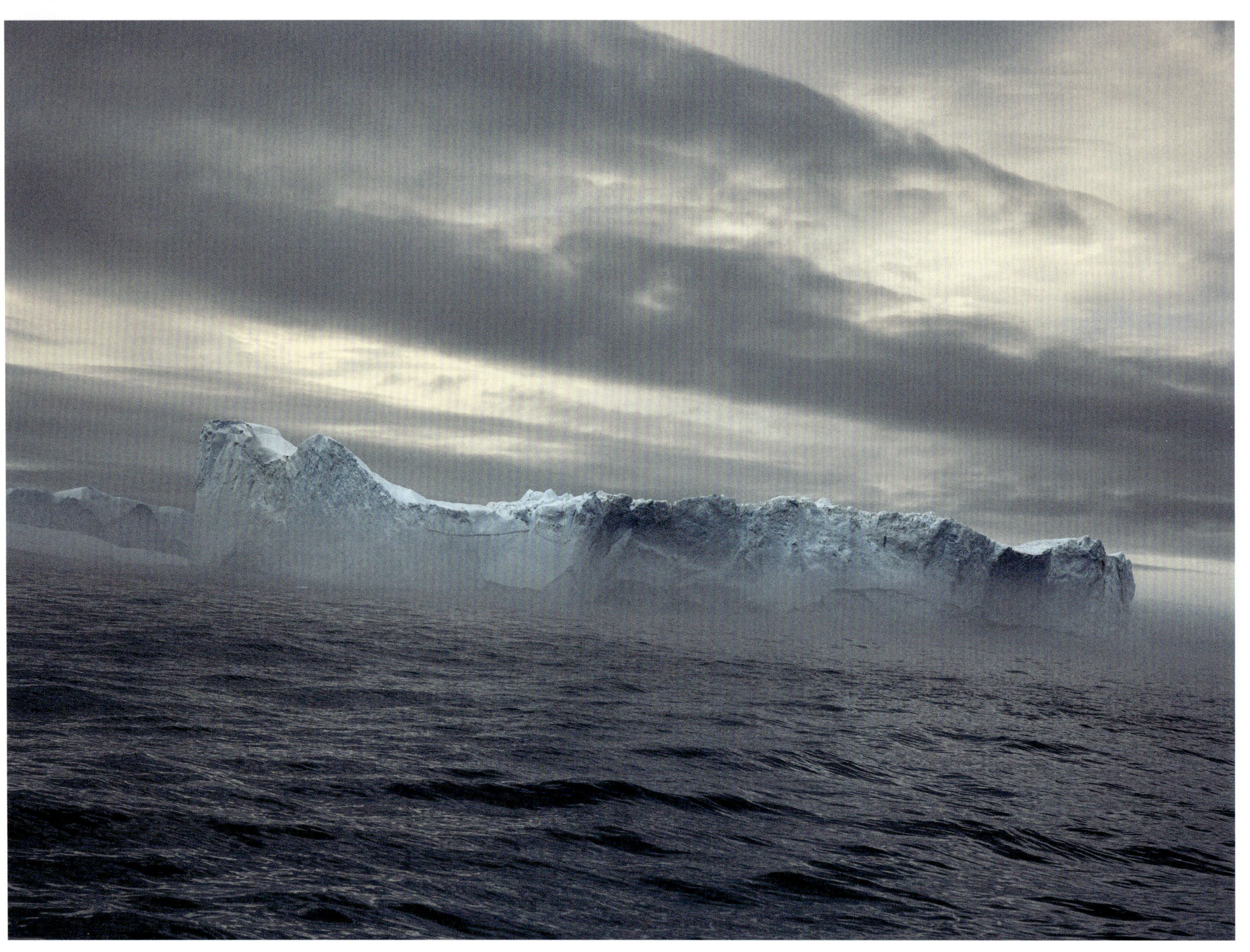

109 Disko Bay, Ilulissat, Greenland, 2021

Kyoto, Japan, 2019

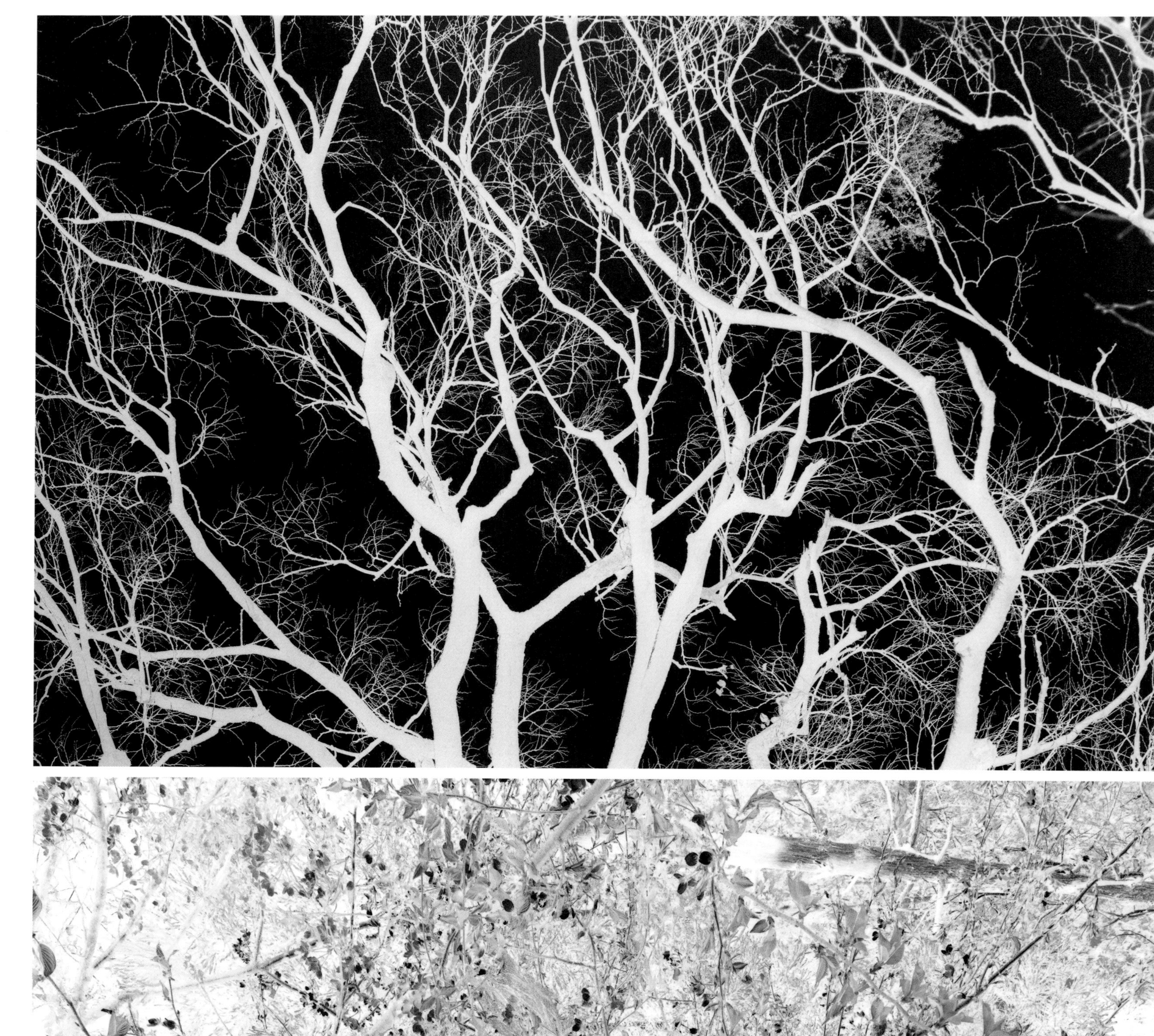

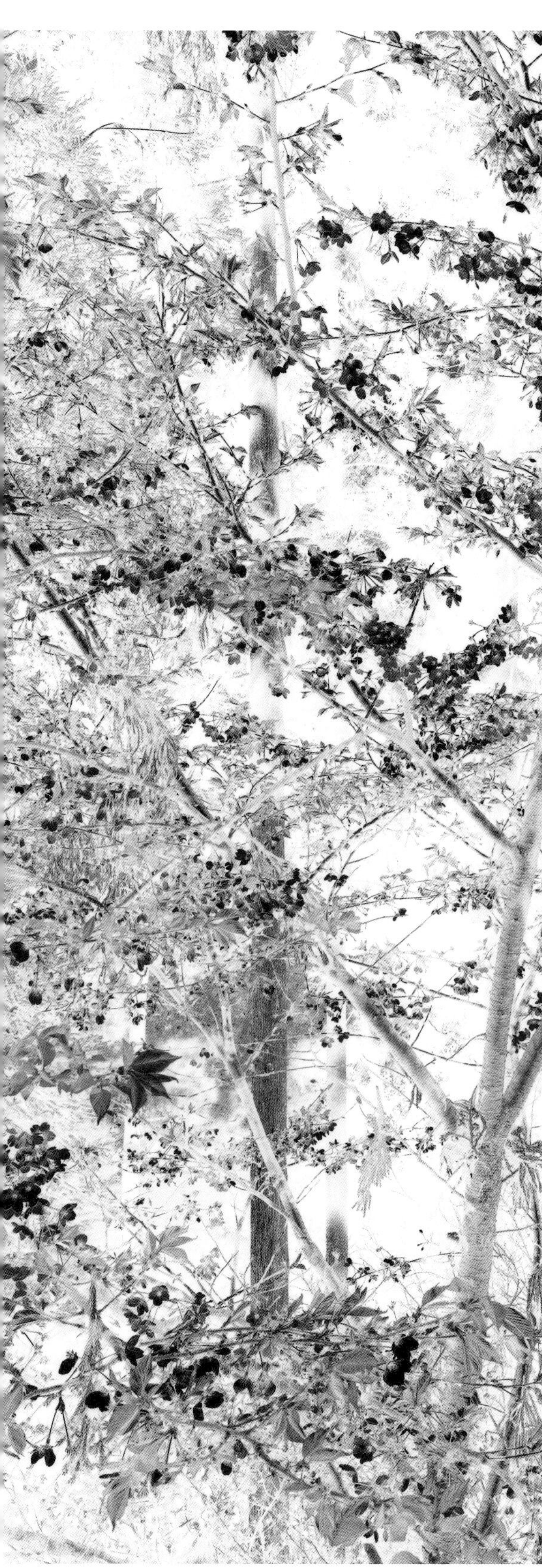

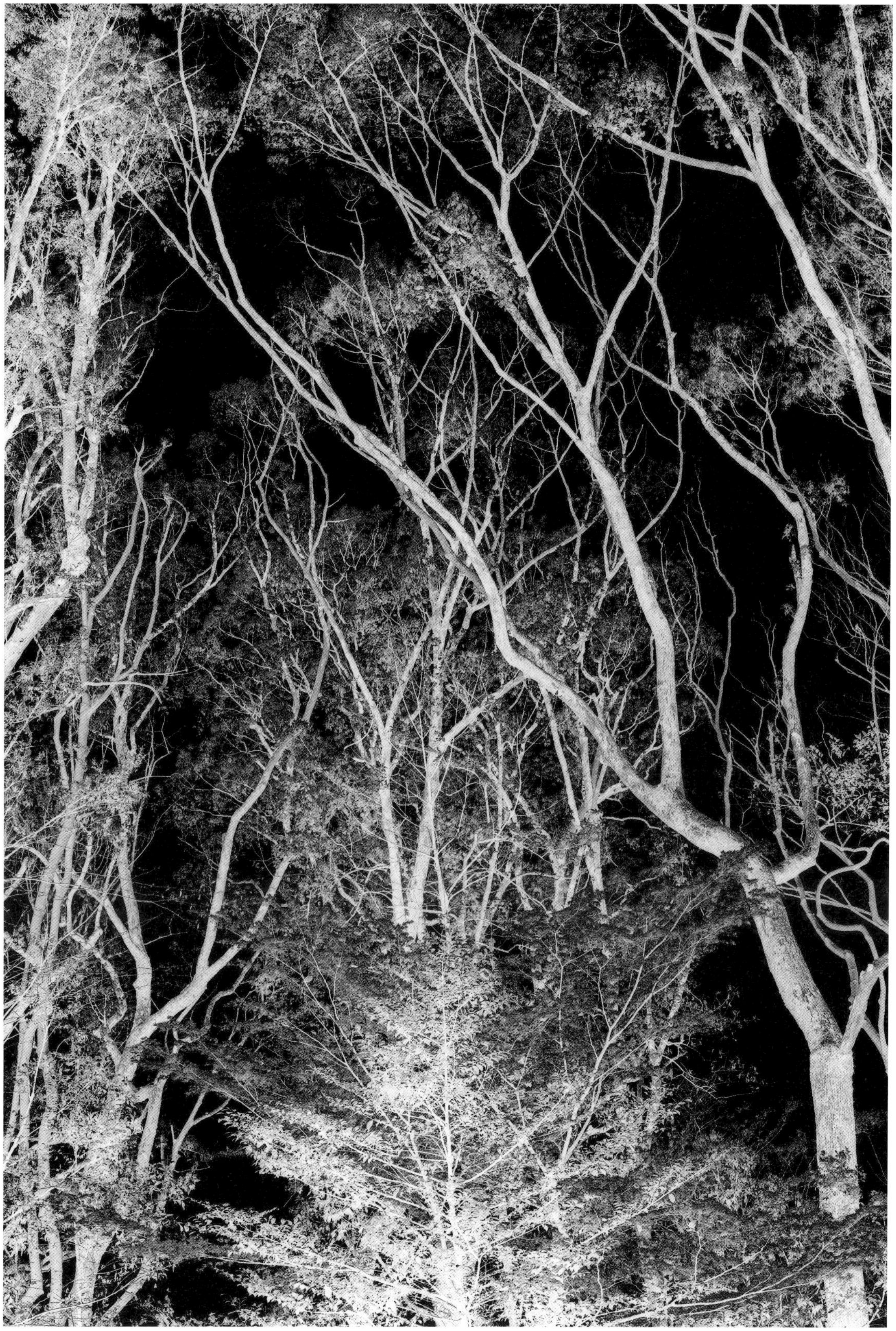

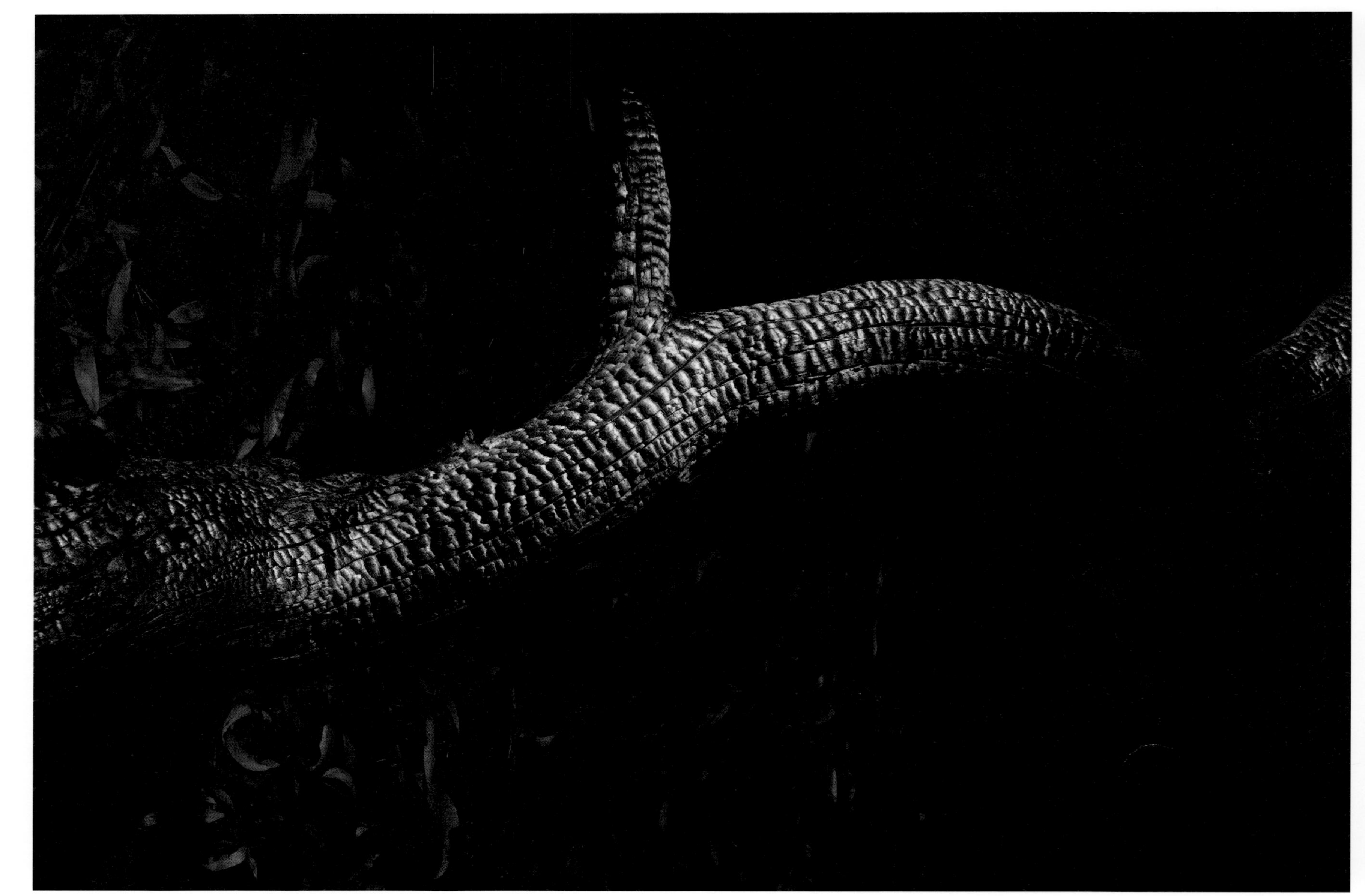

113 Kosciuszko National Park, New South Wales, Australia, 2020

Mount Etna, Sicily, Italy, 2021

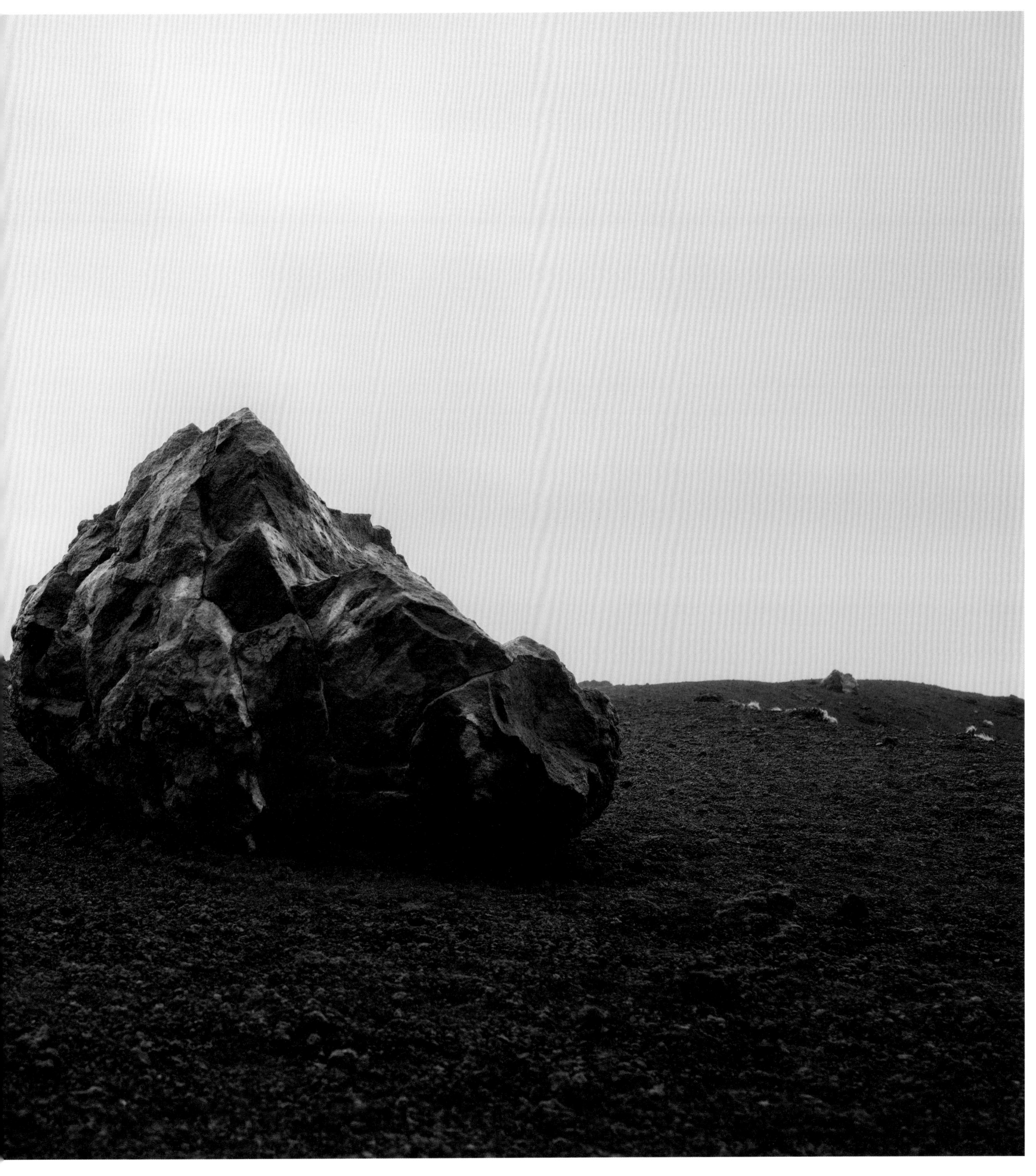

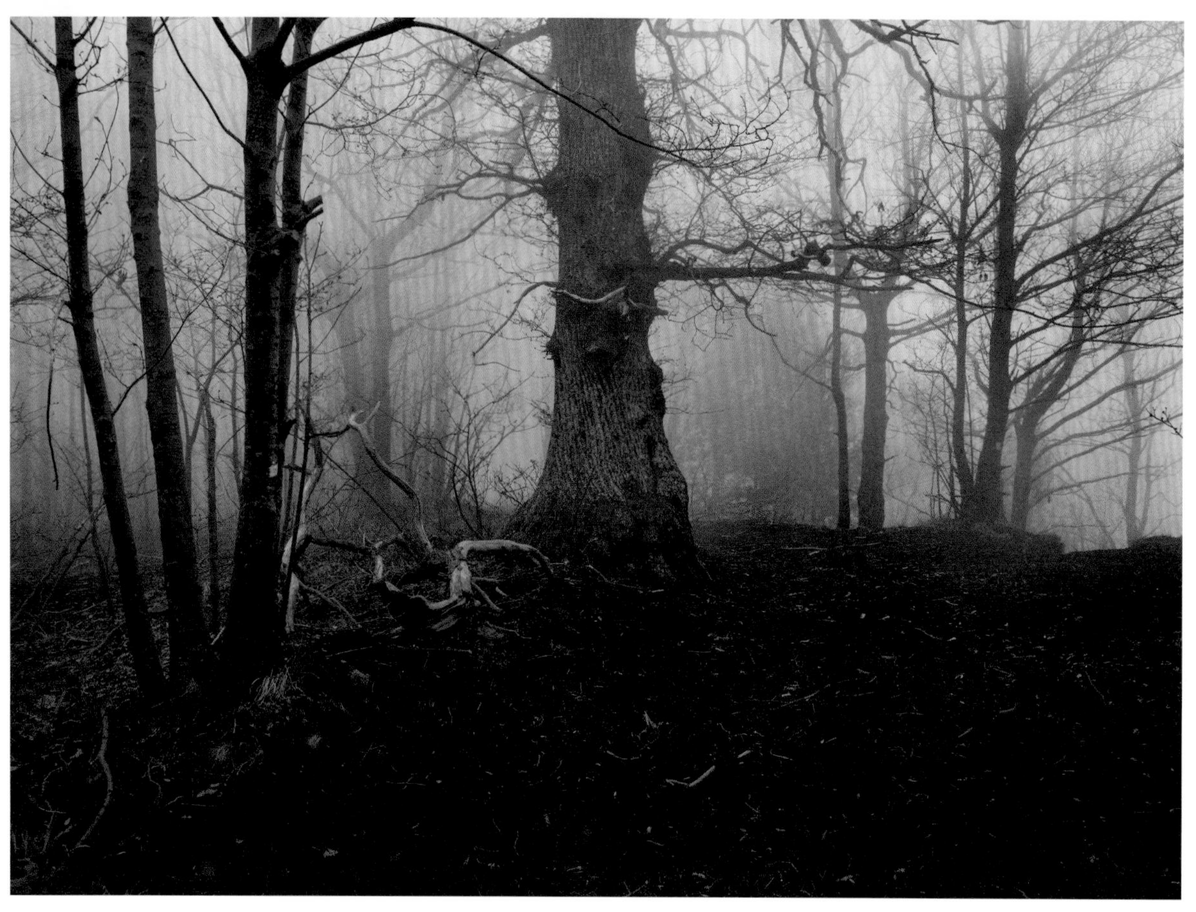

117 Mount Etna, Sicily, Italy, 2021

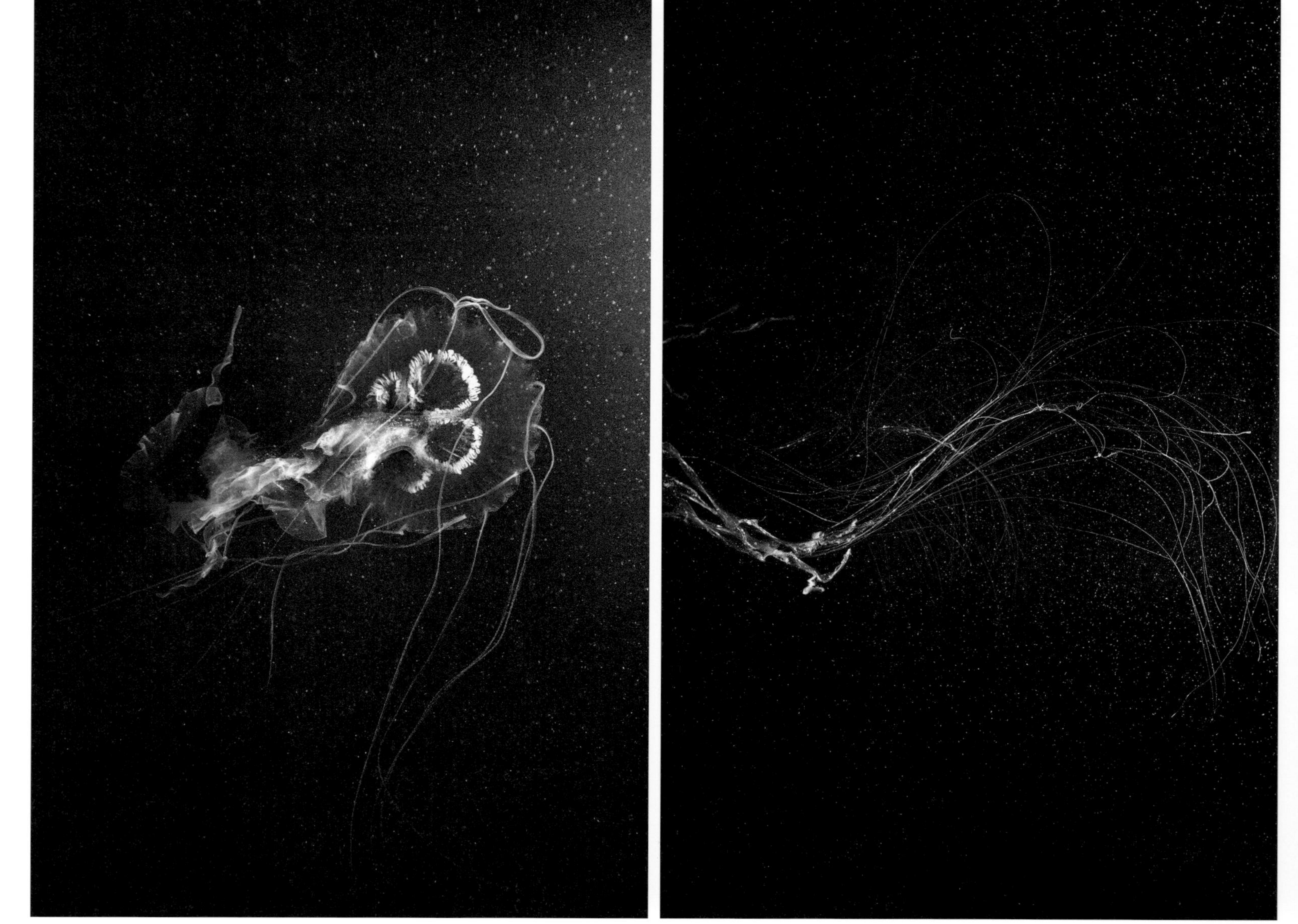

Jellyfish Museum, Kyiv, Ukraine, 2019

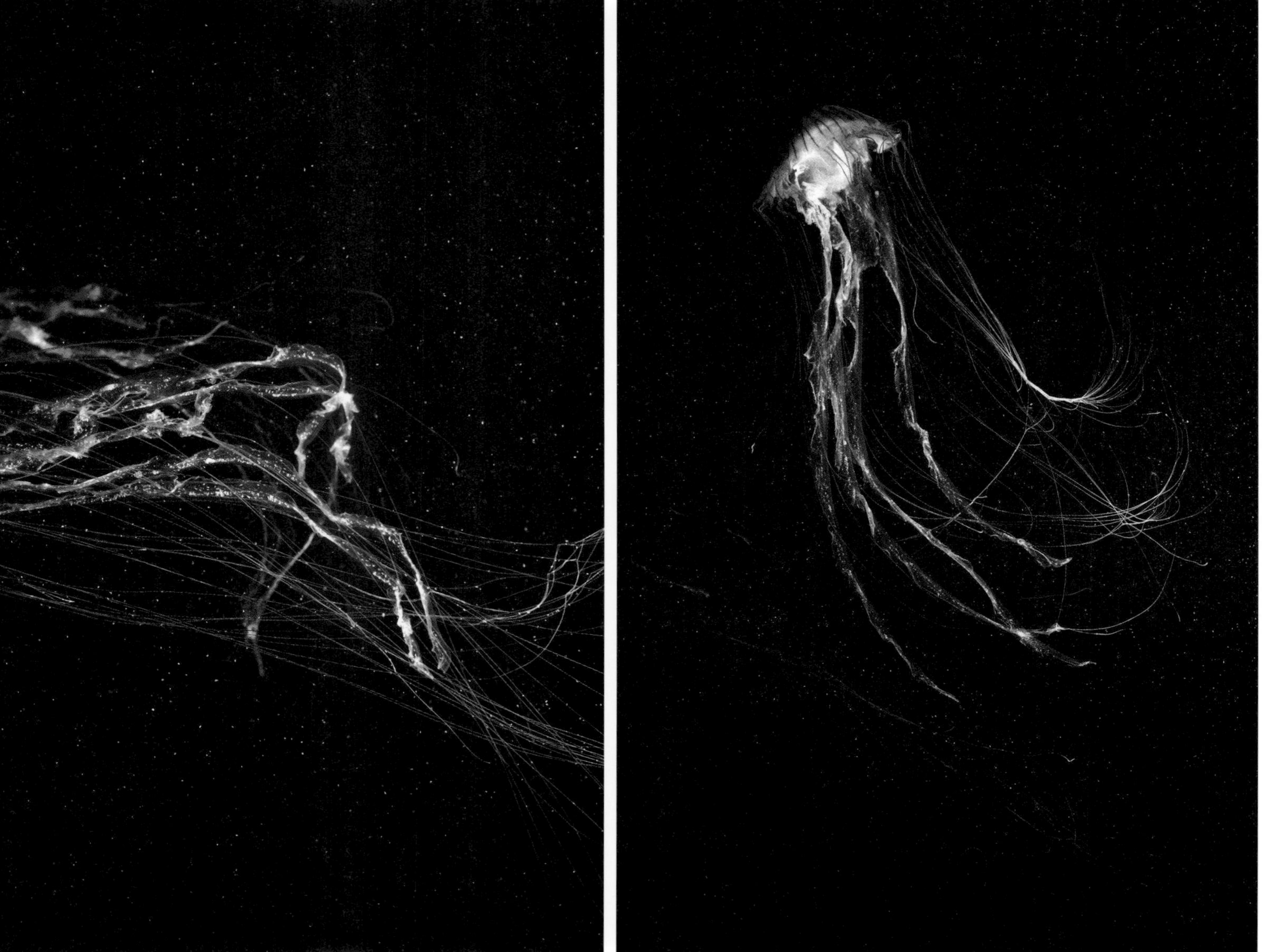

120 Vatnajökull Glacier Area, Iceland, 2021

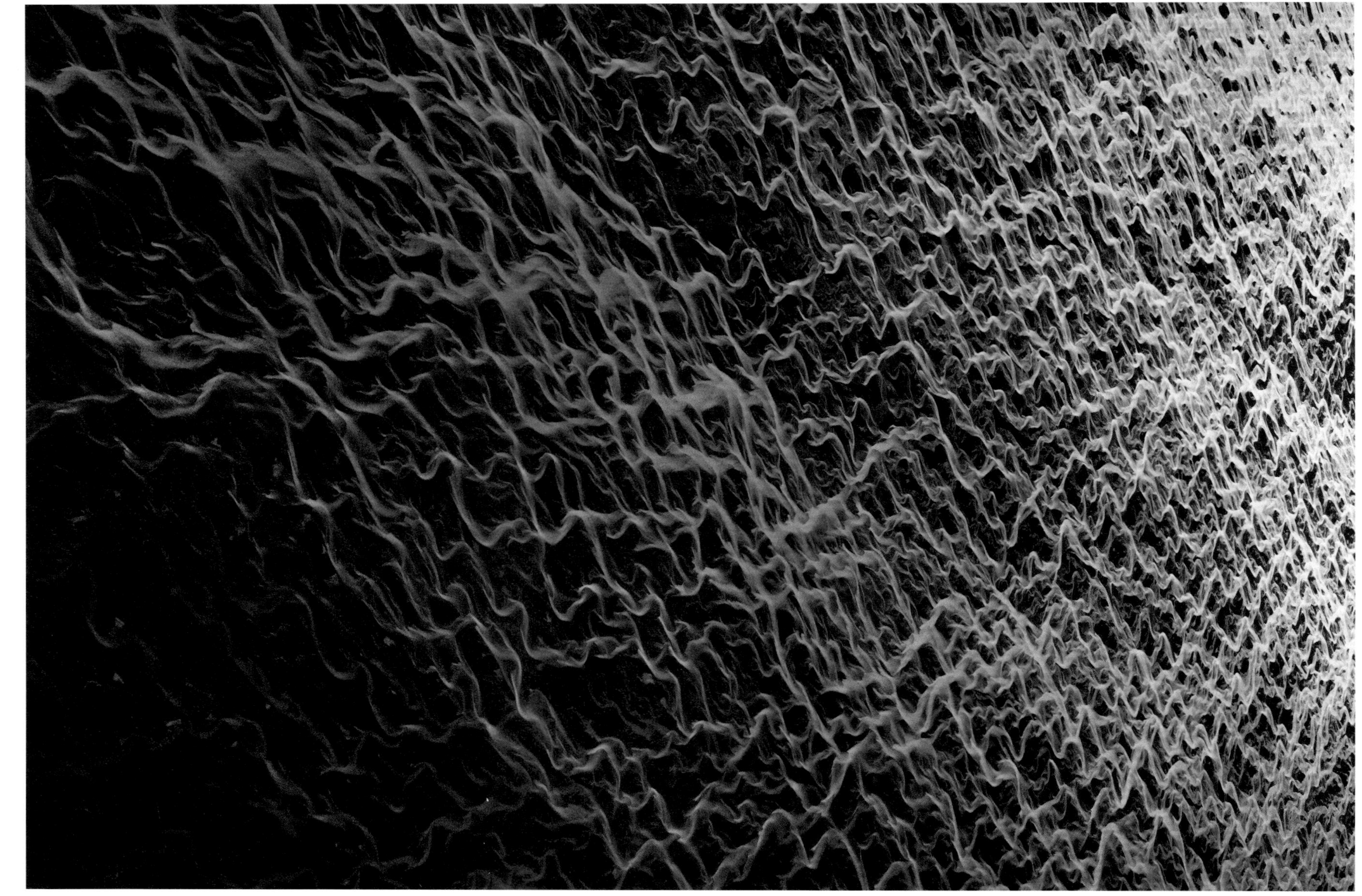

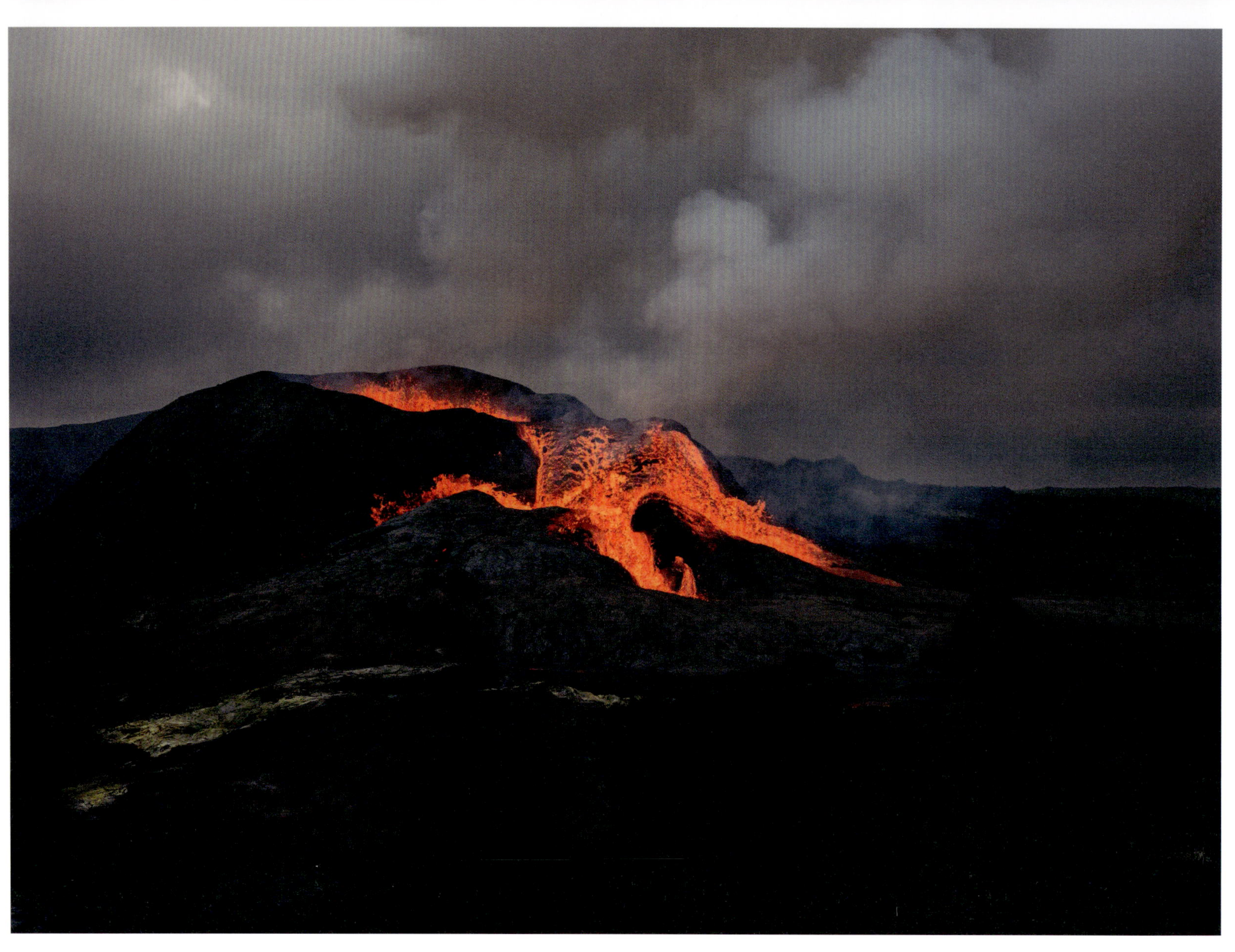

123 Fagradalsfjall Volcano, Reykjanes Peninsula, Iceland, 2021

Disko Bay, Ilulissat, Greenland, 2021

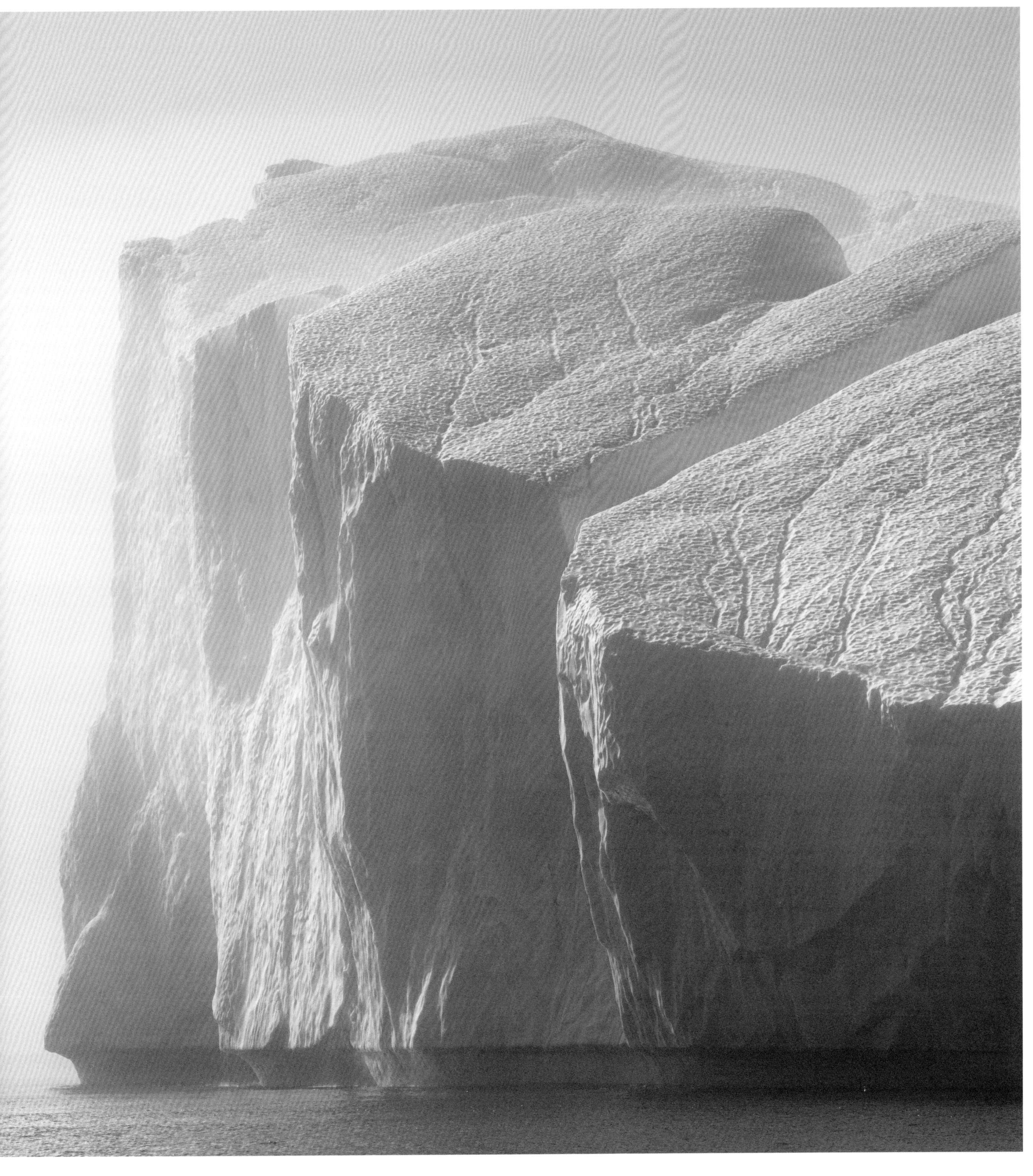

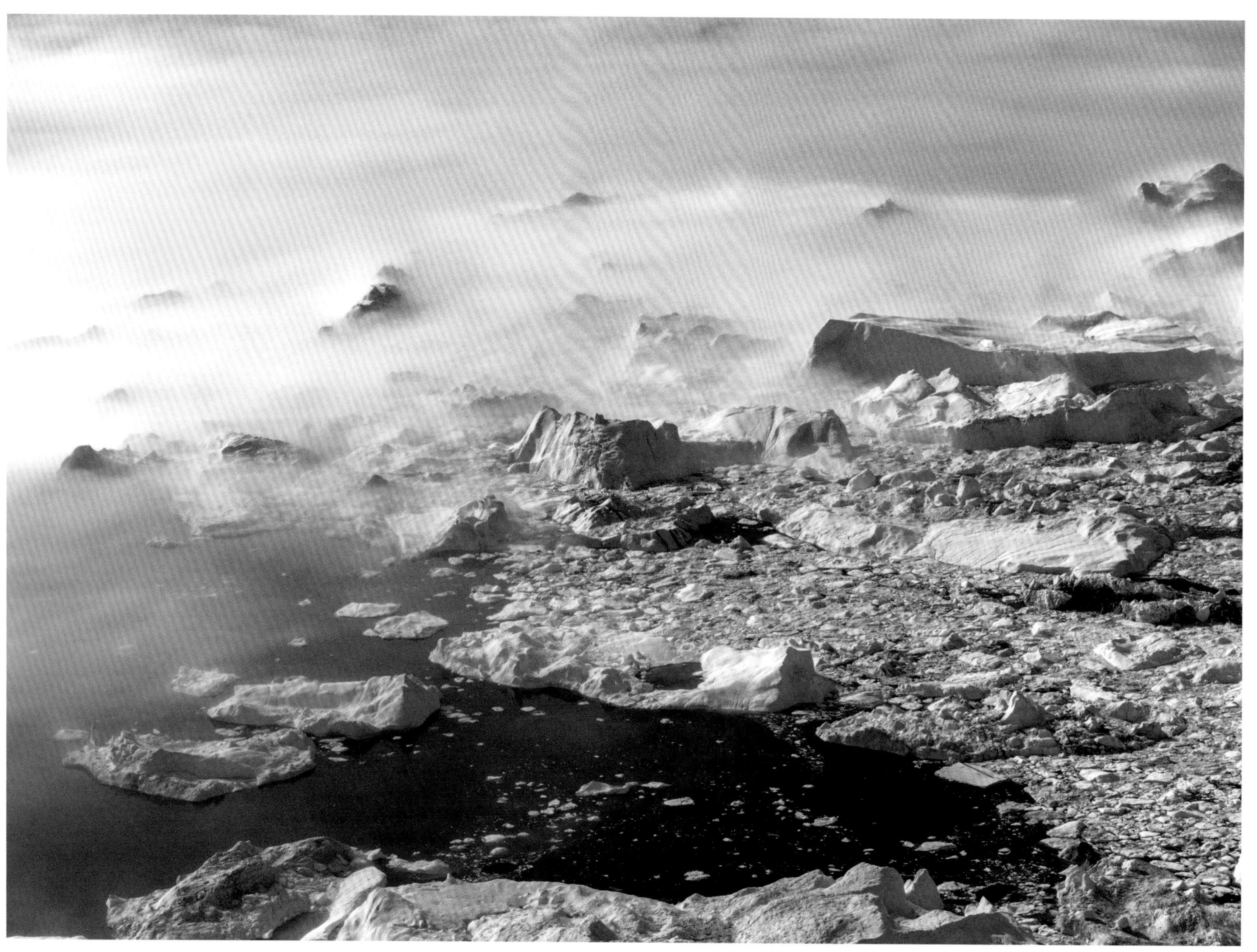

 Disko Bay, Ilulissat, Greenland, 2021

Vatnajökull Glacier Area, Iceland, 2021

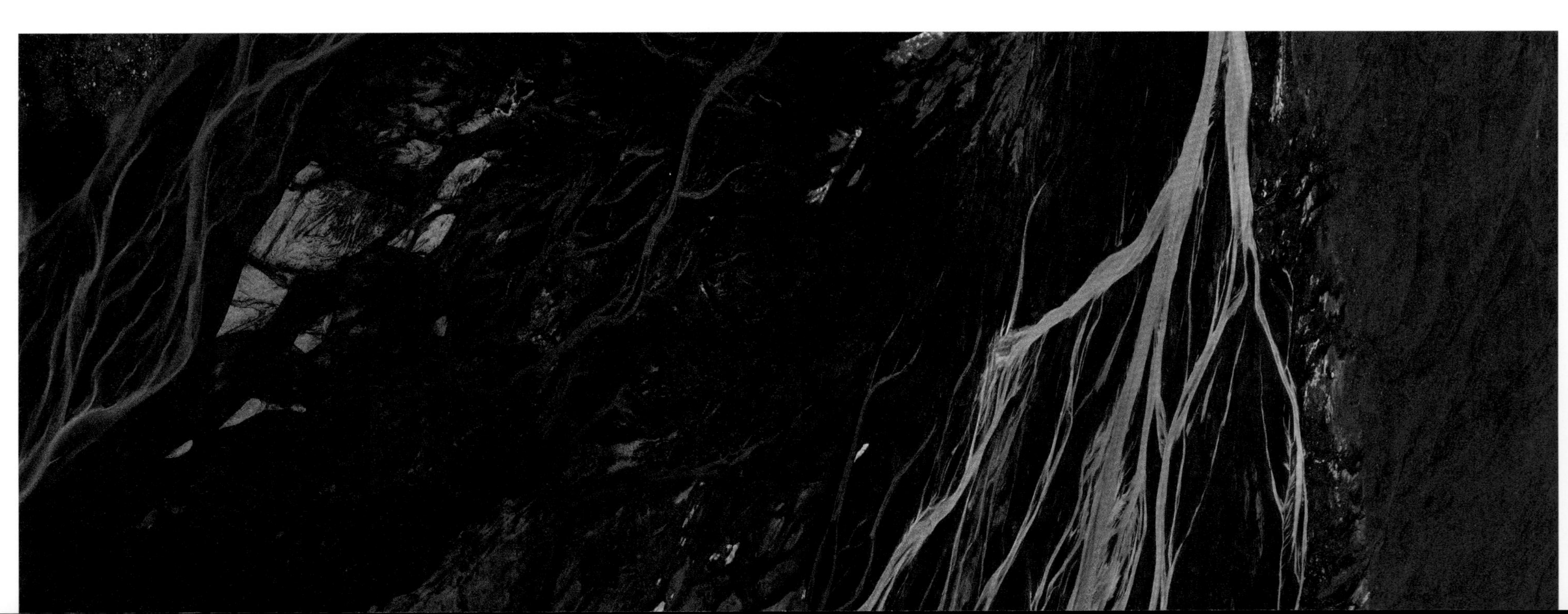

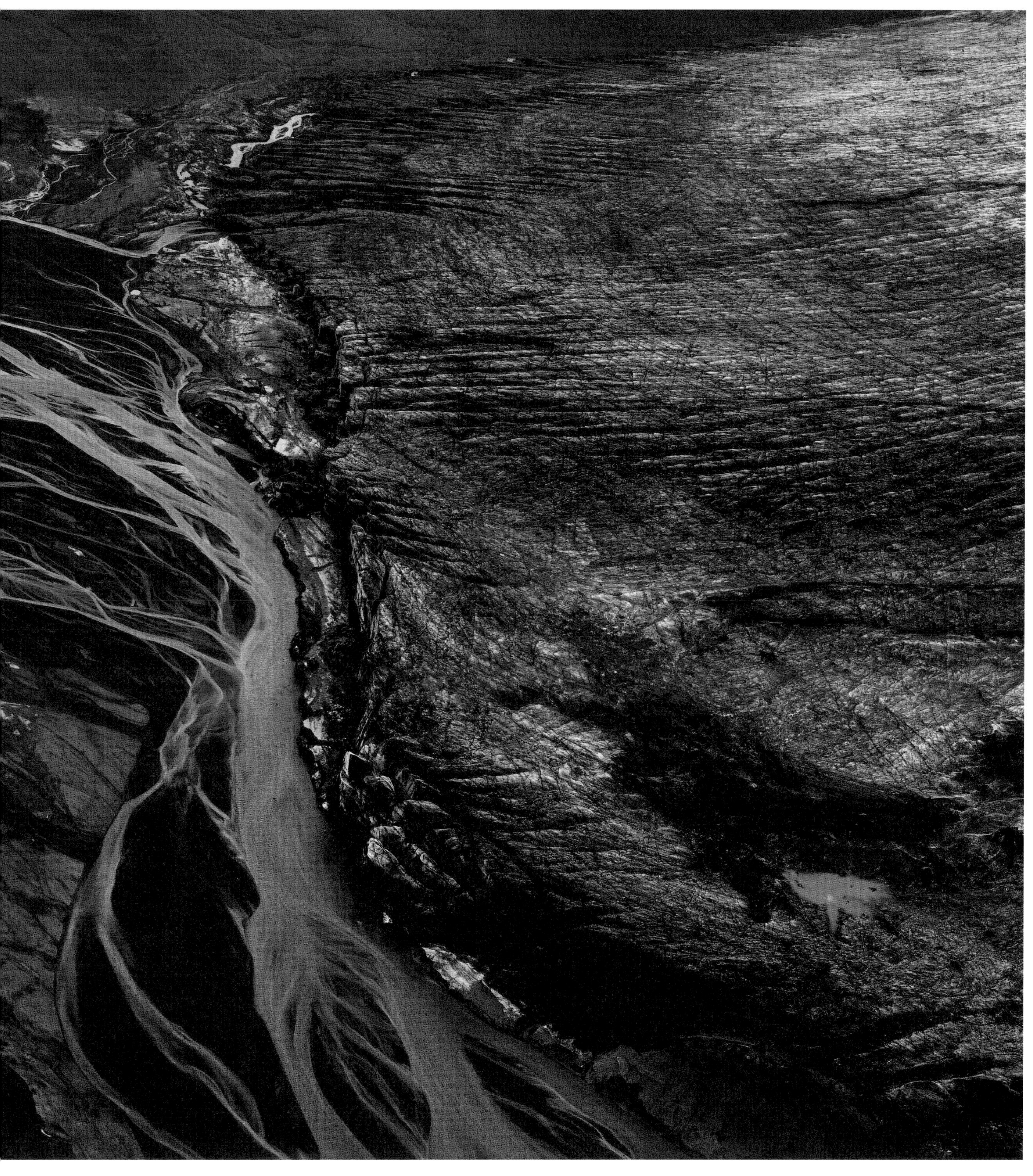

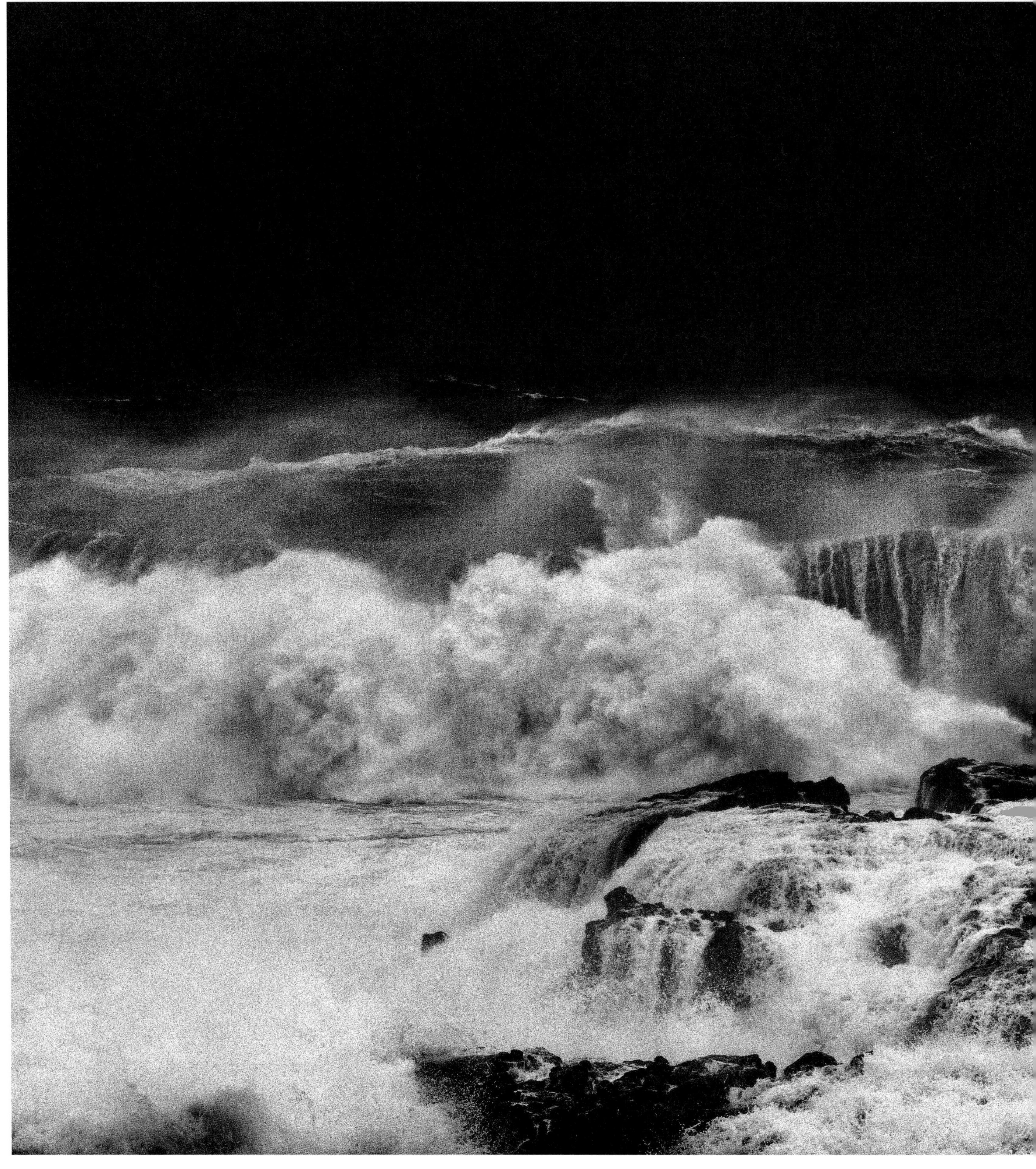

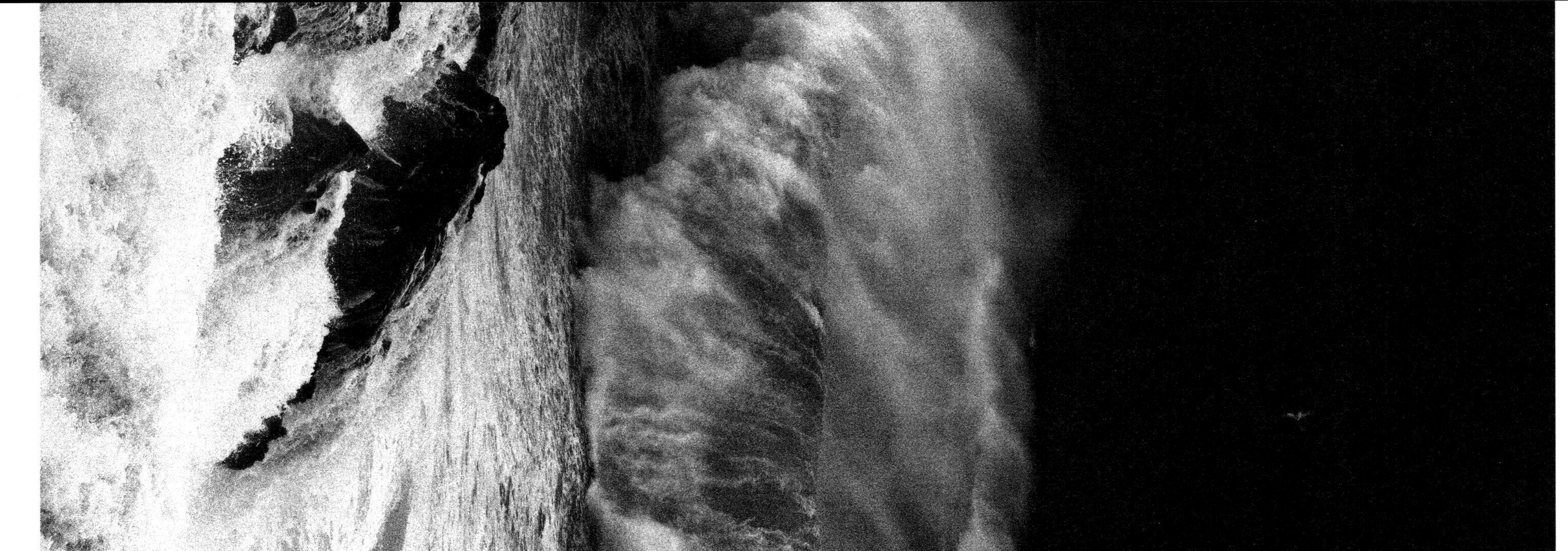

Reynisfjara Beach, Vík, Iceland, 2021

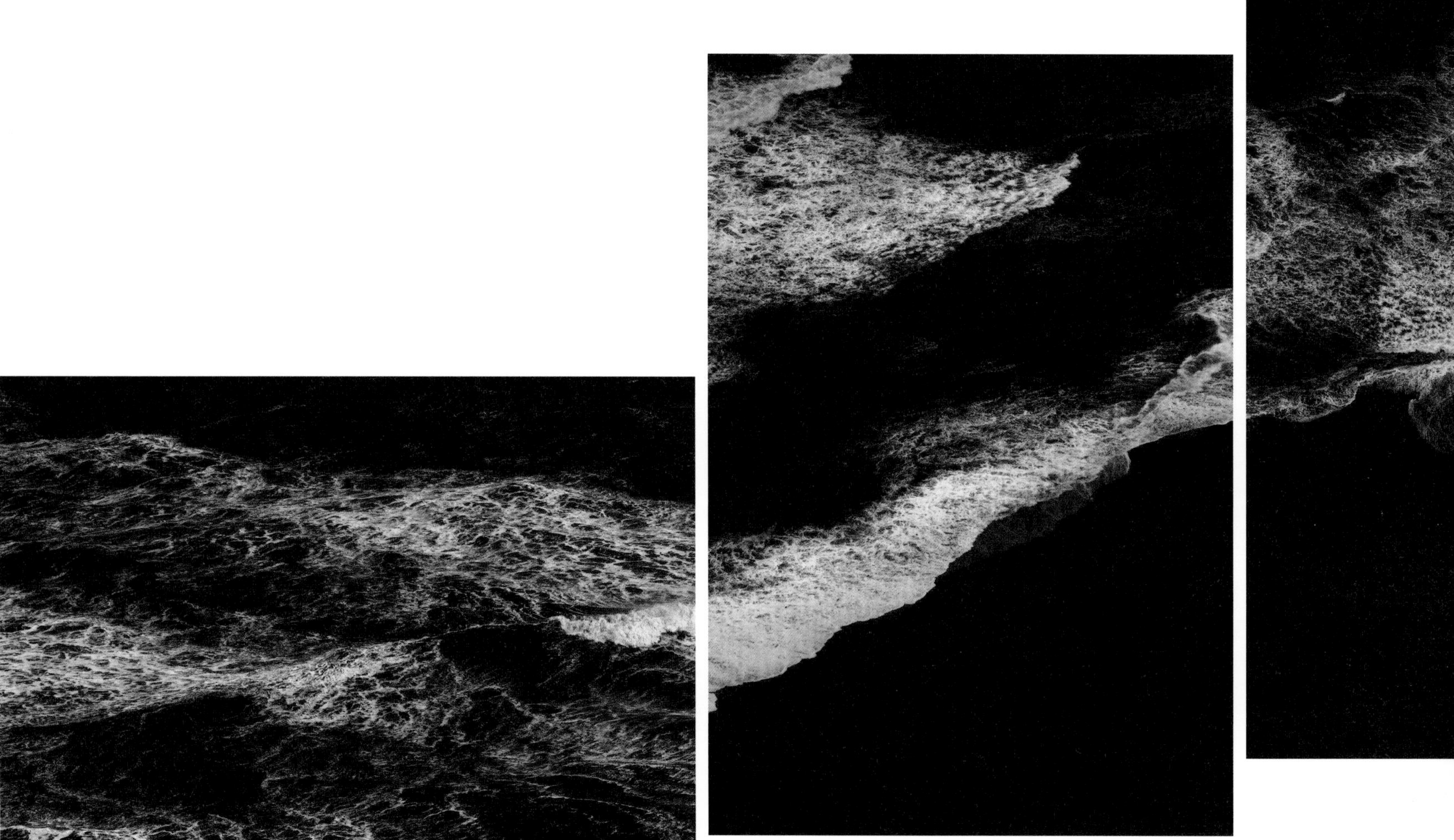

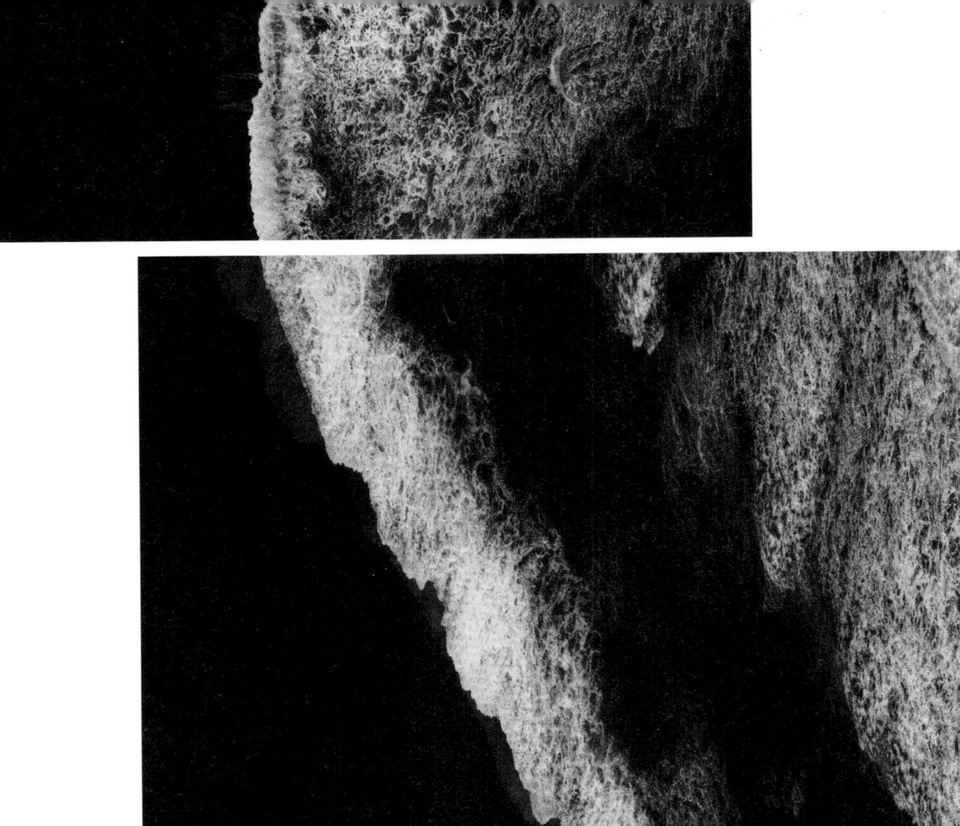

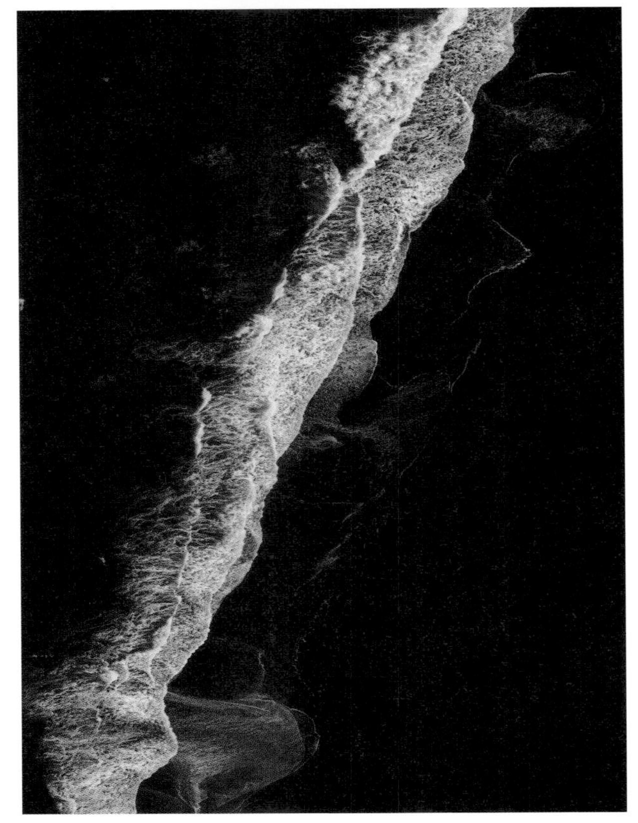

Reynisfjara Beach, Vík, Iceland, 2021

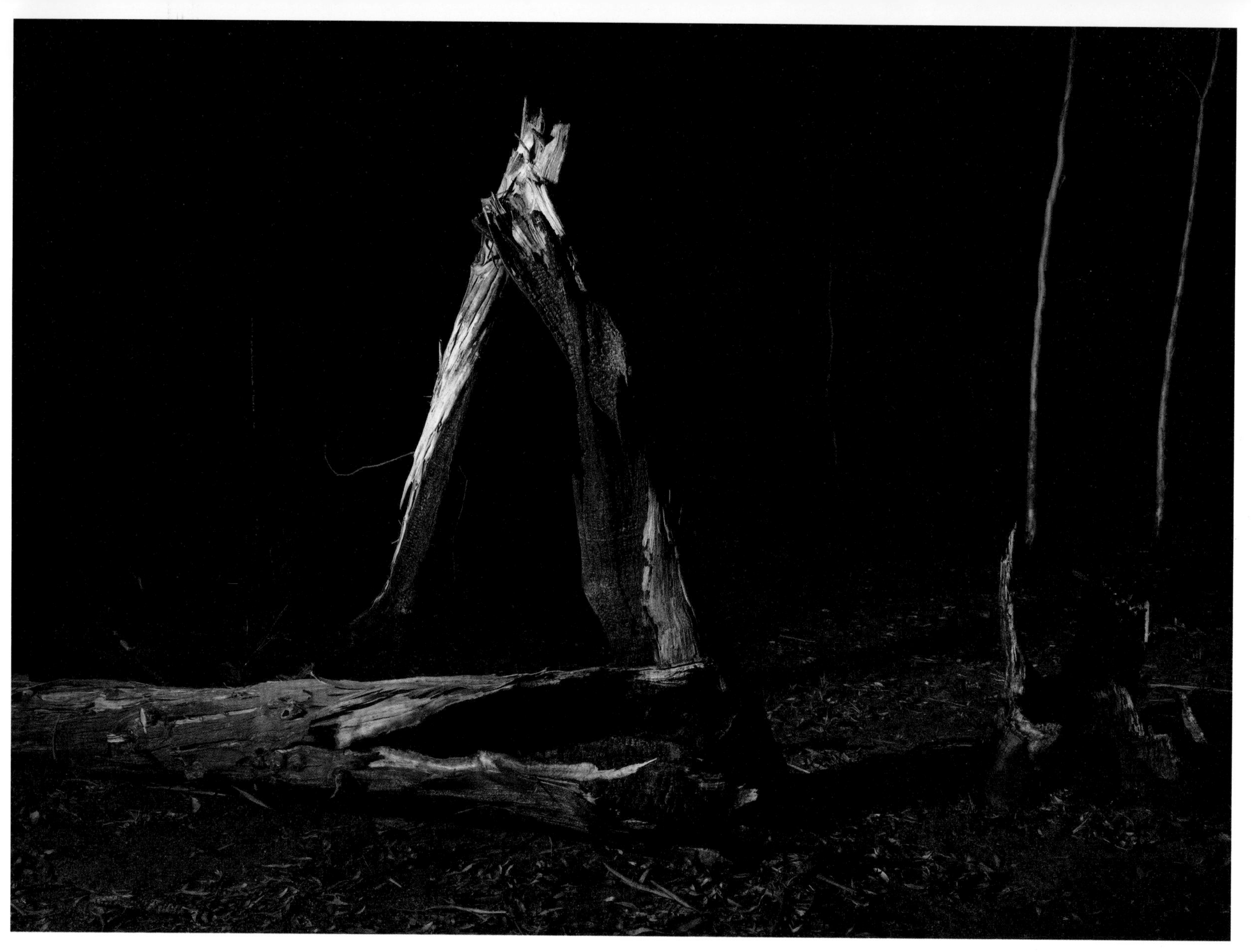

135 Kosciuszko National Park, New South Wales, Australia, 2020

136 Bondi State Forest, New South Wales, Australia, 2020

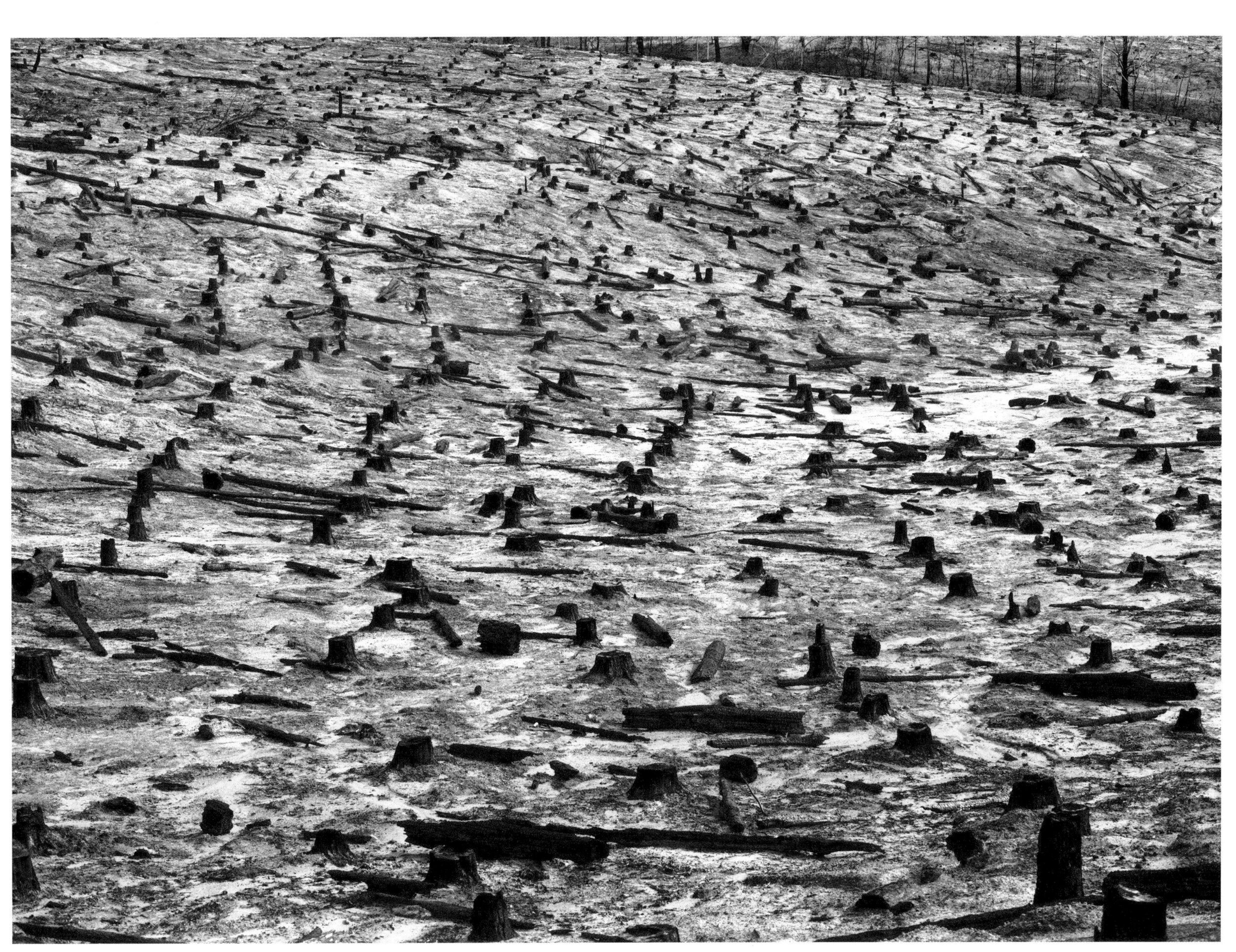

Eden, Victoria, Australia, 2020

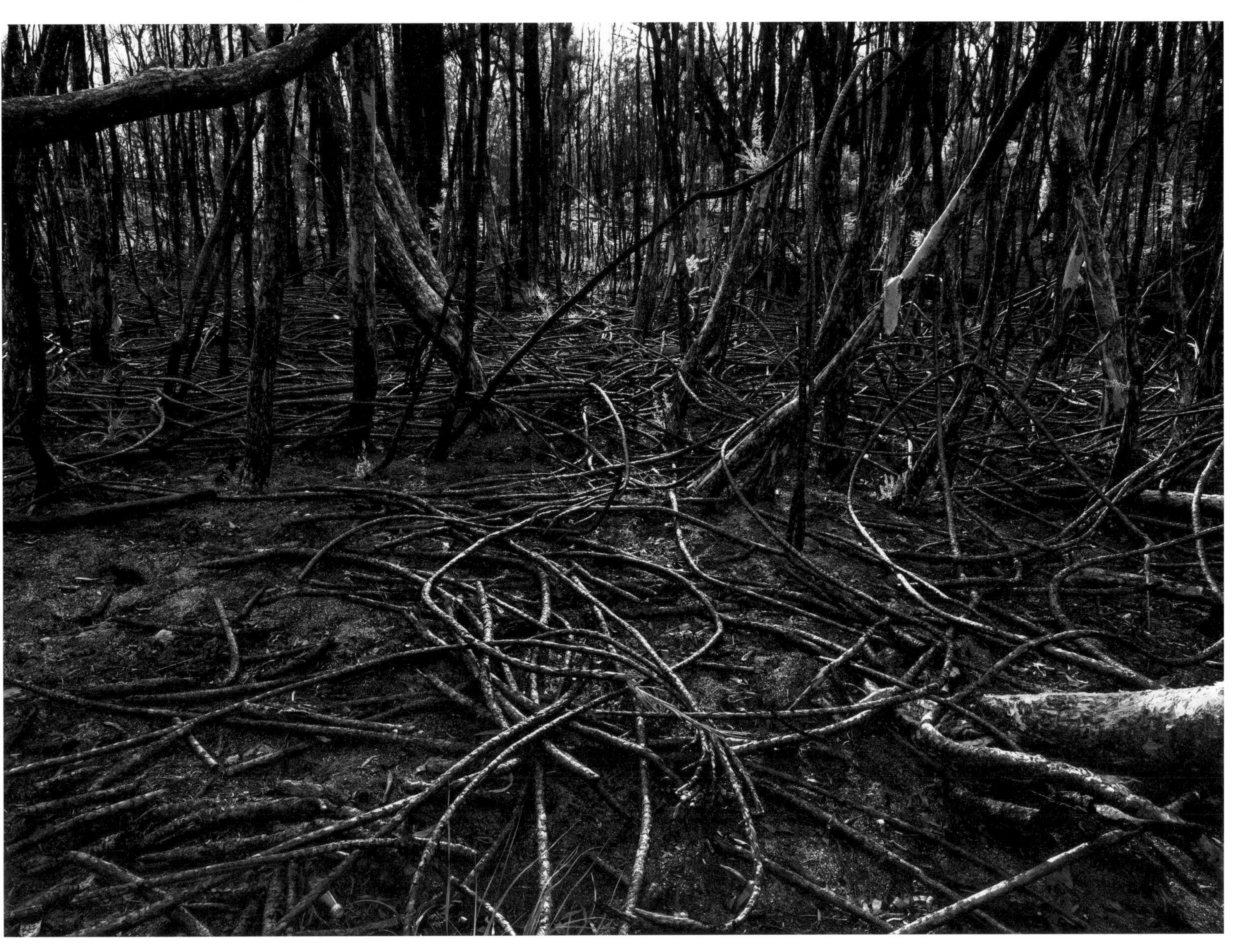

140 Sella Valley, Trentino, Italy, 2019

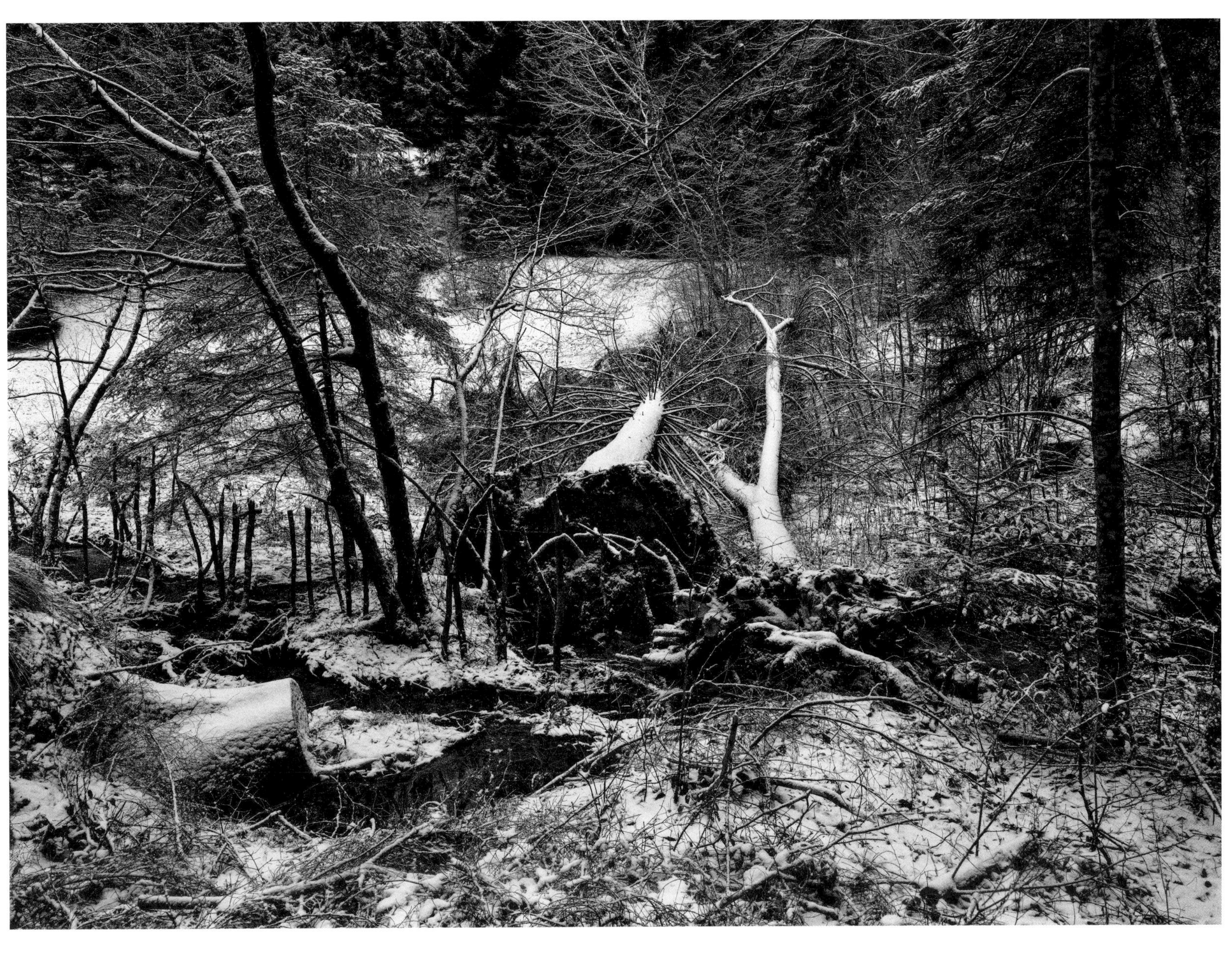

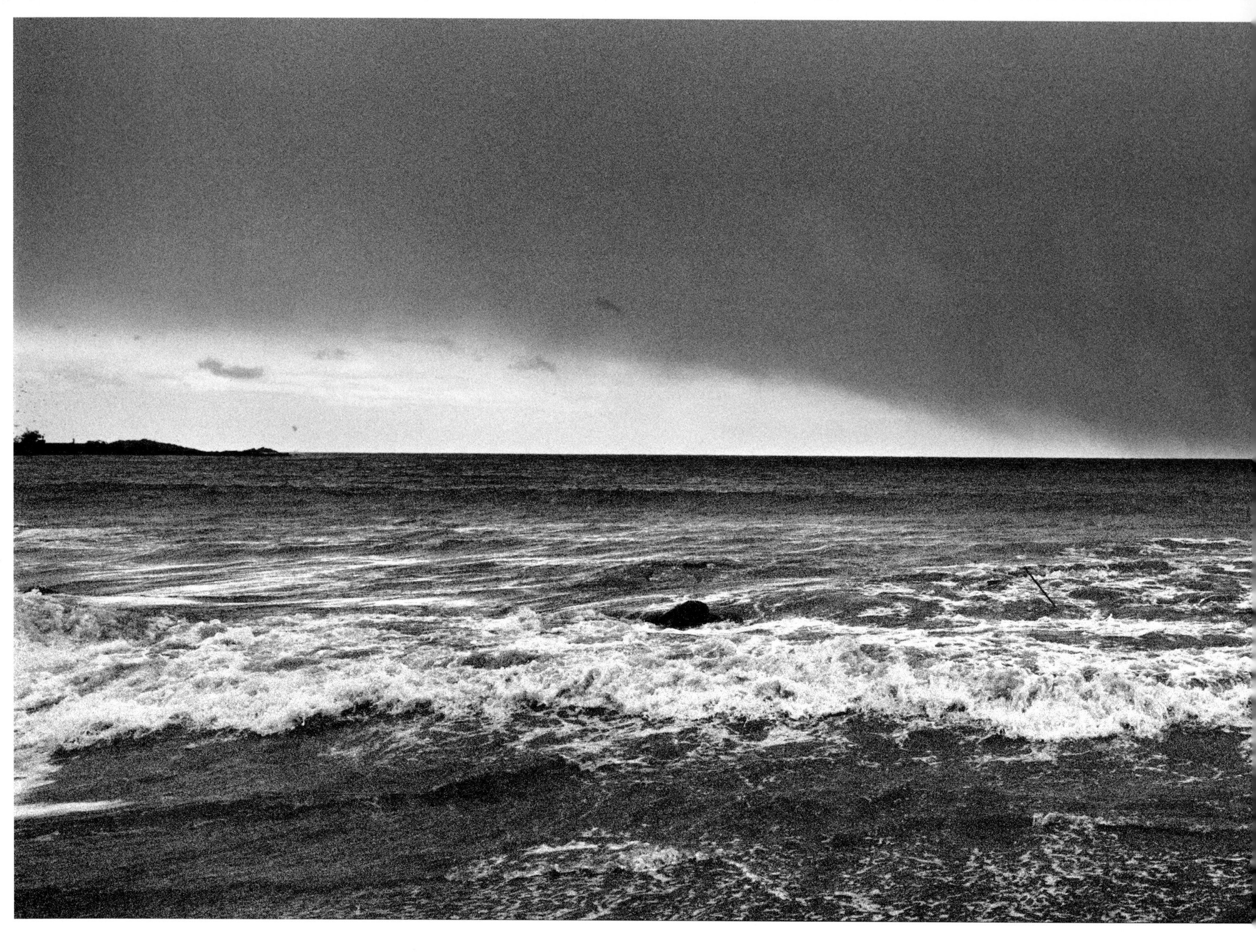

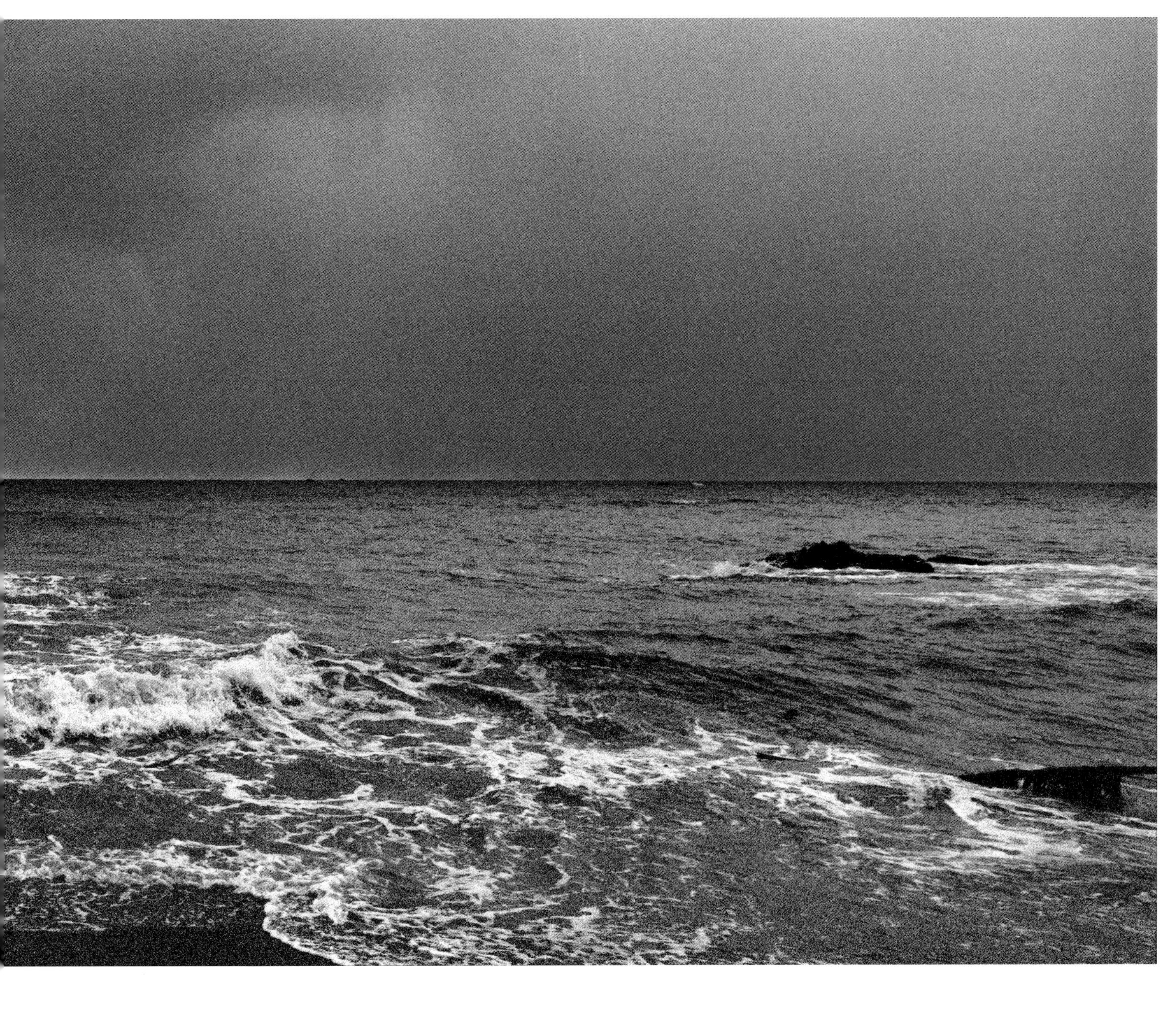

Rikuzenhashikami, Kesennuma, Japan, 2011

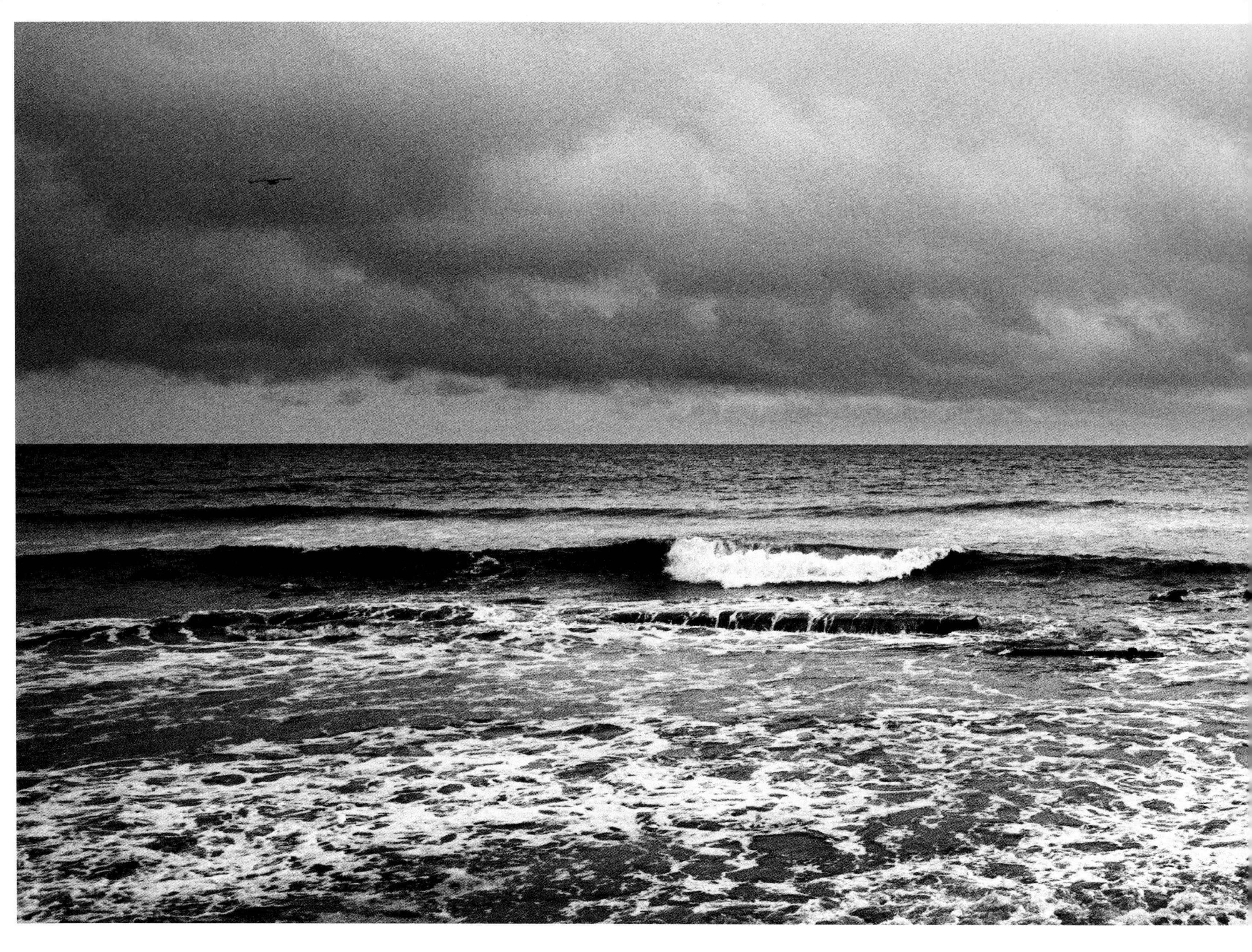

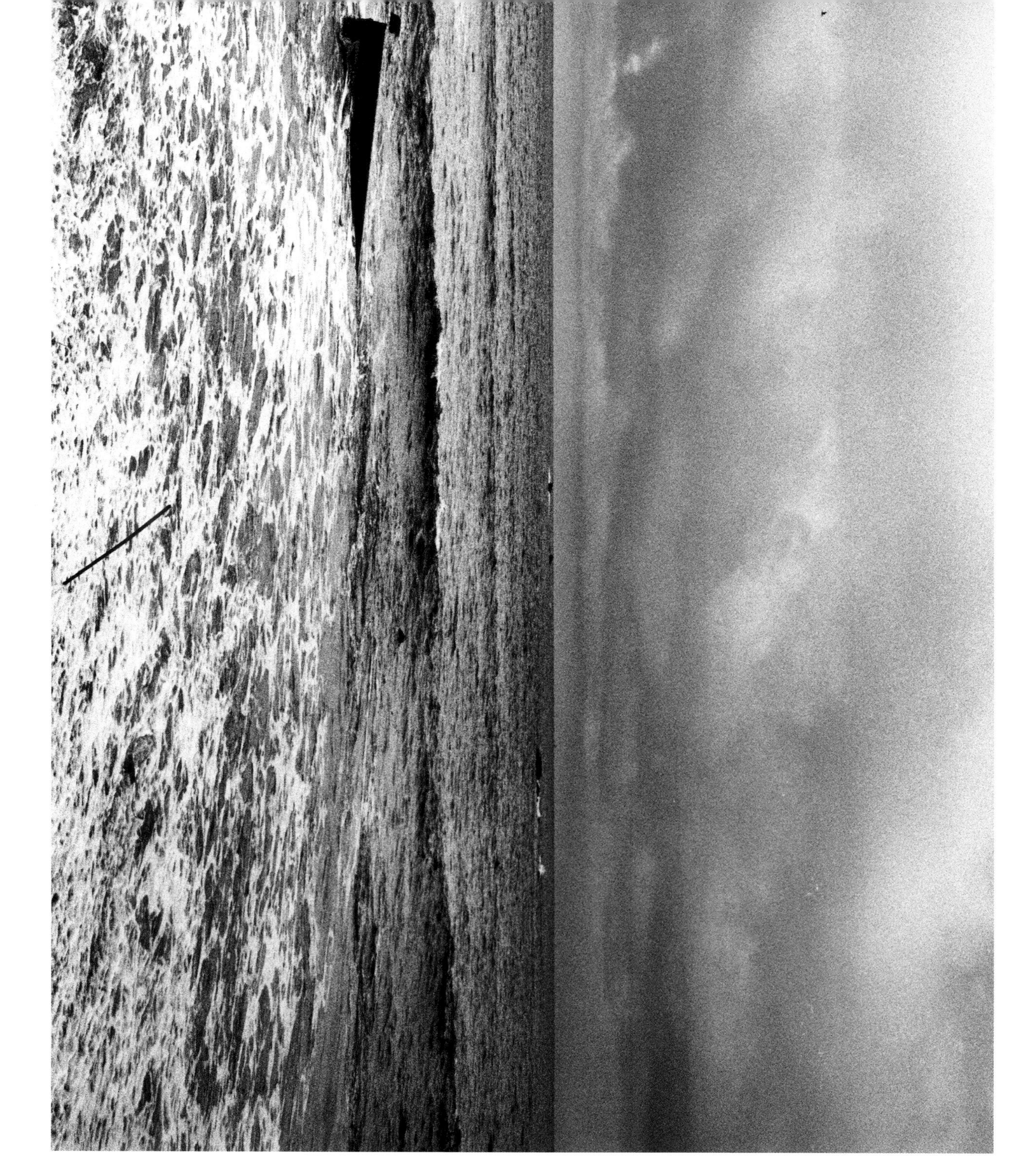

Mishima, Kesennuma, Japan, 2011

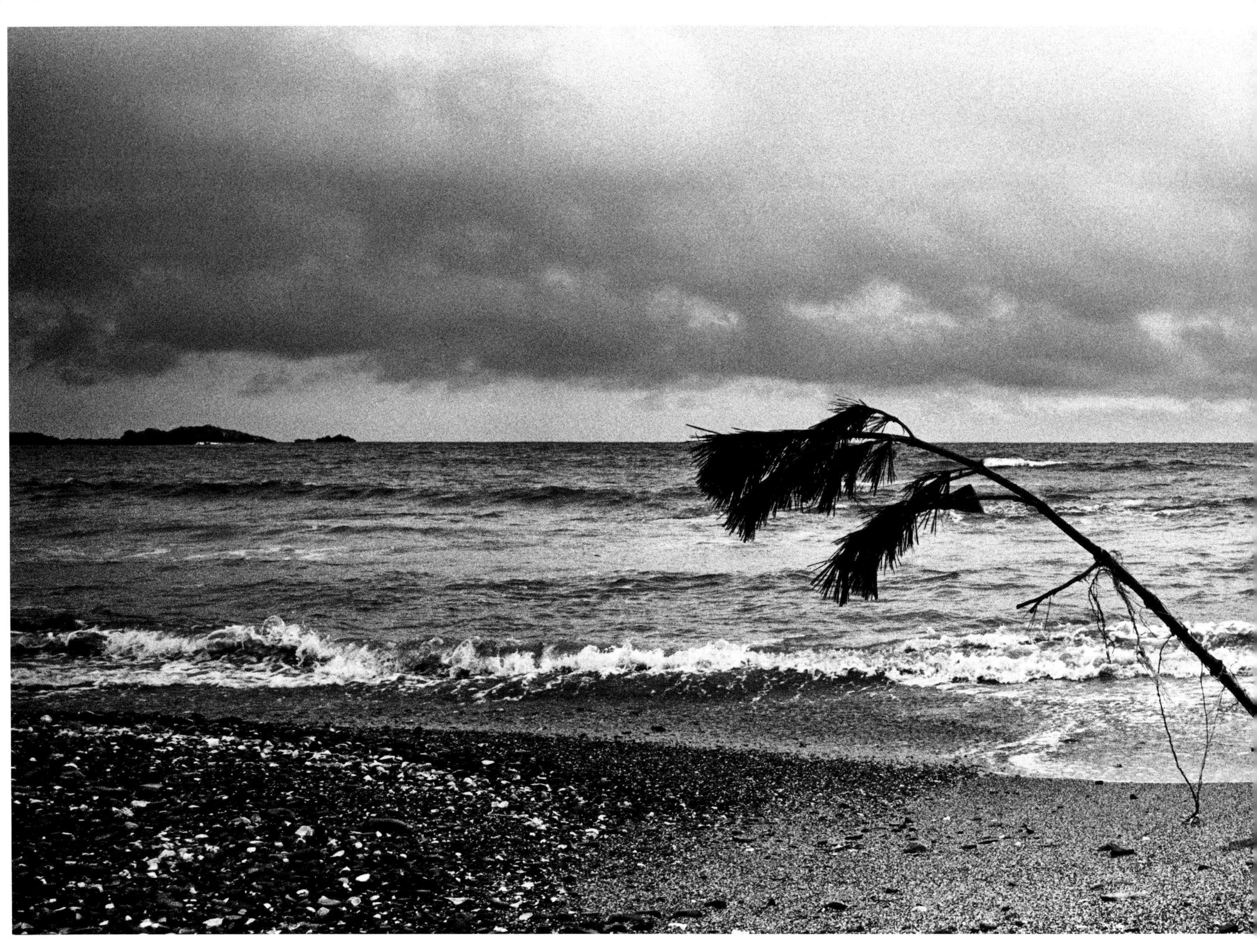

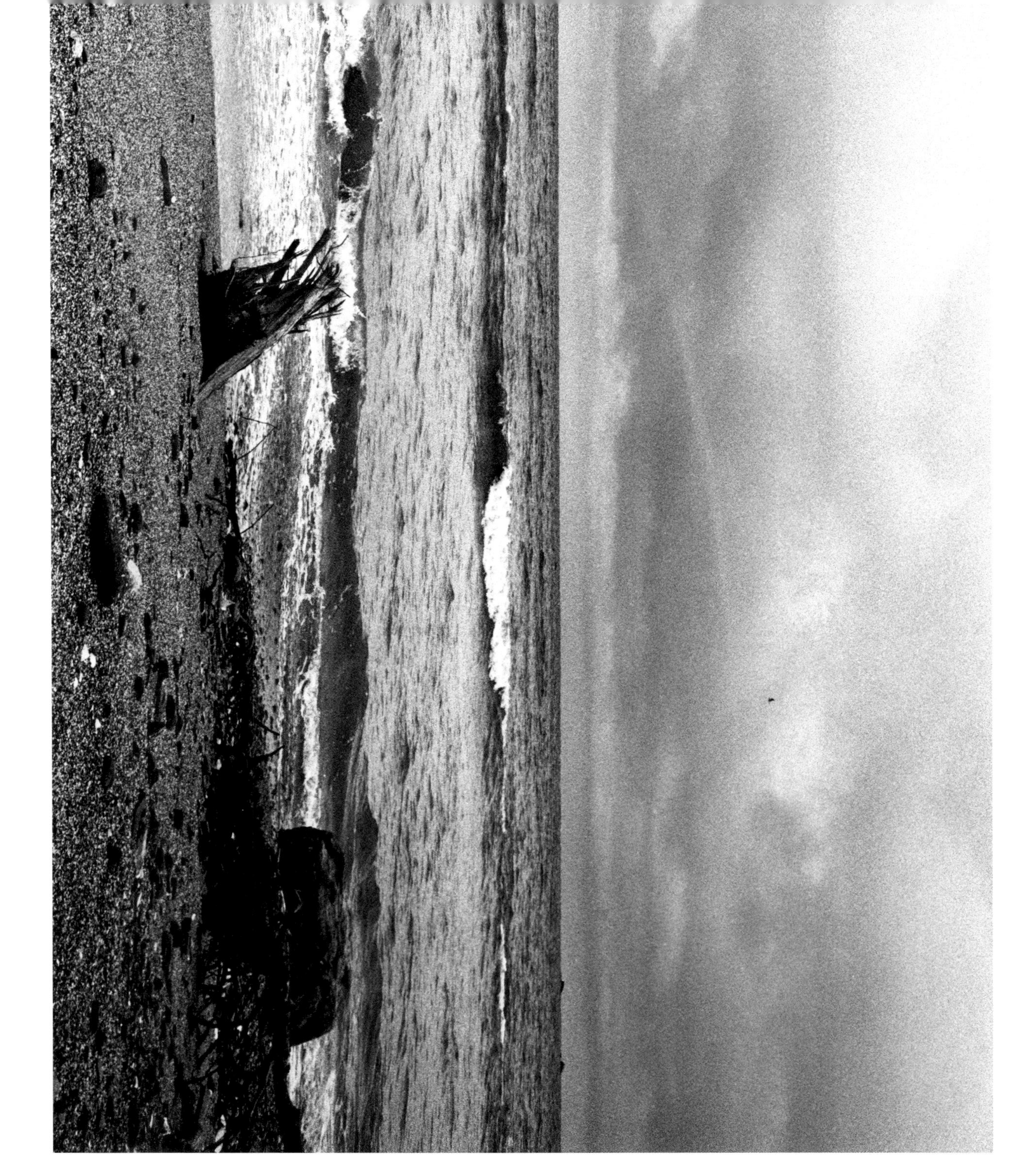

Mishima, Kesennuma, Japan, 2011

Fagradalsfjall Volcano, Reykjanes Peninsula, Iceland, 2021

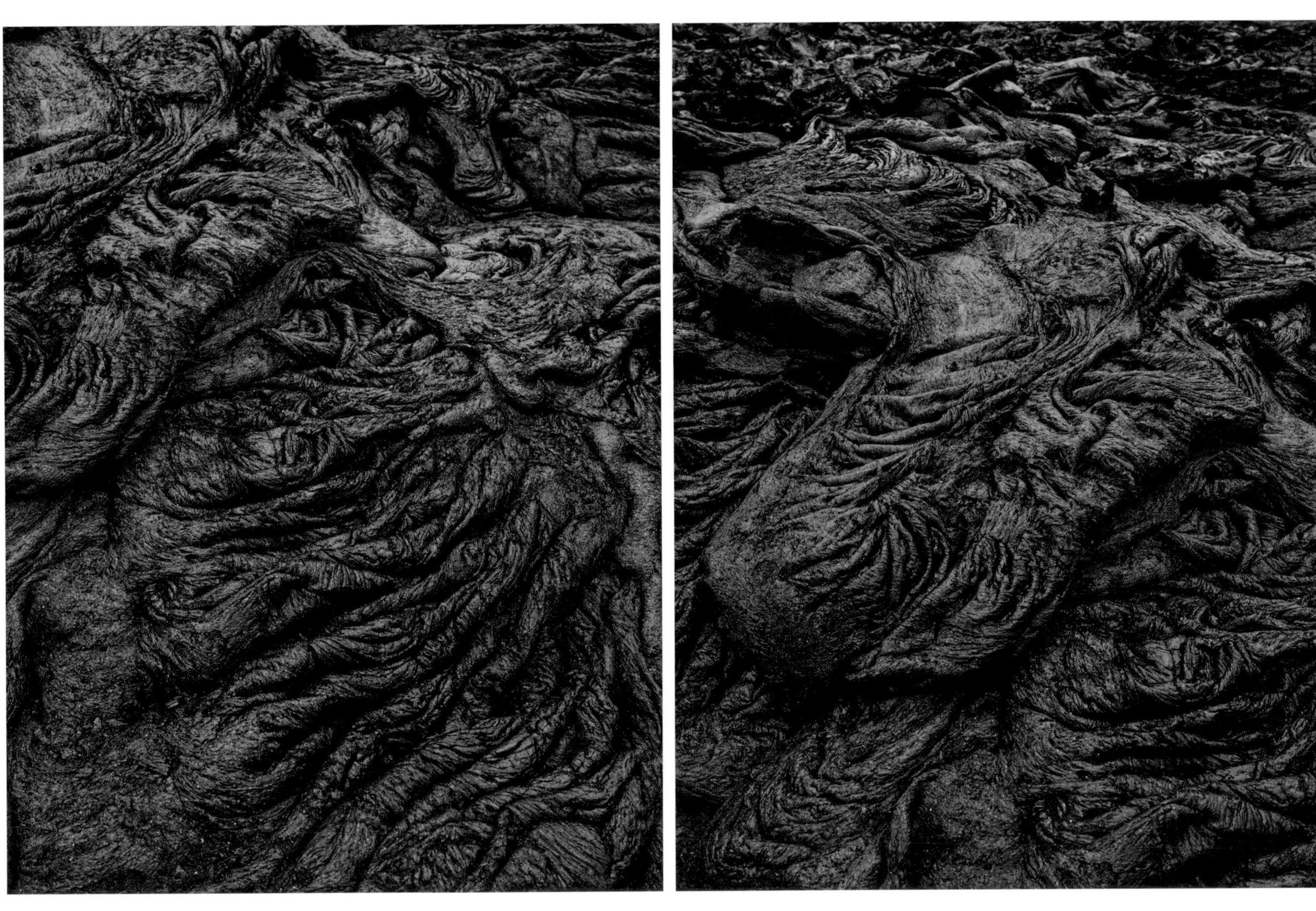

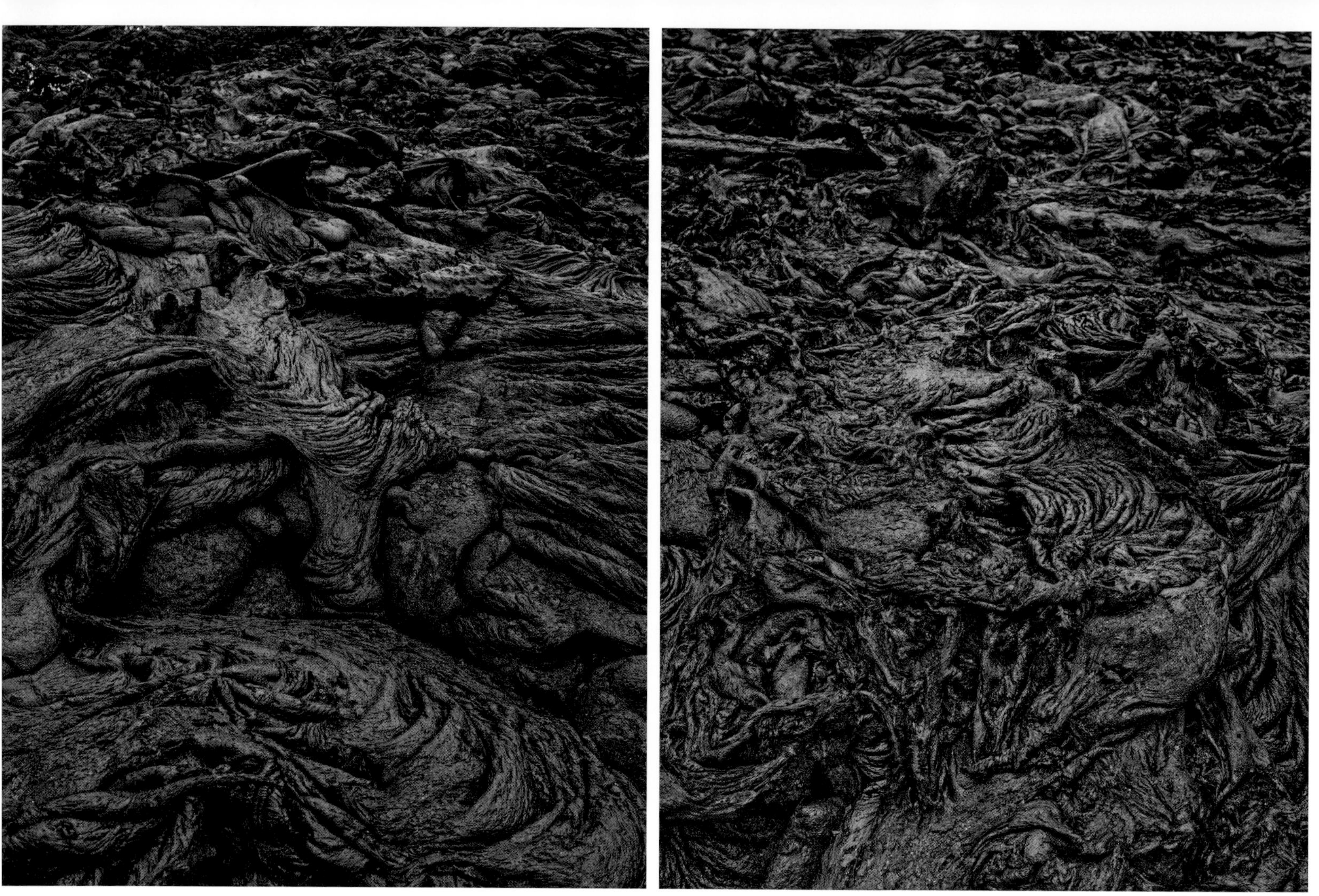

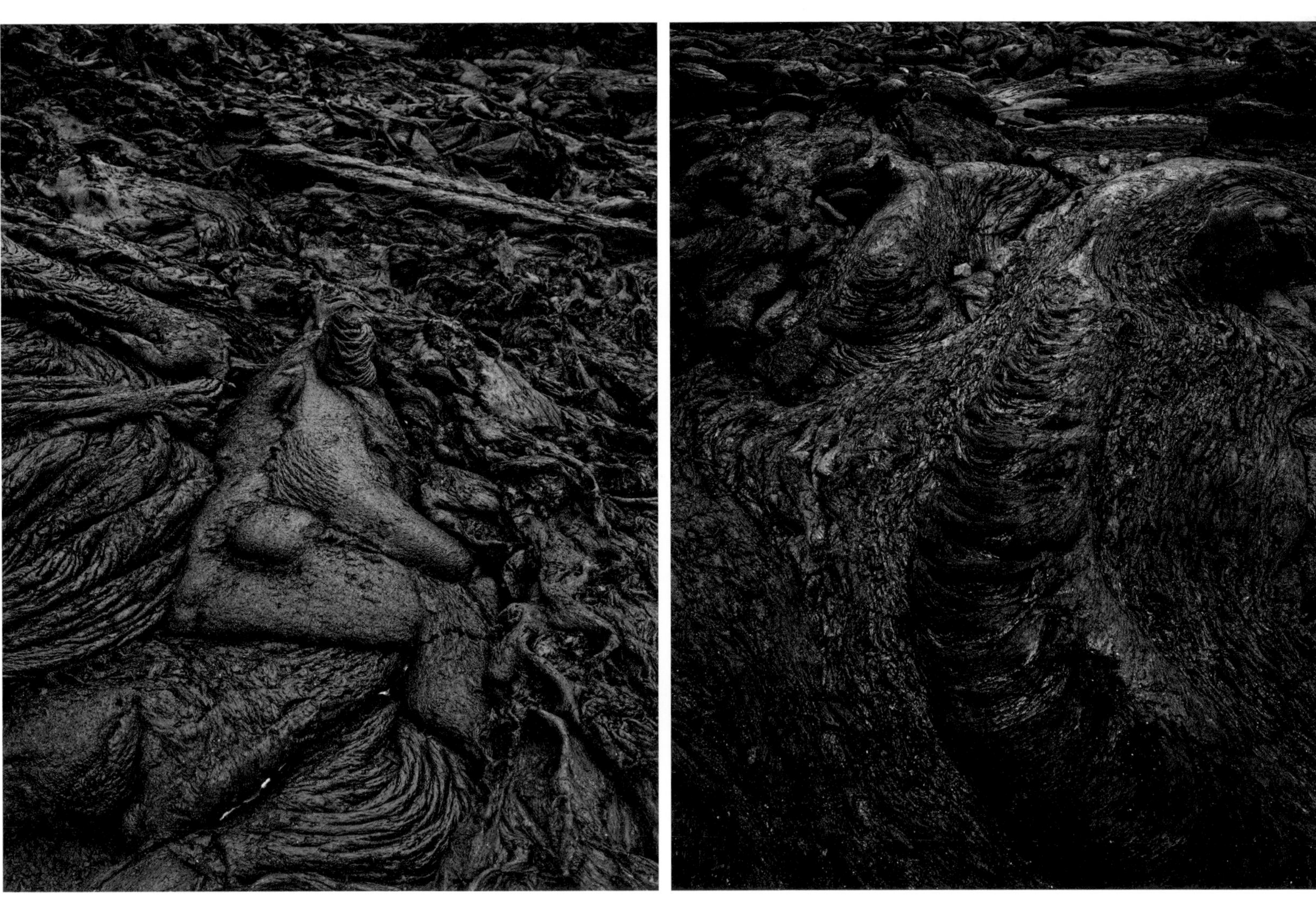

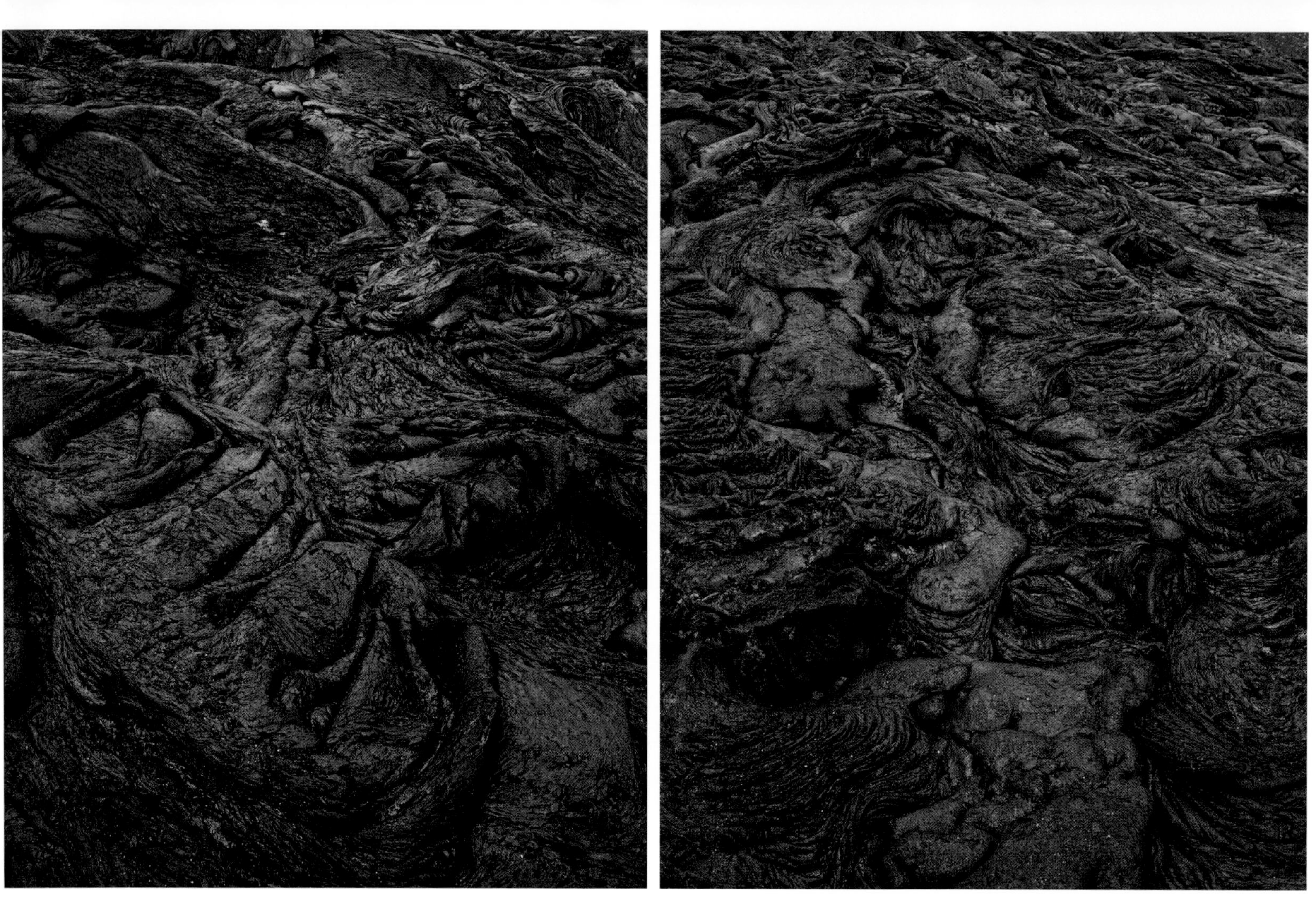

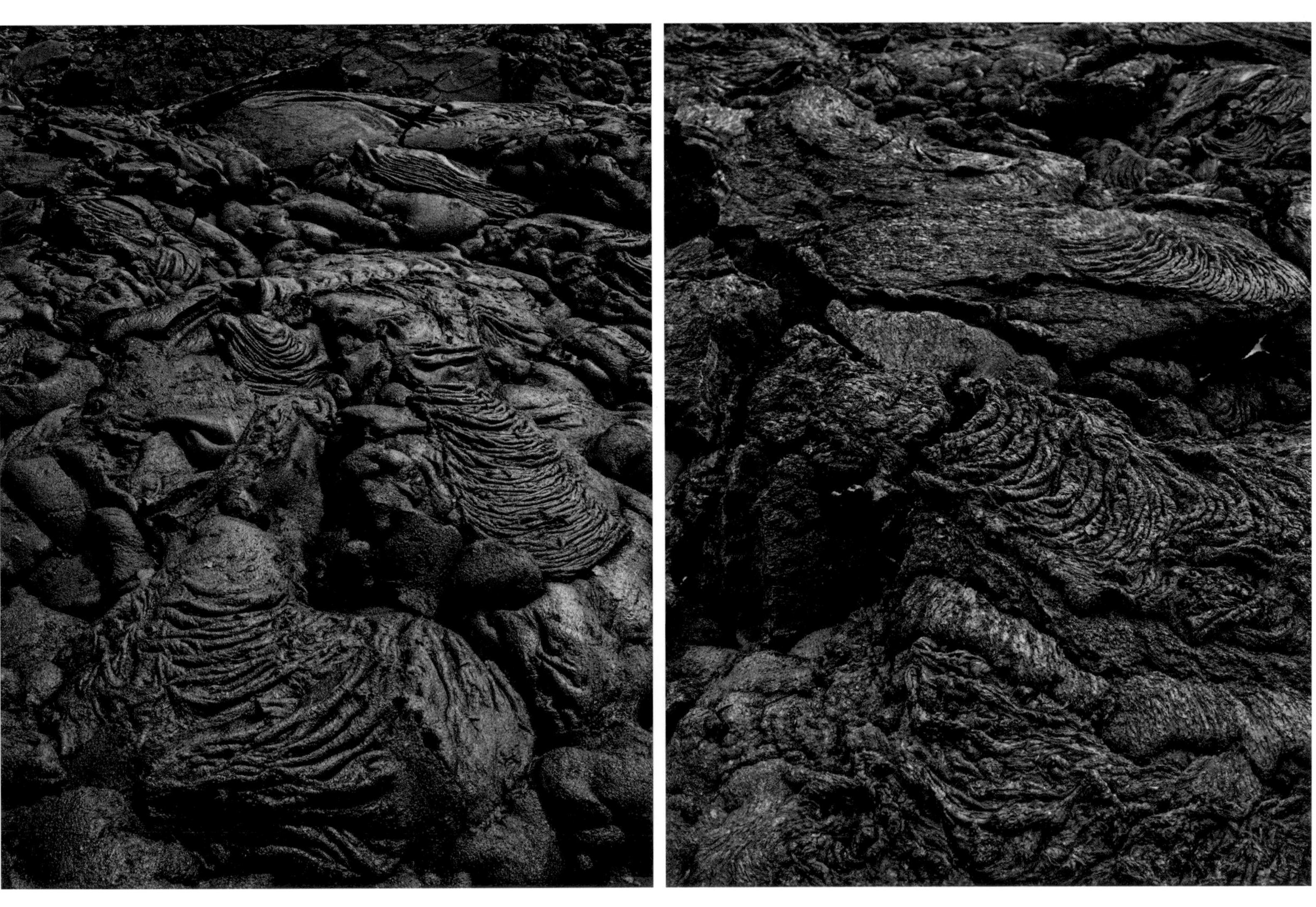

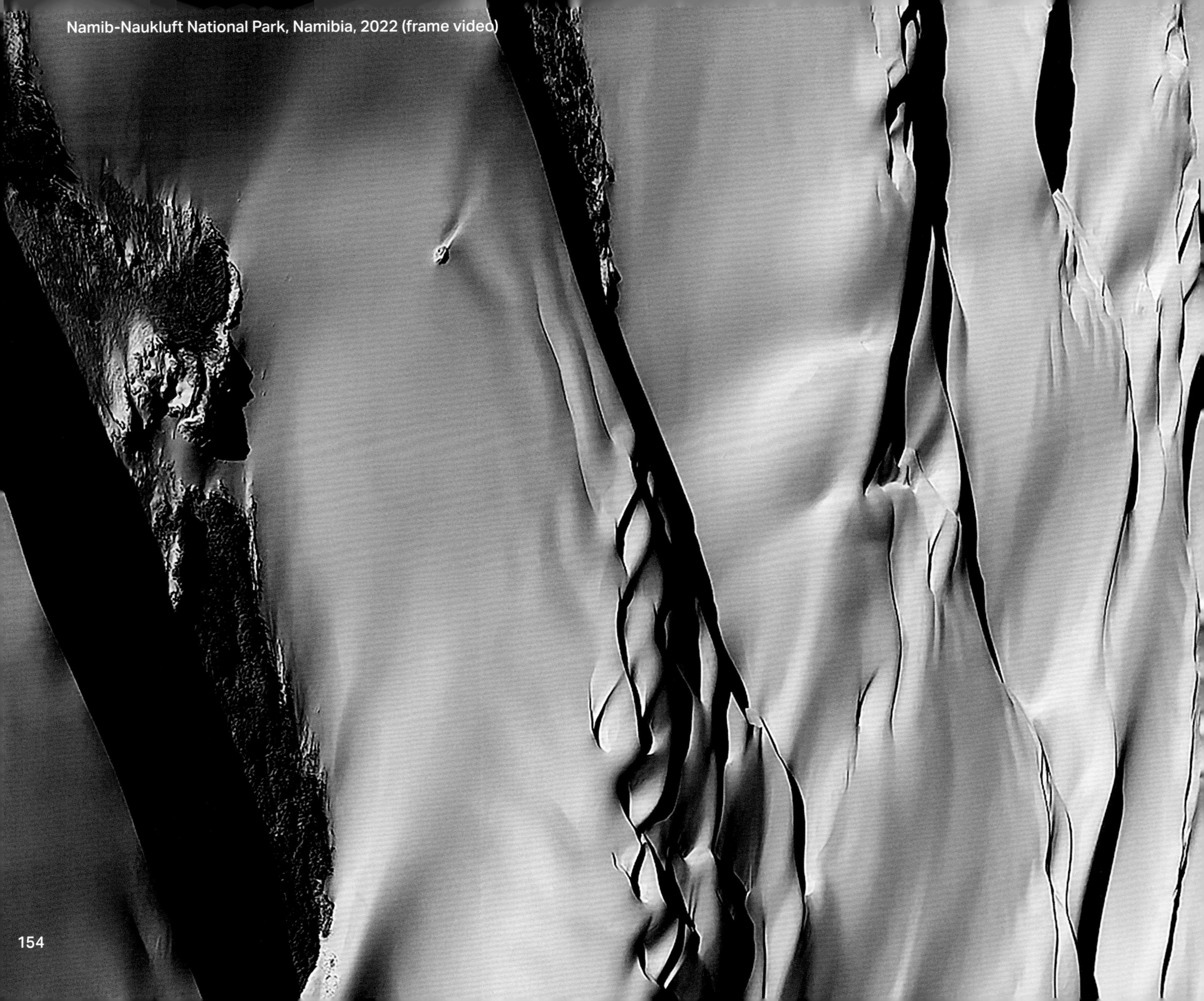

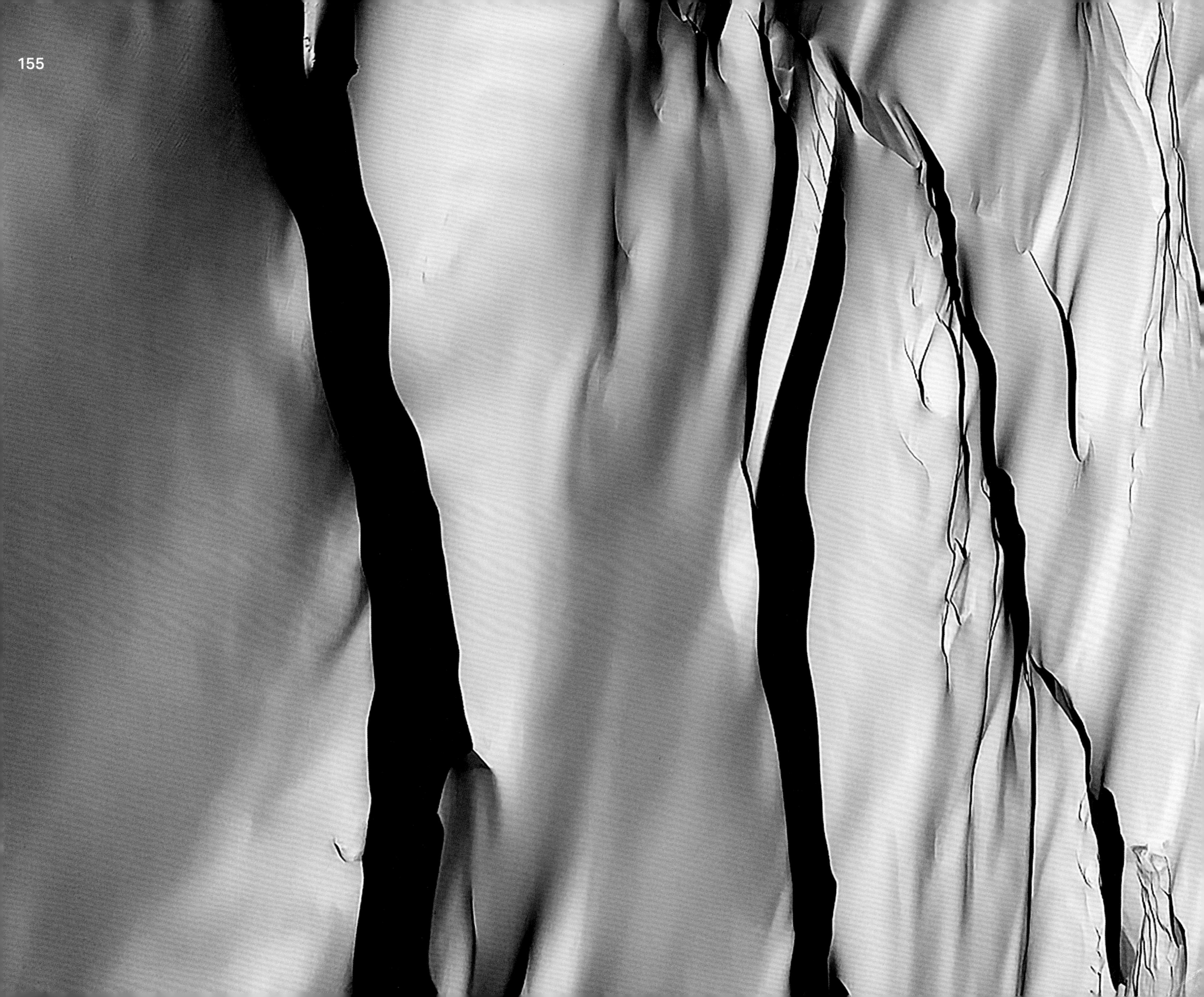

Intesa Sanpaolo

Giovanni Bazoli
Chairman Emeritus

Gian Maria Gros-Pietro
Chairman

Carlo Messina
Managing Director and CEO

Paolo M. Grandi
Chief Governance Officer

Paolo Pellegrin
Fragile Wonder:
A Journey through
Everchanging Nature

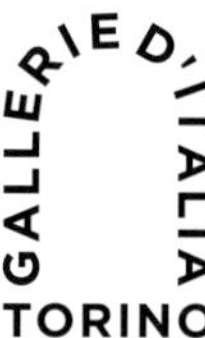

Gallerie d'Italia – Turin
17 May – 4 September 2022

Exhibition project by
INTESA SANPAOLO

as part of
Progetto Cultura

Under the patronage of

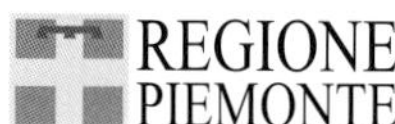

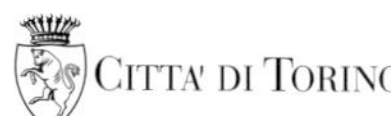

Concept and Organization

Intesa Sanpaolo
Art, Culture, and Historical Heritage
Executive Director
Gallerie d'Italia
Director
Michele Coppola

Historical Artistic Heritage and Cultural Activities
Silvia Foschi
Historical Archives
Barbara Costa
Artistic Heritage
Laura Feliciotti
Cultural Initiatives and Exhibition Projects
Antonio Ernesto Denunzio
with Francesca Dal Cortivo
Exhibition Set-Ups
Mariangela Taliento

Cultural Promotion, Marketing, and Partnership
Laurence Aliquot
Cultural Promotion and Marketing
Simona Cantone
with Davide Rossini,
Alessandro Spagnoli
and Antonella Pellegrino,
Silvia Stabile
Editorial and Music Coordination
Rosanna Benedini
with Laura Tombola,
Valeria Tortosa
Artistic and Cultural Partnerships
Tiziana Antonella D'Amico
with Giulia Borroni,
Luca Saporiti

Gallerie d'Italia – Turin
Deputy Director
Photographic Projects and Commissions
Antonio Carloni
with Maura Dettoni,
Michela Garosi
and Antonella Belli,
Sonia Schellino

Administration Support
Raffaele Franzoni
with Gianluigi Perani

Thanks to

Real Estate and Logistics
Luca Tedesi,
Simone Sprecapane,
Massimo Pignatelli,
Maurizio Perello,
Sergio Scovazzo,
Antonio Tedesco

Media and Associations Relations
Matteo Fabiani
Institutional, Social, and Cultural Activities
Elisa Ferrio
with Andrea Alessandro Ferro
and Silvana Scannicchio

Special thanks to the departments of the Intesa Sanpaolo Group

Administration and Tax
Communication and Corporate Image
Legal Affairs
Corporate Bodies and Corporate Affairs
Procurement
Internal Communication

Production

Exhibition Curator
Walter Guadagnini

with the contribution of
Mario Calabresi

Studio Pellegrin

Production
Annalisa D'Angelo

Coordination
Alessandro Vitali

Consulting
Chiara Pellegrin

Layout Design
Architect Sergio Bianchi
with Fiorella Campodonico,
Mariangela De Meo,
Silvia Perobelli

Video Installation
Paolo Freschi

Graphic Design Project
Etaoin Shrdlu Studio

Image Post-Production
Paolo Lecca

Prints
Davide Di Gianni /
Digid'a, Rome

Silk-Screen Prints
Arturo Amitrano – 56fili

Frames
Martinelli Cornici, Rome

Photo Mounting
Plastifoto, Rome

Exhibition Texts
Alessandro Vitali

Translation of the Exhibition Texts
Arkadia Translation

Guided Visits and Educational Workshops
Civita Mostre e Musei

Catalogue

Edited by
Walter Guadagnini

Essays
Walter Guadagnini
and Mario Calabresi

Publisher
Gallerie d'Italia | Skira

Cover
Venable 01A, Antarctica, 2017

Pages 1–3, 158–60
Aerial views, 2017–22
Silk-screen prints

Design
Etaoin Shrdlu Studio

Image Post-Production
Paolo Lecca

Photographs of the Making of
Vincenzo Labellarte

Production
Alessandro Vitali

Copy Editing
Carlotta Santuccio

Translations
Karen Tomatis on behalf
of Scriptum, Rome

First published in Italy in 2022
by
Skira editore S.p.A.
Palazzo Casati Stampa
via Torino 61
20123 Milano
Italy
www.skira.net

Printed and bound in Italy.
First edition

ISBN: 978-88-572-4831-8

Distributed in USA, Canada,
Central & South America by
ARTBOOK | D.A.P. 75 Broad
Street Suite 630, New York,
NY 10004, USA.
Distributed elsewhere in the
world by Thames and Hudson
Ltd., 181A High Holborn,
London WC1V 7QX, United
Kingdom.

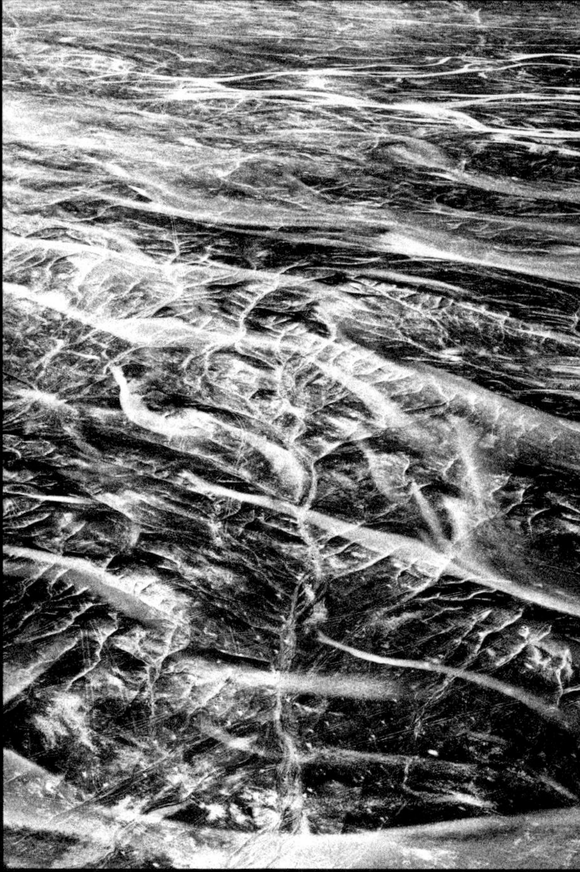

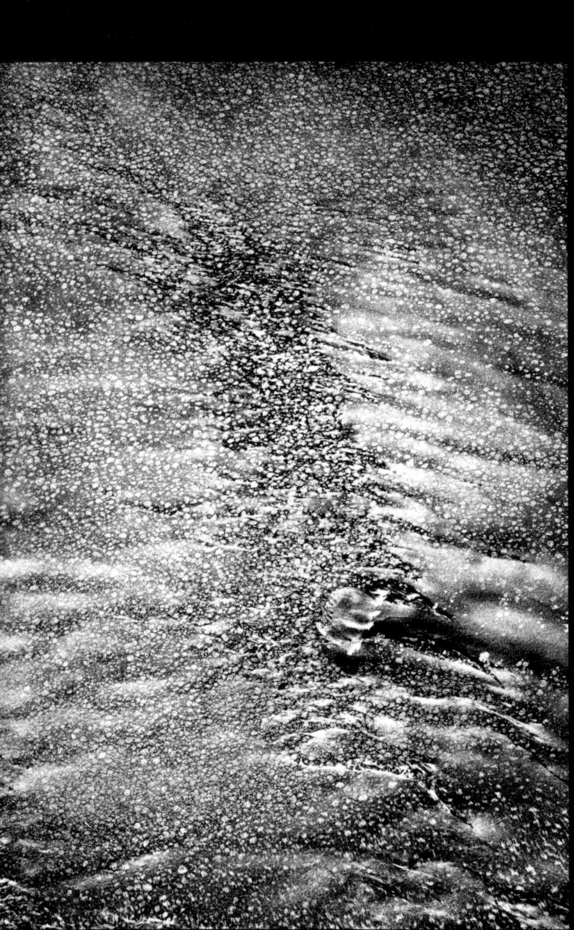

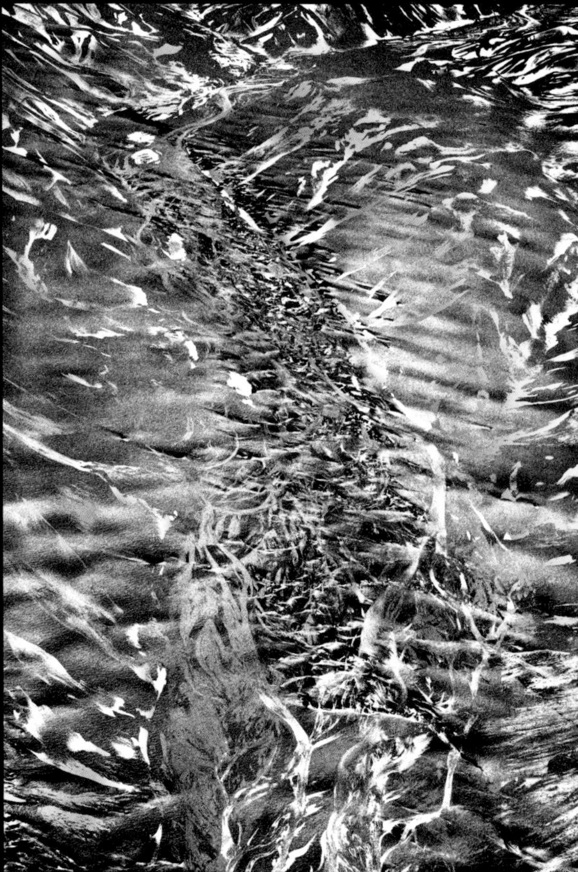

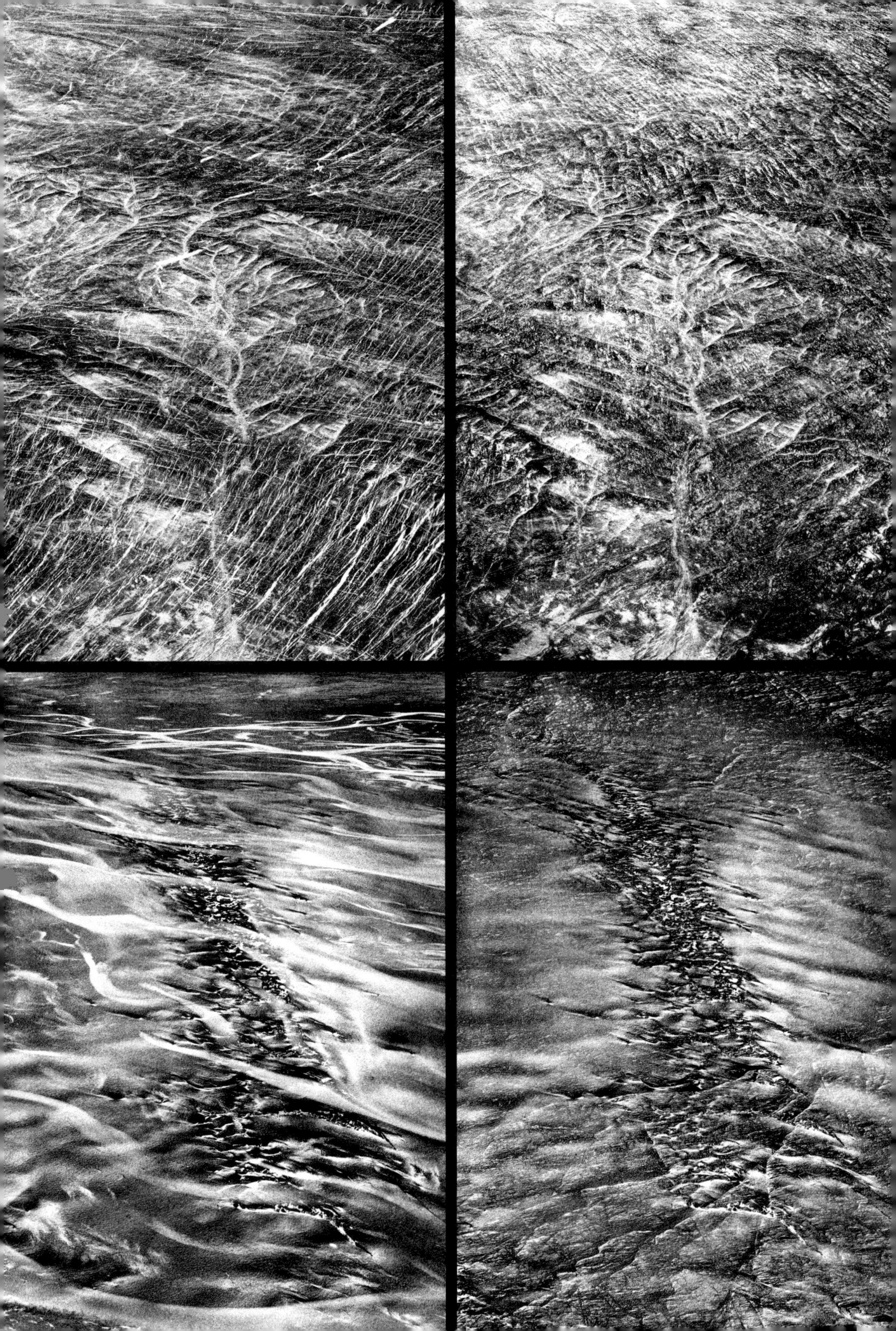